BRAZIL: RESPONSES TO THE DEBT CRISIS
IMPACT ON SAVINGS, INVESTMENT, AND GROWTH

James Dinsmoor

Published by the Inter-American Development Bank
Distributed by The Johns Hopkins University Press
March 1990
Washington, D.C.

The views and opinions expressed in this publication are those of the author and do not necessarily reflect the official positions of the Inter-American Development Bank.

Brazil: Responses to the Debt Crisis

Impact on Savings, Investment, and Growth

© Copyright 1990 by the Inter-American Development Bank

Inter-American Development Bank
1300 New York Avenue, N.W.
Washington, D.C. 20577

Distributed by
The Johns Hopkins University Press
701 West 40th Street
Baltimore, Maryland 21211

ISBN: 0-940602-30-X

PREFACE

This report presents an updating and extension of a similar study prepared by the author in May 1987 entitled "Brazil: Responses to the Debt Crisis." Besides taking into account much new information, including substantially revised national income accounts, and incorporating the results of new research by economists on different aspects of Brazil's adjustment process, the present study expands the previous analysis to focus more explicitly on savings and investment and on the obstacles that must be overcome for a sustained recovery to occur.

The author gratefully acknowledges the valuable comments and guidance provided by his colleagues at the Inter-American Development Bank, especially Messrs. Willy Van Ryckeghem and Gerald Malovany. Mr. Malovany painstakingly reviewed the entire first draft and offered numerous suggestions. Assistance was also forthcoming from José Roberto Nováes de Almeida of the International Monetary Fund in the interpretation of economic policy issues; David Garlow of the WEFA Group in analysis of the interrelationships between monetary correction and financial savings; and Persio Arida, who reviewed a very early draft of Chapter V. Valuable detailed and incisive observations were also received from two anonymous referees. They are not responsible, of course, for any remaining factual errors or for opinions expressed in the text. Finally, special debts of gratitude are owed to Mrs. Ibelyse Larrea Barrios of the Country Studies Division Secretarial Pool, who competently typed the manuscript and to José Nuñez del Arco, Paul Raimondi, and Barbara Rietveld who rendered invaluable assistance in preparing the book for publication.

TABLE OF CONTENTS

	Page
I. Summary and Conclusions	
Savings and Investment in the Context of Economic Adjustment	1
Domestic Adjustment and Its Impact on Savings and Investment	3
Economic Policies and Their Impact on Savings and Investment	7
The Implementation of Economic Policy After 1982	7
The Effects of Economic Policies on Savings and Investment: Major Conclusions	13
II. An Overview of Savings, Investment, and Growth from the Post-War Period to the First Oil Shock	
Introduction	17
Brazil's Economic Performance in the 1964–74 Period	20
III. The Impact of the Debt Crisis and External Adjustment on Savings, Investment and Growth	
The Growth and Structure of the External Debt	27
Trends in the 1974–81 Period	27
The 1982 External Debt Crisis	31
The Balance of Payments and the External Adjustment Process Through 1985	33
The Restrictions Imposed on the Balance of Payments by the 1982 Debt Crisis	33
The 1983 External Sector Program and the IMF Accord and Their Combined Impact on Balance of Payments Adjustment in the 1983–85 Period	35
Import Substitution Investment and Brazil's Adjustment Process	39

The Characteristics of Brazil's Import Substitution Policies	39
An Evaluation of Brazil's Import Substitution Investments and Their Impact on the Balance of Payments Adjustment Process	41

IV. Analysis of the Domestic Adjustment and its Impact on Savings, Investment, and Growth

The Nature of Domestic Adjustment	51
An Overview of the Domestic Adjustment in Terms of the Savings-Investment Identity	55
The Process of Brazil's Domestic Adjustment	57
Introduction	57
Analysis of Investment	63
Analysis of Savings	68
Conclusions	71

V. Analysis of Policy Instruments Used to Effectuate Economic Adjustment and Their Impact on Savings, Investment and Growth

Policy Instruments and the Strategy of Adjustment	73
The Role of Fiscal Policy in the Adjustment Process	74
The Role of Monetary and Credit Policy in the Adjustment Process	76
The Role of Wage Policy in the Adjustment Process	77
The Implementation and Effects of Policy Instruments on the Domestic Adjustment Process in 1983–85	77
The Implementation and Results of Fiscal Policy	78
The Implementation and Results of Monetary and Credit Policy	83
The Implementation and Results of Wage Policy	83
A Quantitative Analysis of the Impact of Brazil's Economic Adjustment Policies on Output and Inflation	87
Between the Charybdis of Indexation and Continued Inflation and the Scylla of Restrictive Demand Management Policies	93
Economic Policy in 1985 and the Cruzado Plan	95
Economic Performance and Policy Formulation in the Post-Cruzado Plan Era: Inflation and Stagnation	102
The "Summer Plan" of January 16, 1989	108
The Effects of Economic Policies on Savings and Investment: A Synthesis	109
Statistical Appendix	115
Annex	135
Bibliography	147
Index	153

List of Tables in the Text

Table		Page
II-1	Structure of Principal Fixed Yield Financial Assets of the Public and Participation in Current GDP in Selected Years (Percentages)	22
II-2	Savings and Investment Indicators (Percentages of GDP)	24
III-1	External Debt Indicators, 1978–1988	30
III-2	Balance of Payments, 1978–1988 (Millions of Dollars)	32
III-3	Latin America and the United States. Indicators of Openness (Percentages of GDP and GNP)	39
III-4	Exports and Imports of Capital Goods and Basic Inputs in the Balance of Payments (Millions of Dollars)	42
III-5	Selected Indicators of Substitution in the Energy Sector	44
III-6	Output and Imported Input Declines in 1980–1983 (Percentages)	47
IV-1	Indicators of External and Domestic Adjustment	54
IV-2	Income-Expenditure Matrix	58
IV-3	Income-Expenditure Matrix (Percentage of GDP)	60
IV-4	Investment Indicators	62
IV-5	Investment in Manufacturing, 1987	69
IV-6	Indicators of State Enterprise Finances, 1980–1987 (Percentages of GDP)	71
IV-7	Domestic Savings, National Savings and Net Factor Payments (Percentages of GDP)	71
V-1	Public Sector Borrowing Requirements as Percentages of GDP	78
V-2	Federal Domestic Debt in Bonds and Treasury Bills (Millions of Cruzados)	81
V-3	Indicators of Money and Quasi-Money	82
V-4	Trends in Income Distribution of the Economically Active Population	84
V-5	Trends in Growth Rates of Credit to the Private Sector, Minimum Wages and the Real Effective Exchange Rate (Percentage Change)	89
V-6	Actual and Predicted Changes in Output and Prices, 1973–1985 (Percent Growth)	91
V-7	Selected Macroeconomic Indicators, 1986–1989 (Percentages)	100

List of Graphs in the Text

Graph		Page
II-1	Savings and Investment (Percentages of GDP)	19
III-1	Total External Debt, 1970–1988	29
III-2	Average Propensities to Import (Percentages)	47
IV-1	Relationship Between the Resource Gap and Economic Growth (Three Year Moving Averages)	52
IV-2	Savings and Investment Indicators, 1980–1988 (Percentages of GDP)	56
	PANEL A: Total Investment = National Savings + External Savings	
	PANEL B: National Savings = General Government Savings + Private Savings (Households + Businesses)	
IV-3	Real Price Indexes of Selected Public Enterprises Goods and Services (1980 = 100)	64
	PANEL A: Petroleum and Derivatives	
	PANEL B: Telephone, Steel, Electricity, and Postal Rates	
V-1	Inflation versus Idle Capacity (Percentages)	92
V-2	Average Percentage Change in Consumer Prices, 1946–1988	106
V-3	Gross and Net Financial Savings as Percentages of Current GDP	111

CHAPTER I

SUMMARY AND CONCLUSIONS

Savings and Investment in the Context of Economic Adjustment

Economic adjustment refers to the process by which a nation responds to significant changes in its economic environment either beyond or within its boundaries. In this sense, not only is economic adjustment continuously occurring but also the stimuli giving rise to the need to adjust vary significantly over time in terms of their impact and, consequently, condition the magnitude and type of response required by the economy. This study analyzes Brazil's economic response to the 1982 external debt crisis, primarily in terms of the effects of this response on Brazilian savings, investment and growth. The present crisis was clearly a long time in the making and was strongly influenced by the nation's institutional setting, by its chronic inflationary problems, and by its heavy reliance upon industrialization policies based on import substitution, and it has affected Brazil in fundamental ways. Moreover, with the passage of time, the nature of the problems stemming from the initial shock has also changed markedly, owing both to alterations in international financial conditions and to shifts in domestic economic policy.

The problems posed by the onset of the debt crisis were similar throughout the Latin America. The countries' most immediate need was to adjust their balance of payments to the abrupt contraction of commercial bank lending after mid-1982. During the first months of the crisis, this objective was met primarily by an unprecedented drawdown of the countries' international reserves. At the same time, however, vigorous efforts were initiated to reduce the current account deficit. Given the high level of interest payments on the external debt, the lack of external financing required the attainment of substantially higher trade surpluses through higher exports, lower imports, or some combination of both. Because the deepening international recession largely precluded a rapid growth of exports in the short run, most countries drastically cut imports in order to achieve the needed improvement in their trade accounts.

At the same time, the initiation of external adjustment (changes in the structure of external trade and payments) triggered a simultaneous process of far-reaching domestic adjustment (changes in the structure of domestic production, savings, and investment), which affected virtually all economic sectors. In broad terms, production had to be reoriented from domestic to export markets as rapidly as possible in order to ease the balance of payments constraint. In turn, this required the implementation of stringent wage and monetary policies in most of the adjusting countries in order to reduce domestic demand. Moreover, if capital formation were not to be sacrificed unduly, it was also clear that domestic savings would have to increase substantially, not only to offset the abrupt cessation of capital inflows that had triggered the crisis but also to meet the hike in debt-servicing obligations caused by soaring international interest rates.

A basic objective of this study is to analyze how Brazil's ongoing economic adjustment has been accomplished. To this end, national accounts, balance of payments, economic policy, and movements in the price level are examined in detail, including their interactions during the 1982–88 period. Four rather clearly defined phases of the adjustment process can be discerned. Attention is first given to the recessionary phase, which lasted from 1982 until approximately mid-1984. The second phase can be characterized as one of export-led recovery and expansion; this phase began in the second half of 1984 and continued through most of 1985. The third phase, characterized by a strong recovery in investment and by consumption-stimulated growth, commenced in February, 1986, and continued until year-end. The recovery in domestic demand proved unsustainable, however, and during the 1987–88 period, Brazil's economic performance was adversely affected by the stagnation of output and the steady escalation of inflationary pressures.

Brazil's balance of payments response to the debt crisis through year-end 1988 was, in most respects, the most successful in the region. Many positive accomplishments can be cited, but perhaps the most important was the dramatic growth of the nation's trade surplus, which, after averaging less than $1 billion in the 1981–82 period, jumped to nearly $12 billion in the 1984–86 period and in 1988 jumped to $19.1 billion. Both in relative and absolute terms, this was by far the largest increase in the region, and it enabled Brazil during most of the period since 1983 to nearly cover—or more than cover in 1984 and 1988—not only the interest payments on its massive external debt but also other debit items in its service accounts as well.

Various factors contributed to these impressive results in Brazil's merchandise trade. In the first instance, very early in the adjustment process the country gave highest priority to stimulating exports, despite the recession in international trade. In part, this export stimulation was accomplished by substantially depreciating the cruzeiro in early 1983 and—with the exception of 1986, when a fixed exchange rate was maintained during most of the year—continuing a policy of frequent minidevaluations in line with domestic inflation. At the same time, the nation was able to compress its already modest import ratio to one of the lowest levels in the world in the 1983–84 period, without the highly disruptive effects on production that occurred in most of the other countries of the region. Brazil's continuing ability to operate its economy as well as it did despite the imposition of comprehensive import controls was in large measure attributable to sustained increases in its domestic petroleum production, to falling world prices on its oil imports, and to its ability to substitute effectively a wide range of other imports. In this regard, many of the large import substitution investments in energy, capital goods, and basic inputs initiated in the aftermath of the first oil price shock—investments whose financing had contributed to the rapid buildup of Brazil's burgeoning external debt—were completed and had initiated production by the early 1980s.

With respect to minimizing the adverse effects of the adjustment process on economic activity, Brazil likewise achieved positive results with respect to the rest of the region. By mid-1984, in fact, the nation was already beginning to recover from the deep recession of the previous year, primarily because of the sharp growth of exports. In 1985, the economic growth rate, spurred by resurgent domestic demand, jumped by more than 3 percentage points to 8.4 percent, the largest increase in five years. Although spearheaded by a recovery in real investment, the rise in domestic demand also reflected higher private consumption outlays, which resulted from the lagged multiplier effect of the surge in export earnings, amplified by a more expansive wage policy. Average real wages in manufacturing rose about 14 percent during the year and enabled workers to recoup about half the loss in purchasing power that had occurred in the 1982–84 recession. The economic recovery continued in 1986, and by year-end not only had real GDP expanded 7.6 percent but also open unemployment had plummeted to less than 3 percent. Thus, between 1984 and 1986 Brazil's real GDP expanded more than 16 percent, substantially more than the increase for the rest of Latin America.

B. Domestic Adjustment and Its Impact on Savings and Investment

Notwithstanding the highly satisfactory results in improving its trade surplus and in returning to rapid growth, Brazil's economic adjustment process was not without problems. In the first instance, the measures utilized to effectuate external adjustment—dramatic though they were—were far from optimal in terms of their consequences for the rest of the economy. To offset the increase in net factor payments, for instance, the preferred response would clearly have been an incremental growth in exports, greater than what actually occurred. Because exports did not respond in the desired way, however, especially in the early part of the adjustment process, significant cuts in imports were ultimately required to produce the needed trade surpluses.

Domestic adjustment, in turn, was strongly conditioned by the nature of this suboptimal external adjustment.[1] In this regard, the most satisfactory

---

[1] In simple macroeconomic terms, the domestic adjustment that corresponds by definition to the external adjustment is determined by the following *ex post* identity:

(footnote continues next page)

domestic response would have been a rapid expansion in output (fueled by external demand), accompanied by an increased savings effort that would, as a minimum, offset the fall in external savings while leaving capital formation unchanged from its previous levels. Even at the outset of the debt crisis, however, it seemed unlikely that this objective would be accomplished. First, the need to cut imports (as opposed to increasing exports) made it largely inevitable that the investment ratio would fall, at least in the short term. Second, because a rising share of Brazil's overall savings effort (that is, domestic savings) had to be diverted to cover interest payments, the level of national savings available to finance investment began declining after 1982.

The aforementioned factors were fully in evidence by 1983, when investment, after averaging a relatively stable 22.4 percent of GDP in the 1980–82 period, plunged 4.5 percentage points in 1983 and an additional 1.2 percentage points in 1984, to 15.3 percent of GDP, the lowest level since 1956. In part, the decline in capital formation reflected an anticipated downturn in the investment cycle, since many of the large-scale projects initiated during the mid-1970s had been completed by the early 1980s, thus endowing Brazil with ample productive capacity in most sectors. Despite this, the nation's investment ratio was also progressively impacted by the same problems affecting the rest of Latin America. In addition to the disappearance of external savings, for instance, capital formation was also constrained by the imposition of comprehensive import controls, rising real interest rates, and a deepening domestic recession.

With respect to timing, the experiences of state enterprises differed somewhat from those of private firms. State enterprise investment outlays had already begun to drop in 1982, a year before the generalized decline in Brazil's investment ratio became evident. This decrease, from 6.1 percent of GDP in 1981 to 3.8 percent in 1984, reflected a variety of factors, including the following: the acute shortage of foreign exchange; constraints on foreign and domestic borrowing; falling revenues because of price controls and because of weak demand for selected goods and services produced by the public sector (for example, steel and electric energy); and numerous import restrictions

---

$$\frac{\text{External Adjustment}}{(M - X) + R} = \frac{\text{Domestic Adjustment}}{I_T - S_N}$$

where

$(M - X)$ = The resource balance (M and X correspond to imports and exports of good and nonfactor services, respectively)
R = Net factor payments (made up principally of interest payments)
I_T = Total investment, including variation in stocks and
S_N = National savings.

Thus, in terms of this identity, the basic characteristic of Brazil's external adjustment was that the trade surplus covered a rising share of interest payments during most of the 1982–88 period. This is reflected on the right-hand side of the identity by the fact that national savings (domestic savings less net factor payments) covered an increasing part of total investment because of the decline in external savings. In theory, the savings–investment gap could be closed through an increase in national savings, a reduction in investment, or a combinaton of the two.

and prohibitions. The decline in private sector capital outlays was also steep, as the investment ratio (excluding the state enterprises) dropped from a 14.6 percent average of GDP in the 1981–82 period to 10.8 percent of GDP in 1984. By 1985, however, private investment began to recover, largely in response to the renewed opportunities in export markets precipitated by the real devaluation of the cruzeiro.

Thus, although the contraction of capital formation occurred at different rates for private firms and for state enterprises through 1985, both groups were severely impacted by the adjustment process. In some respects, however, the state enterprises may have been confronted by more constraints than were their private sector counterparts; in addition to the factors already noted, for example, some state enterprises were also obliged to incur unwanted external debt for balance of payments support, and others were constrained by government policy in implementing desired increases in prices and rates and in cutting current expenditures. This is not to say, however, that the situation of private firms was markedly better; corporate indebtedness, both to the domestic financial system and to external creditors, was at such high levels that further borrowing for capital formation became infeasible, especially as real interest rates continued to escalate. Consequently, to continue operations—even at reduced levels—private firms were forced increasingly to generate their own cash requirements; by early 1986, the ratio of internally generated financial requirements to total financial requirements exceeded 50 percent, dramatically above the 14 percent level of 1983.

Another result of the various official measures adopted in Brazil in the 1982–85 period to limit and redirect expenditure (rapid devaluation, tax rebates to exporters, and so forth) was an increase in the amount of investment—and output—directed toward export-related activities. Even import prohibitions, which had become increasingly commonplace after the mid-1970s and which in principle were designed to provide renewed impetus for import substitution, often favored in practice those firms producing inputs needed for exports. As a result, most public and private enterprises producing for the domestic market fared poorly, at least until 1985, when real wages began to recover in the industrialized Center-South.

In 1986, real wages continued to rise rapidly because of the temporary control of inflation and interest rates achieved by the implementation of the Cruzado Plan. These developments, coupled with the fact that industrial capacity rapidly rose to near-maximum utilization levels, triggered an increase in investment—especially by small and medium-sized firms, which responded quickly to the hike in domestic demand. Most of the investment increase was accounted for by construction; the construction sector's share in total fixed investment for 1986 reached 69.8 percent, up from 60.5 percent in 1980. In contrast, state enterprise investment outlays continued to stagnate, largely because of continuing debt-servicing constraints, aggravated by the fact that the price freeze ruled out rate hikes. Large domestic and foreign enterprises for the most part also postponed new investment, preferring to strengthen their cash balances while evaluating the longer-term effects of the Cruzado Plan on demand and inflation control. On the whole, however, the 1986 measures had a nearly immediate positive effect on capital formation. In real terms, total investment rose 16.8 percent, despite a significant drawdown on stocks, and in relation to current GDP, the investment ratio rose one percentage point over 1985, to 18.3 percent.

In 1987, the ratio of investment to current GDP apparently continued to recover, jumping 3.8 percentage points to 22.1 percent, only fractionally below the 22.4 average of the 1980–82 period. For the most part, however, this apparent increase was actually just a reflection of adjustments in relative prices; that is, with the return of rapid inflation, costs in the construction sector had escalated by rates above the increase in the general price level. Hence, once adjusted for inflation, total fixed investment in Brazil, after rising 22 percent in 1986, dropped about 0.4 percent in 1987. The decline of fixed investment was even greater than this in the key manufacturing sector, where real outlays decreased in eleven of the nation's twenty-one major industrial subsectors, or by an average of 3.6 percent. Finally, preliminary data suggest that this situation worsened considerably in 1988, since the inflation rate more than doubled, to an unprecedented 934 percent, while industrial output continued to decelerate despite a remarkable surge in exports.

With the onset of the debt crisis, Brazil's use of external savings plummeted, falling from a rather stable 4.7 percent average of GDP in the 1980–82 period to 2.7 percent in 1983. Thereafter, with the exception of a small upturn in 1986, external savings essentially disappeared, averaging −0.2 percent of GDP in the 1984–88 period. As a result, Brazil's investment ratio since 1984 has been determined by the availability of national savings (that is, domestic savings minus net factor payments). In this regard, the striking feature of Brazil's national savings was that they declined as little as they did especially during the earlier part of the adjustment period and despite increasing dissavings of the general government (0.7 percent of GDP in 1980 to a 10.0 percent average in the 1985–88 period).

The rapid deterioration in savings of the general government reflected various factors. First, the government was forced to assume responsibility for large amounts of external debt that could no longer be serviced by state enterprises after mid-1982 because of the latters' deteriorating financial situation. At the same time, Brazil's net tax burden was progressively eroded by the combined effects of collection lags and inflation and by the steady growth of tax rebates to exporters and of other current transfers. Additional forms of expenditure likewise contributed to the deteriorating fiscal imbalance, including the steep growth of the wage bill, as a result of the hike in public employment after 1985, and soaring interest (including exchange and monetary correction payments) on Brazil's mushrooming domestic debt, which escalated from a 2 percent average of GDP in the 1980–81 period to around 6 percent by 1987.

The primary beneficiary of the large growth in domestic debt service payments was the private sector, whose share in national savings rose rapidly, especially after 1983. It is difficult to perform a precise breakdown of how this growth in savings was allocated between households and businesses. Available data indicate, however, that most of the increase was attributable to households, in part because firms supplying the domestic market, which constituted the vast majority of all firms and accounted for most of the sector's value added, tended to have low savings rates compared with the savings rates of firms able to export. Savings by households themselves, despite rising substantially in absolute and relative terms, showed wide variations according to household income level. Not surprisingly, most of the increase was attributable to the wealthier classes, which were in a far better position to invest funds in domestic debt instruments than were poor families, whose shrinking real incomes increasingly approached absolute poverty levels and were, of necessity, directed toward consumption, not savings. Thus, in Brazil's case the growth of household savings during the 1980s was probably accompanied by a further deterioration in an already serious income distribution problem. The magnitude of the problem is illustrated by the fact that in 1984 the richest 5 percent of the population accounted for about one-third of national income, compared with only approximately one-sixth of national income for the entire poorer half of the population.

Distributional considerations apart, the increase in private sector savings more than offset the growing dissavings of the general government. National savings were therefore able to recover from a period low of 17.6 percent of GDP in 1983 to 22.0 percent of GDP by 1987, above the 18.7 percent average of the 1980–81 period. Still left unanswered, however, is the fundamental question of why domestic savings did not increase more than they did during the period under consideration. Certainly, a major explanation lies in the severity of the recession that gripped Brazil (and most other countries) during the 1982–84 period, the effects of which, in turn, have been subsequently exacerbated by the probable deterioration in income distribution, extreme inflationary pressures, and a largely uncontrollable fiscal deficit. These attendant problems, which accompanied the formulation and implementation of economic policy, suggest that Brazil had to make a significant effort simply to achieve modest gains in domestic savings during the last several years.

In short, perhaps the major finding stemming from the analysis of Brazil's domestic adjustment is the inadequacy of the savings effort to date. In particular, what occurred through 1988 can be characterized more appropriately as an "accommodation" to the disappearance of external savings rather than as a structural increase in savings capacity. Clearly, a structural increase in savings constitutes a necessary condition for the recovery of investment from its current levels and for the resumption of sustained growth. As examined later, however, unless fundamental changes in economic policy are forthcoming—and vigorously implemented—such increases will be difficult to achieve.

Economic Policies and Their Impact on Savings and Investment

The Implementation of Economic Policy after 1982

Brazil's inability to achieve the desired increase in domestic savings was closely linked to the effects of the economic policies implemented after 1982, as noted earlier. The principal objective of policy formulation from the beginning of the crisis was to lower the public sector deficit. The fiscal imbalance, which had not become apparent until the 1970s, was the result of several factors. In the first place, current and capital expenditures at all levels of the public sector consistently outstripped revenues, and by widening margins. Part of this expenditure increase was attributable to the state enterprises, whose outlays progressively exceeded federal budget allocations and whose external borrowing and import requirements contributed to the rapid deterioration in the balance of payments, distortions in the allocation of investment resources, and pressures on the price level. Another factor contributing to the fiscal imbalance was the exceptional growth of credit subsidies, both to mortgage holders through Brazil's extensive housing finance system and to other borrowers through special credit programs used increasingly as economic policy instruments to benefit the import substitution and export promotion investments initiated after the first oil price shock.

Vigorous measures were therefore initiated in late 1982 to cut government expenditures and increase revenues. Simultaneously, monetary and demand management policies were significantly tightened to dampen demand, as part of the overall adjustment program agreed to with the International Monetary Fund (IMF) in January 1983. The results achieved by these measures, however, were mixed. For instance, significant progress was initially achieved in lowering the so-called "operational" or real component of the public sector deficit, but this reduction could not be sustained. Meanwhile, the nominal fiscal deficit (defined as the operational plus accrued exchange and monetary correction payments on the domestic debt) rose steadily throughout the adjustment period, accompanying the escalation of inflation.

To a large extent, the inability to reduce the nominal deficit reflected the widespread and institutionalized use of indexation procedures in the economy, which provided nearly automatic mechanisms for increasing nominal values of exchange rates, wages, bonds, and other economic variables in the current period to maintain their real values in the previous period. By year-end 1984, this tendency of past increases in the price level to be ratcheted forward to successively higher plateaus had commonly become known as inertial inflation.

The increasingly inertial nature of Brazil's inflationary process severely constrained efforts to reduce the fiscal imbalance. One basic problem was that the expenditures and financial liabilities of the public sector tended to be adjusted almost instantaneously in domestic currency terms to reflect inflation, while tax receipts and other sources of public revenue lagged behind increases in the price level because of delayed collections, tax rebates, and the like.

By early 1986, the interrelated problems of the fiscal deficit and inflation had reached critical proportions. Large wage settlements, a drought-induced hike in food prices, and growing capacity constraints in industry contributed to a 35 percent increase in consumer prices through February and to a projected 400 percent rise by year-end. Confronted by this steady drift toward hyperinflation, the authorities declared a bank holiday on February 28, 1986, and announced a sweeping economic program, the Cruzado Plan, to halt spiraling prices. The plan did create a new monetary unit, the cruzado, equal to 1,000 cruzeiros, but its basic objective was to rid the inflationary process of its inertial component. Toward this end, monetary correction on most types of financial instruments was abolished. This included replacing the Readjustable Treasury Bond (ORTN), which had undoubtedly been the key indexed security in the economy and which in many ways had substituted the cruzeiro as a means of exchange and, especially, as a store of value; the ORTN was replaced by the nonindexed National Treasury Bond (OTN), the unit price of which was frozen, effective March 1, 1986, for one year. At the same time, a comprehensive freeze on prices, including most public utility rates, was introduced for an indefinite period. The cruzado was also pegged at an initially fixed rate of 13.8 per U.S. dollar, but with the understanding that it could be devalued in the future as deemed necessary. Finally, wages were converted into cruzados on the basis of their average—as opposed to "peak"—real value during the preceding six months; this adjustment to the average real wage was necessary, since otherwise, workers who had received adjustments immediately prior to implementation of the plan would be better off in real terms than those who had received their adjustments six months earlier.

The highly disparate effects of the Cruzado Plan on Brazil's economic performance during 1986 continue to be felt even in 1990. The plan did drive down inflation significantly during the second and third quarters of the year, but it also triggered a boom in consumer expenditures, since real wages increased and the cost of consumer credit declined. In addition, the growth of fixed investment, despite rising 22.2 percent, was insufficient to alleviate mounting capacity constraints; consequently, price pressures once again began to build at a rapid pace by year-end 1986. The balance of payments was also adversely affected, since surging domestic demand, coupled with a fixed exchange rate and a poor agricultural harvest, precipitated an increasing diversion of potential exports into the domestic market and higher import demand. As a result, the trade surplus dropped from its 1984–85 average of nearly $12.8 billion to only $8.4 billion in 1986.

In an attempt to address these problems, the authorities sought to dampen demand and to correct distortions in relative prices, primarily through raising taxes and adjusting public sector prices. Nevertheless, Brazil's economic situation became increasingly unsettled. Interest rates soared to more than 400 percent by year-end 1986 (compared with an average growth of 142 percent in the general price index) and continued to rise at an even more accelerated pace in early 1987 as the dwindling trade balance and the imponderables that surrounded economic policy set the stage for a new price spiral. Inflationary expectations were fueled especially by legislation in late 1986 that largely reinstituted monetary correction in the economy (including the indexation of the OTN) and by the additional wage increases granted to industrial workers. Consequently, when Brazil's year-old price freeze was lifted in February 1987, prices of many goods immediately jumped between 30 and 40 percent. Of even greater significance was the fact that inflation was again rising at an annualized rate of around 400 percent—or at approximately the same rate as on the eve of the Cruzado Plan.

The uncertainty that emerged after late 1986 was also accentuated by developments in the external sector. The drying up of capital flows, the decreasing levels of reserves, and the steady deterioration of the trade balance placed Brazil in an untenable debt-servicing situation. For these reasons, on February 21, 1987, the government suspended interest payments due on about $68 billion of medium- and long-term debt with commercial banks.

Faced with this deteriorating environment, Brazil's economic performance weakened in 1987. In the first instance, real GDP growth decelerated to a 3.6 percent rate, as the stimulus to consumer spending provided by the Cruzado Plan through rising real wages and the price freeze could not be sustained. The price freeze would have posed problems under the best of circumstances; too short a period would have failed to break the automatic link between past and current inflation, but conversely, if the freeze were too long, the resulting distortions would have affected investment decisions, the mobilization of savings, and the entire adjustment process itself in undesirable ways, perhaps including the implementation of complex rationing. In any event, the failure of the plan to break inflationary expectations was inevitable, since price controls remained in place well beyond the time frame originally envisioned. The Cruzado Plan also greatly aggravated the already serious financial disarray in the public sector, since, as noted, prices of most public goods and services had been fixed at unrealistically low levels. Coupled with a rising wage bill, this caused a cost-revenue squeeze that led to a significant expansion of public sector borrowing requirements.

Consequently, the process of phasing out the price freeze and adjusting public sector prices that was initiated in early 1987 unleashed a renewed—and virulent—escalation of prices and real interest rates, especially during the first half of the year, when the economy rapidly returned to the fully indexed status that had existed prior to the Cruzado Plan. By year-end, consumer prices had risen by an average of 232 percent, the largest increase in Brazil's history. Moreover, with the exception of most federal government and major state enterprises, inflation outstripped wage gains by wide margins, despite settlements sometimes above those permitted by existing policy. Another stabilization program failed at mid-year, and the deteriorating economic environment was also complicated by the uncertainties surrounding the drafting of Brazil's new constitution, further eroding business confidence.

During 1988, highly divergent trends continued to characterize Brazil's economic performance. On the positive side, substantial progress was achieved in normalizing the country's relationships with the international financial community, strained following Brazil's imposition of the moratorium on interest payments. Of particular importance was the agreement reached with private banks to refinance $62.1 billion in loans to Brazil originally scheduled to fall due by 1993. Signed in late September, this comprehensive accord lowered interest rates, restructured principal payments over a ten-year period beginning in 1995, and provided $5.2 billion in so-called new loans to finance interest payments.

To a large extent, the agreement with the banks was facilitated by Brazil's successful rapprochement with the IMF, following three years of estrangement from that institution. By mid-year, Brazil had already presented a macroeconomic program to the IMF, which was intended to provide the basis for a new accord. The ensuing negotiations culminated on June 29, 1988, in the approval of a nineteen-month stand-by for the equivalent of $1.4 billion. The new agreement was viewed by some analysts as being considerably more flexible (and realistic) than the previous letter of intent signed in January 1983 and subsequently modified five times, because of Brazil's inability to meet the different targets. The principal provisions were to reduce the so-called operational public sector deficit to 4 percent of GDP for 1988 (down from about 6 percent projected early in the year) and to 2 percent in 1989; to limit inflation to 600 percent in 1988, a target applied implicitly in the 1988 federal budget and other public expenditure items; to limit the expansion of the monetary base in 1988 to 375 percent; to achieve a trade surplus of $12.6 billion; to increase net international reserves to $4.2 billion; to roll over 75 percent of the external debt obligations of the states and municipalities; and to limit real growth of the domestic debt to 5 percent.

The measures just summarized provided important relief to Brazil's onerous debt-servicing problems. In addition, the overall balance of payments situation benefited during 1988 from a significant improvement in the trade accounts. By year-end, the trade surplus reached $19.1 billion—by far the largest in the nation's history. This increase in the trade surplus more than compensated for a $1.7 billion increase in the service deficit caused by higher interest payments and profit remittances and brought the current account to an unprecedented $4.8 billion surplus. This surplus more than offset the net capital outflow, resulting in part from the settlement of arrears during the previous year, and it enabled net international reserves to rise an estimated $2.1 billion.

Despite the exceptionally positive results in Brazil's external accounts, the country's real GDP declined 0.3 percent in 1988, as economic activity was depressed by widespread uncertainty and the escalation of inflation. By year-end, consumer prices had risen 934 percent—by far the highest inflation in the nation's history. The explosion in prices was apparently fuelled by an extraordinary net transfer of resources abroad, which jumped from zero in 1987 (when the debt moratorium was in effect) to an estimated 7.5 percent of GDP in 1988. This additional claim on real resources, which was simultaneously reflected by the record trade surplus, was only partially offset by a decrease in the operational fiscal deficit, so that there was considerable pressure on private savings to increase through a process of forced savings. Efforts to resist this pressure ignited higher wage demands as well as frequent price markups and pushed inflation up to a new and dangerously high level.

As a result of these developments, price pressures again reached unmanageable proportions by year-end 1988. In December, the money supply soared 50 percent and, with inflation approaching 30 percent a month, or an annualized rate of around 1,900 percent, confidence in the nation's currency had essentially disappeared. Faced with this deepening crisis, the authorities declared bank holidays for January 16 and 17, 1989, and announced the so-called Summer Plan. The main elements of the new plan were the following:

- A general price freeze was announced on all goods and services, with the exception of some public sector prices. Although the duration of the freeze was to be "indefinite," it was expected to be shorter than in the case of the Cruzado Plan.
- A new monetary unit, the new cruzado, was introduced to replace the cruzado. Equal to 1,000 cruzados, the new cruzado was also devalued by 17 percent, making one new cruzado equal to $1. The plan did not indicate how or when the new cruzado would be devalued in the future.
- The indexed-linked National Treasury Bond (OTN) was formally abandoned; as was the case of the OTN's predecessor, the Readjustable Treasury Bond (ORTN), which was abolished when the Cruzado Plan was announced, abandonment of the OTN was considered to be the key measure for de-indexing the economy. To avoid a flight of capital into non-new-cruzado assets, monetary policy was significantly tightened to raise interest rates. The OTN and the Fiscal OTN were to be abolished by the end of January. In contrast, passbook savings would continue to be corrected by inflation plus 0.5 percent per month in interest.
- If foreign exchange reserves (estimated at $7 billion) fell below an unspecified level, a moratorium would again be instituted on interest payments to foreign banks. Debt-equity auctions were also to be canceled for the near term.
- In the public sector, several categories of measures were announced. First, a number of prices were increased prior to implementing the general price freeze including air fares, alcohol fuel for cars, gasoline, electricity, postal rates, and telephone charges. Second, the ministries of Housing, Science and Technology, Agrarian Reform, and Irrigation were abolished. Third, an unspecified number of public sector employees were to be dismissed, and an ambitious privatization program was proposed. The most important, however, was the government's declaration that expenditures were to be kept in line with revenues.

Regarded by the authorities as the most stringent set of economic policies ever adopted at one time in Brazil's history, the Summer Plan attempted to correct the errors of the Cruzado and subsequent stabilization plans in several fundamental ways. Safeguards were incorporated to prevent another eruption in domestic demand, primarily through limiting adjustments in nominal wages and increasing the cost of consumer credit. Moreover, because of the frequent increases implemented during 1988, it was believed that the prices of public sector goods and services were much closer to equilibrium levels than had been the case when the preceding plans had been announced; this conviction supposedly would preclude any surge of "corrective" inflation of the type that had occurred when the previous price freeze ended in February 1987. By limiting expenditure to resource availability, reducing redundant employment, introducing institutional streamlining, and offering a privatization program for selected state enterprises, the new measures also adumbrated significant reforms in the public sector.

Only five months after the Summer Plan was initiated, however, popular support for it collapsed. After being held to low levels through April, inflation jumped to almost 10 percent in May and to 25 percent in June. With prices continuing to accelerate, the authorities were forced to reindex the economy in early July through the creation of a new financial instrument, the National Treasury Bill (BTN), to replace the 1986 National Treasury Bond, or OTN. The return to rapid inflation was fueled by a large adjustment in the minimum wage (70 percent), the informal reindexation of key economic variables (including most wage contracts) even before the creation of BTN in July, and, especially, the lack of resolve in lowering the fiscal deficit, which, instead of decreasing to around 2 percent of GDP as had been intended, was projected to have increased substantially by year-end.

As a result of these factors, inflation spiraled increasingly out of control; by December 1989, the growth in prices (measured by the government's official cost of living index) reached an estimated 53.6 percent, or more than the rate usually regarded as the threshold for hyperinflation, and for the year as a whole the increase was 1,765 percent. Despite the surge in prices, real GDP is estimated to have expanded between 3 percent and 4 percent. The recovery in output was due primarily to higher consumption outlays, which were fueled by an inflation-induced flight into goods (despite high real interest rates) and also by mounting concerns about the stability of the financial markets. The trade surplus declined $3 billion from the previous year's record to $16.1 billion, but was still sufficient to generate a current account surplus of around $380 million, notwithstanding increased interest payments and record profit remittances. At the same time, the capital account was expected to deteriorate because of reduced capital flows, a sharp drop in direct foreign investment, and capital flight. After mid-year, these factors also gave rise to strong pressures on Brazil's reserves as the nation was forced to delay scheduled interest payments to its creditors.

The Effects of Economic Policies on Savings and Investment: Major Conclusions

With regard to domestic adjustment in general and the implementation of economic policy in particular, Brazil's most fundamental problem since the onset of the debt crisis has been the failure to reduce its fiscal deficit. Even before the dislocations of 1982, the nation had an increasingly serious imbalance in its public finances—a legacy of many years of deficit spending by all levels of government and by state enterprises. By the end of 1986, it was clear that neither an approach of "gradualism" to achieve reduction of the deficit nor "heterodox" experiments such as the Cruzado Plan, which attempted, over a period of several months, to eliminate the memory of past inflation from the economy, would produce the desired results. For these reasons, technicians were increasingly in agreement that future stabilization efforts must take into account, and indeed emphasize, some form of traditional (or "orthodox") fiscal adjustment program, comparable to those carried out in Jamaica and Chile during the 1980s, in order to restore fiscal equilibrium and reverse the unacceptable growth of inflationary expectations. Among other features, the Jamaican and Chilean adjustment programs featured sweeping tax reforms, deep cuts in expenditure (including reduction of redundant personnel), privatization, reduction of subsidies, and comprehensive administrative reform. Although the programs were initially painful and they required time to implement, their success in restoring the basis for improved economic growth has been borne out in both countries in recent years.

The analysis of Brazilian economic policy also reveals that efforts to reduce the fiscal imbalance have been constrained by the increasingly inertial nature of the inflationary process created by indexation. In the context of efforts to achieve public sector adjustment, a major problem has been that expenditures and financial charges are adjusted almost instantaneously to reflect inflation, while revenues, for a variety of reasons, have lagged. These problems are compounded by massive sales of indexed domestic debt instruments through the open market in an increasingly futile attempt to neutralize the expansionary pressures resulting from Brazil's huge trade surpluses.

As a result, not only has fiscal management become progressively intractable but it is also clear that, from the standpoint of implementing economic policy, Brazil's external adjustment process has become increasingly incompatible with concomitant attempts to foster domestic adjustment. The magnitude of the latter problem is indicated by the fact that Brazil's nominal fiscal deficit, as measured by the public sector borrowing requirements to cover the operational deficit plus monetary correction on the domestic debt, expanded steadily from 16.6 percent of GDP in 1982 to an estimated 48.5 percent in 1988.

In view of the problems just summarized, a number of important conclusions can be drawn with respect to savings and investment. First, given the present heightened state of inflationary expectations and assuming no fundamental changes are forthcoming in economic policy, little basis exists for expecting a sustained recovery in fixed capital formation in the short term. Investor uncertainty has simply become too pronounced.

Perhaps the most important consequence of the sharp intensification of the inflationary process, however, has been the further erosion of the nation's already weakened savings capacity, which has occurred despite the institutional hypertrophy in the financial sector. Several critical problems can be identified. First, as was the case in the early 1960s, long term sources of financial savings have again virtually dried up. By late 1988 and continuing through 1989, most government backed savings instruments, especially Treasury Bonds (OTNs, Fiscal OTNs, and the like) had extremely short maturities. As a result, economic agents, including some of Brazil's best minds, were utilizing increasing amounts of time and energy in an ongoing effort to protect the real value of financial assets (or in speculative activities of a distinctly nonproductive nature), as willingness to undertake new productive investment steadily waned.

The main reasons for high interest rates, inflation, and capital flight, with their negative implications for savings and investment, may well lie in political problems: Brazil has thus far failed to decide how to distribute the costs of adjustment and make the decision stick. Any viable solution to this impasse would be greatly facilitated by a distribution of the adjustment costs that is perceived to be equitable by all segments of society; such a solution would also, of course, necessitate building a strong concensus on medium-term goals and achieving agreement as to the means both to achieve them and to provide for the more equitable distribution of the fruits of future growth than heretofore has been the case.

At the same time, the results just summarized constitute a major indictment of the long-term effects of indexation on the mobilization of savings. In the first instance, the results suggest that an important consequence of such procedures is simply to enhance the economy's capacity to tolerate inflation rather than to contribute to the expansion of the nation's real savings capacity, even though increasing savings capacity was its original intention and has been a fundamental objective of economic policy since the early 1960s. Indexation has also tended to make overall economic management increasingly difficult; in particular, the preceding analysis demonstrated that stabilization programs as applied in the 1980s have served essentially to depress economic activity and worsen income distribution, while inflation, in the absence of a frontal attack on the underlying causes of the fiscal deficit and driven by inertia, has continued its inexorable march to successively higher levels.

All things considered, in order to establish a suitable environment for a sustainable upturn in savings and investment, Brazil continues to require a fundamental correction of its fiscal imbalance as well as the de-indexation of the economy. These measures are imperative for restoring confidence and reversing the government's negative contribution to national savings. In principle, the Summer Plan of January 1989 contained important elements of fiscal reform as well as measures for de-indexation; as noted, however, these provisions were not implemented. In this regard, it should also be noted that the ultimate success or failure of the future stabilization efforts will depend not only upon the resolve of the president but also upon the Brazilian Congress, which, under the nation's new constitution, is now required to approve the federal budget, establish expenditure priorities, and adopt legislation in politically sensitive areas such as wage policy and privatization.

The prospects for success of future reforms initiatives could also be greatly enhanced if external and domestic interest rates could be lowered from their present levels. The problems posed by large interest payments are not limited to the latters' adverse consequences on the balance of payments, capital markets, and investment: the problems also concern basic credibility in the implementation of economic policy. It becomes extremely difficult, for instance, to generate widespread support for unpopular fiscal reforms, such as the dismissal of public employees, when it recognized that financial charges constitute an exceptionally high percentage of total public outlays and, moreover, that selected economic minorities have benefited considerably from the purchase of domestic debt instruments, especially during periods of high interest rates such as existed in early 1989.

For these reasons, the credibility of fiscal reforms could be improved by a lowering of interest payments. In the case of the domestic debt, interest reduction could perhaps be accomplished through a restructuring of the present maturity profile of existing obligations over a substantially longer time horizon. At the same time, if a thorough revamping of the public sector were clearly under way and all segments of society were participating in the adjustment, external creditors might be willing to provide additional debt relief to Brazil, perhaps in the form of reductions in interest rates or capitalization of interest. In this regard, a principal objective of the failed Summer Plan was precisely to set the stage for a new round of negotiations with external creditors.

Even though such measures as the restructuring of domestic debt maturities and capitalization of interest on the foreign debt might be politically difficult to achieve and would not directly solve the problems of ultimate repayment to creditors, important benefits could nevertheless result. In the case of the external sector, for instance, significantly lower net factor payments would permit Brazil to maintain a smaller trade surplus and would enable imports to rise. This result would provide an important stimulus to capital formation and economic growth, which in turn would be beneficial to Brazil and, ultimately, to the banks, whose likelihood of recovering past loans would improve. Second, this decreased need for a large trade surplus would also reduce pressure on the open market and hence would decrease the need to expand the growth of the domestic debt at such a rapid rate. Such a result would do much, in turn, to eliminate the fundamental incompatibility that currently exists between external and domestic adjustment, and it would free up additional resources for productive purposes at lower cost to borrowers and facilitate the implementation of more consistent, growth-oriented economic policies.

CHAPTER II

AN OVERVIEW OF SAVINGS, INVESTMENT, AND GROWTH FROM THE POSTWAR PERIOD TO THE FIRST OIL SHOCK

Introduction

This study analyzes Brazil's economic response to the 1982 debt crisis, primarily in terms of the effects on savings, investment, and growth. This crisis was a long time in the making. Many of responses observed since 1982 have been strongly influenced by the nation's pre-existing institutional setting, chronic inflationary problems, and heavy reliance upon import substitution industrialization policies—all of which had their origins in earlier periods. The import substitution strategy, which received its initial impetus during the 1930s in the wake of depressed foreign exchange earnings from the coffee sector, was particularly important. In Brazil's case, this strategy was characterized by erection of high tariff barriers, use of foreign exchange controls, rising government outlays in physical and social infrastructure, direct government investment in basic industry, special incentives for foreign investors, and the creation of various nonbank financial intermediaries.

These policies provided a considerable stimulus to investment during most of the postwar period. As shown in Graph II–1, for example, the ratio of investment to current GDP rose steadily from a 13 percent average in the 1947–50 period to 23.3 percent in the 1962–66 period (See also Statistical Appendix, Tables 1 and 2). The required increase in savings was generated primarily by the private sector, which responded strongly to fiscal and credit incentives in order to take full advantage of the large and highly sheltered domestic market. The private sector also transferred resources to the general government, because the latter's current savings were usually insufficient to finance its growing capital outlays, especially after the mid–1950s. Finally,

Brazil made only modest use of external savings, which averaged less than 1 percent of GDP through the mid–1960s. The importance of external savings is easily underestimated, however, since they provided key inputs and technologies needed for industrialization, especially capital goods, and in critical subperiods they served also to offset declines in savings by the private sector.[2]

The steady increase in capital formation associated with the nation's import substitution policies also exerted a positive effect on economic growth. Real GDP, for instance, expanded at a 6 percent average annual rate in the 1948–67 period, high in terms of most international comparisons over the same period. Not surprisingly, the most rapid growth was achieved by industry, which grew by rates averaging 9.4 percent through 1962 and by almost 8 percent for the entire 1948–67 period. Growth in the agricultural sector, in contrast, was markedly lower—averaging only 4.5 percent in the 1948–67 period—as a consequence of unfavorable pricing and exchange rate policies, insufficient credit, and inadequate incentives for modernizing agricultural production techniques to achieve higher productivity.

Despite the high national economic growth, important distortions were developing throughout the 1950s, that interacted to depress output in subsequent years. Thus, after expanding at a 10 percent average from 1960 to 1961, real GDP slowed to rates of only 3.2 percent in the 1962–64 period. In part, the generalized decline in economic activity reflected the cumulative effects of pursuing import substitution "at whatever cost".[3] In particular, as the initial phase of import substitution drew to a close during the late 1950s, the economic consequences of such policies and of the misallocation of investment resources began to emerge. For some inefficient and high-cost industries to continue operations, for instance, additional tariff protection and subsidies were required. At the same time, the nation's industrialization process also contributed to a weakening in the balance of payments, since the net foreign exchange savings from substituted imports was often less than what had been anticipated, while, simultaneously, interest payments and profit remittances increased steadily. These problems were exacerbated by the protracted decline in the terms of trade and the continual overvaluation of the cruzeiro throughout the postwar era, which stimulated imports of capital and intermediate goods, but strongly hampered export growth and diversification.

The economic stagnation and ensuing political turmoil of the early 1960s were also accompanied by an increasingly serious inflation problem. Measured by the general price index, prices accelerated from a 16 percent average rate of increase in the 1950–55 period to 28.9 percent in the 1956–61 period and to 64.8 percent in the 1962–65 period. Several factors contributed to this result. First, the stagnation of fiscal revenues, combined with rising current expenditures, reduced government current savings from around a 2.5 percent average of GDP in the 1947–60 period to only 0.5 percent in the 1961–64

---

[2]A thorough analysis of Brazil's early import substitution industrialization process and its financing is provided in Werner Baer, *Industrialization and Economic Development in Brazil*; (Homewood, Ill: Richard D. Irwin, Inc., 1965).

[3]Mario Henrique Simonsen, *Brasil 2001* (Rio de Janeiro: APEC Editora, 1969), p. 42.

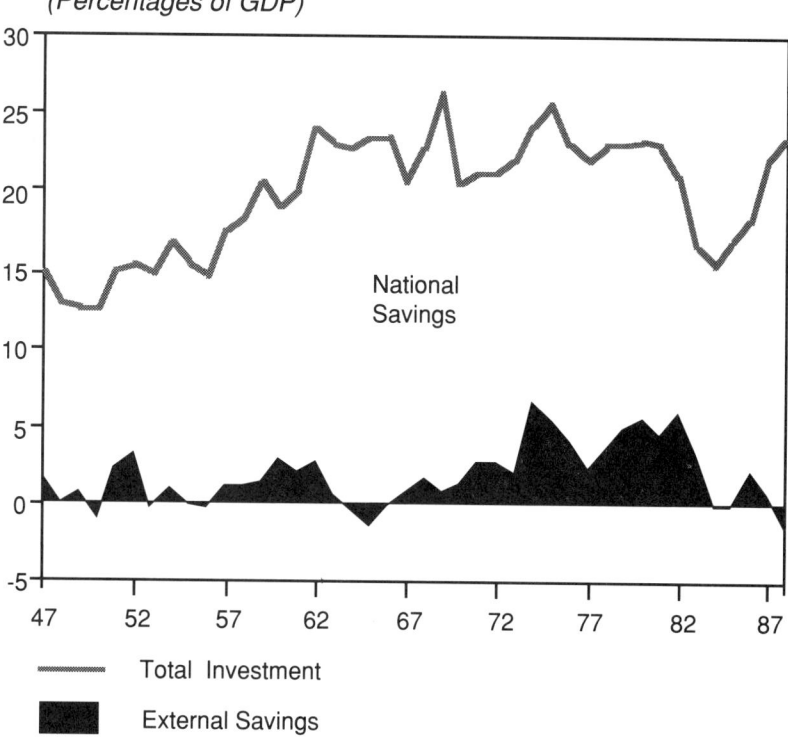

Graph II-1. BRAZIL. Savings and Investment
(Percentages of GDP)

- Total Investment
- External Savings

Source : Country Studies Division, based on Statistical Appendix, Table 2.

period; the reduction in savings in turn triggered an acceleration in the already substantial growth rate of domestic credit and, ultimately, the money supply. This was especially the case since government capital expenditures rose strongly after the mid-1950s, in part because of the construction of Brasilia and numerous other public sector investments. At the same time, officially dictated increases in nominal wages—often far in excess of productivity gains—contributed both to the price spiral and to the disarray in the business sector, where the profitability of even the most efficiently operated enterprises was affected.

Despite the stagnation of output, investment remained at surprisingly high levels during the difficult 1961–64 period, averaging 22.4 percent of current GDP. The high inflation rates, however, aggravated existing distortions in the pattern of private sector investments, since many of the outlays made in this period were directed toward speculative rather than productive purposes. Likewise, investment lagged in key sectors such as housing and basic services, owing partially to government policies that limited adjustments in rents and public utility tariffs. Finally, to maintain capital formation at such high levels, gross domestic savings had to increase significantly to compensate for the virtual disappearance of external savings in the early 1960s (Statistical Appendix, Table 2). The rise in domestic savings was accomplished primarily by the inflationary process and its impact on real wages, which in turn led to a drop in private consumption, from 81 percent of GDP in 1960 to only 76.5 percent by 1964.

By March 1964, with inflation rising at an annualized rate of 144 percent, many analysts believed that Brazil's traditionally "high tolerance" to inflation had reached its limits.[4] This was especially the case, since, in addition to the inflationary surge, the nation was also experiencing falling output in many sectors and a rising capital flight problem.

Brazil's Economic Performance in 1964–74

The government that assumed power in March 1964 adopted a variety of stabilization and reform measures to alleviate the nation's deteriorating economic situation. The immediate impact of these policies was to worsen an already serious recessionary environment, but they also lowered the rate of inflation and provided the basis for reestablishing rapid economic growth. Consequently, Brazil was able to achieve and sustain one of the highest rates of growth recorded by any developing nation in the era following World War II, as real GDP accelerated from a 3.9 percent average annual growth rate in the 1964–67 period, to a 10.5 percent pace in the 1968–74 period, expanding in per capita terms by more than 8 percent. Substantial gains were registered in real manufacturing value added, which rose by more than 120 percent during the period, and in the dollar value of exports, which increased 446 percent, including almost a doubling in the 1972–74 period. This extremely rapid growth produced a substantial broadening of Brazil's productive base and basic economic infrastructure. As a result, Brazil's share in total Latin American GDP (measured in 1988 dollars) increased from 25.9 percent in 1960 to more than 31 percent by 1974.

Brazil's economic performance in this period was stimulated not only by the implementation of conventional monetary and fiscal stabilization measures but also by the systematic adoption of a wide range of innovative and major economic reforms. Among other objectives, these measures were designed to exploit the buoyant demand for Brazilian exports in world markets, to utilize existing industrial capacity more efficiently, and, especially, to achieve a higher savings rate.

The government's concern with savings was fully justified. In the first instance, agreement existed that the decline of government savings had con-

---

[4]The same views were echoed throughout the 1980s, as inflation, measured by the general price index, escalated from a 98 percent average in the 1980–82 period to 1,000 percent in 1988 and to around 1,780 percent in 1989.

tributed measurably to the intensification of inflation during the early 1960s—a fact that pointed to the need for a sweeping tax reform and rationalization of expenditure policies as basic elements of any recovery program. In a broader sense, however, the economic deterioration also reflected fundamental shortcomings in the nation's financial sector, particularly its inability to mobilize sufficient noninflationary resources to sustain economic development. Institutionally, major deficiencies of the financial sector were readily apparent from even a cursory examination of the sector's structure and operations. In 1964, for example, Brazil's financial system consisted of 336 commercial banks, nearly 150 insurance companies, 26 savings banks, and 134 finance companies. Nine stock exchanges also existed, of which only those of Rio de Janeiro and São Paulo were of economic importance. The finance companies provided high-cost working capital loans to firms and issued short-maturity bills, or letras de cambio, to depositors. The commercial banks were generally small and inefficient, and as inflation intensified after 1960, they were forced to rely almost exclusively upon sight deposits for funds.

By 1964, virtually all sources of long-term development financing had dried up. The severity of the situation was indicated by the decline of the financial interrelationships ratio (that is, the ratio of financial sector assets to national wealth), which provides a widely used measure of the sophistication and depth of a nation's financial superstructure and, hence, of its capacity to mobilize financial savings.[5] In Brazil's case, this ratio had declined to 0.25 percent by 1964, down from already meager levels of 0.40 percent in 1955 and 0.48 percent in 1945, or to levels generally encountered only in the most underdeveloped nations.[6]

Toward correcting these problems, the comprehensive Capital Markets Law (Lei no. 4728) was adopted in July 1965. One major objective of the law was to enhance the ability of the nation's recently created central bank to function as an effective monetary authority, especially in the formulation and execution of monetary policy, and in the regulation of both bank and nonbank financial intermediaries. A second objective of the law was to foster the development of the stock market as a means of increasing the flow of equity finance to businesses in order to alleviate the high levels of indebtedness that confronted many firms in the early 1960s and, additionally, to promote a broader-based distribution of business ownership. In this respect, the Capital

---

[5]Numerous empirical studies have revealed that a basic feature of a nation's financial development is the changing relationship between the size of its financial sector (usually measured by assets) and wealth or GDP. Specifically, during periods of sustained growth, a nation's total stock of financial assets tends to expand more rapidly than wealth (that is, the financial interrelationship ratio rises). It should be clarified, however, that studies of financial development have not been able to determine the direction of causality, that is, if financial deepening must occur before development takes places or vice versa. About all that can be concluded is that a highly positive correlation exists between financial and real development and that the former typically occurs at a more rapid rate than the latter. Perhaps the most comprehensive study on this subject to date is that of Raymond W. Goldsmith, *Financial Structure and Deveolopment* (New Haven: Yale University Press, 1969).

[6]Raymond W. Goldsmith, *Brasil, 1850–1984: Desenvolvimento Financeiro Sob Um Século de Inflação* (São Paulo: Editôra Harper & Rowe do Brasil, 1986), pp. 319 and 325.

Table II-1 BRAZIL. Structure of Principal Fixed-Yield Financial Assets of the Public and Shares of Current GDP in Selected Years
(percentages)

	1964	1968	Average 1969–71	Average 1972–74	1976
I. Composition of Voluntary Fixed Yield Assets					
A. Monetary Assets	91.1	64.3	53.3	42.7	35.6
1. Currency	24.4	12.3	10.1	7.3	6.6
2. Demand Deposits	69.7	52.0	43.2	35.4	29.1
B. Non-Monetary Assets	8.9	35.7	46.7	57.3	64.3
1. Savings Accounts	—	1.0	3.3	7.7	15.3
2. Time Deposits	1.8	4.4	7.8	11.5	10.6
3. Acceptances	3.6	13.8	14.4	15.8	10.8
4. Housing Bonds	—	2.0	3.1	3.1	1.4
5. Government and State Securities	1.8	13.3	17.0	18.5	25.6
6. Others	1.7	1.2	1.0	0.7	0.6
C. Total (A + B)	100.0	100.0	100.0	100.0	100.0
II. Composition of Compulsory Non-Monetary Assets					
1. Job Tenure Guarantee Fund (FGTS)	—	100.0	97.5	71.0	57.0
2. Social Integration Fund (PIS)	—	—	1.5	16.4	28.0
3. Public Workers' Fund (PASEP)	—	—	1.0	12.6	15.0
Total	—	100.0	100.0	100.0	100.0
III. Percentages of Current GDP					
A. Monetary Assets (I-A)/GDP	19.4	17.3	17.0	17.9	15.9
B. Total Fixed Yield Non-Monetary Assets/GDP	1.9	11.2	17.1	29.7	37.6
1. Voluntary Assets (I-B)/GDP	1.9	9.6	14.2	23.8	(28.7)
2. Compulsory Assets (II)/GDP	—	1.6	2.9	5.9	(8.9)
C. Total Assets (I + II)/GDP	21.3	28.4	34.1	47.6	53.5

Source: IDB Country Studies Division, based on various Central Bank annual reports.

Markets Law required, among other things, fuller financial disclosure by firms,[7] protection of the rights of minority stockholders, simplification of stock issue and trading procedures, and the authorization of investment banks to undertake underwriting functions.

In the mid–1960s, the authorities also initiated several important forced-savings schemes. The first and most important was the Job Tenure Guarantee Fund (FGTS), established in 1966 primarily as an unemployment fund held by the National Housing Bank (BNH) and financed by payroll tax of 8 percent. The BNH, in turn, functioned as a central bank for Brazil's Housing Finance System (SFH), a group of specialized nonbank intermediaries established to provide loans for housing and related social infrastructure.

In 1970, two additional compulsory-savings programs were created with the stated objective of accelerating the transfer of the fruits of Brazil's rapid growth in that period to workers. The first was the Social Integration Program (PIS), which required employers to contribute a percentage of their gross sales (starting at 0.15 percent in 1971 and rising to 0.75 percent by 1976) and

---

[7]This measure also contributed to the impressive growth of tax collections in the second half of the 1960s.

5 percent of their income tax liabilities into a fund to be administered by the Federal Savings Bank (CEF); resources from the fund were credited to workers accounts and could be withdrawn for stipulated purposes such as disability and purchase of housing. A similar fund was established for public sector employees (Public Sector Workers' Patrimony Program, or PASEP). At present, most of the jointly administered PIS-PASEP funds are applied in the form of long-term development loans by the National Economic and Social Development Bank (BNDES). Since the 1960s, the BNDES has functioned as Brazil's largest development finance intermediary.

The institutional improvements initiated by the Capital Markets Law, coupled with the creation of new types of non-monetary assets and measures to achieve a real positive interest rate structure, produced impressive results. As shown in Table II–1, total financial system assets grew rapidly, up more than two and one-half times, from 21.3 percent of GDP in 1964 to 53.4 percent by 1976. Moreover, this increase was overwhelmingly in the form of non-monetary as opposed to monetary assets. This fact supports the hypothesis that a significant deepening of Brazil's financial sector occurred after the mid-1960s, thereby enhancing—in principle, at least—the nation's capacity to mobilize domestic funds for investment.

For purposes of analyzing Brazil's difficulties in increasing domestic savings during the 1980s, however, the key point is that much of this rapid growth of financial assets after 1964 was made possible by the progressively more widespread application of monetary correction to the nominal values of savings instruments; in particular, given the chronically high rates of inflation in Brazil, this indexation process was viewed as necessary not only to attract long-term sources of financial savings but also to prevent distortions in relative prices.[8] Within the financial sector, essentially two variants of indexing emerged. For short-term assets with relatively high liquidity, such as certificates of deposit, bills of exchange, and time deposits, ex ante monetary correction was applied. For instruments with longer maturities, such as Treasury Bonds (ORTNs), ex post correction evolved in order to compensate investors for higher risks resulting from the inability to project inflation.[9] Simultaneously, the spread of monetary correction after the mid-1960s directly influenced the evolution of other financial assets, such as consumer acceptances and time deposits, which, although not indexed until 1972, nevertheless registered sharp increases in nominal yields in order to remain competitive. These spillover effects appear to have been important throughout the financial sector in mobilizing additional savings, particularly in those areas where indexation was not practical or where it was resisted on other grounds.

---

[8]With the wisdom of hindsight, it can be argued that instead of stimulating financial savings, the practical effect of indexation, especially after 1973, has been to increase greatly the economy's capacity to tolerate inflation. This point is examined in detail in Chapter V.

[9]Initially, most ex post instruments were tied to the wholesale price index and other inflation indicators published by the Getulio Vargas Foundation. A good overview of the spread of monetary correction is presented in Carlos Langoni, *A Economia de Transformação*, Coleção Brasil em Questão (Rio de Janeiro: 1975).

Table II-2 BRAZIL. Savings and Investment Indicators
(Percentages of GDP)

	1947–59	1960–64	1965–67	1968–74	1975–81	Adjustment Period 1982–1988
Total Investment/Savings	15.3	21.7	22.5	22.6	23.3	19.1
External Savings	0.8	1.6	−0.2	2.4	4.9	1.0
National Savings	14.5	20.1	22.7	20.2	18.4	18.1
General Government	2.5	0.9	3.2	5.5	1.5	−7.4
Private Sector[1]	12.1	19.2	19.5	14.7	16.9	25.5

[1]Businesses and households.
Source: IDB Country Studies Division, based on Statistical Appendix, Table 1.

Although a detailed examination of indexation and of its effects on the financial sector is beyond the scope of the present study, some analysis is nevertheless in order. The consequences of indexation are central to understanding the increasingly complex interrelationship between inflation control and the huge increases in the domestic debt that have been observed since the onset of the debt crisis and that have greatly complicated efforts to increase economic savings. A useful starting point for this analysis is Table II–2, which displays savings components expressed as percentages of GDP for different subperiods. The most striking feature of the table is that total savings remained consistently high from 1968 through 1982, averaging around 23 percent of GDP, suggesting, at first glance, that monetary correction was perhaps positively associated with the high savings rates of this period. Further inspection, however, indicates that important new trends were emerging in the composition of savings.

In the first instance, the table reveals that Brazil's traditionally limited use of external savings was reversed after 1967. In particular, after averaging −0.2 percent of GDP in the 1965–67 period, the nation's use of external savings jumped to a 2.4 percent average in the 1968–74 period and to 4.9 percent in the 1975–81 period.[10] A second fact derived from table is that the general government's current savings improved dramatically to a 5.5 percent average of GDP in the 1968–74 period, well above the 0.9 percent levels registered in the early 1960s. This improvement was attributable to the introduction of far-reaching fiscal reforms after 1964, which resulted not only in significant revenue increases but also in significantly tightened tax administration. Taken together, in fact, the hike in external and general government savings during the 1968–74 period more than offset a 4.8 percentage point decline in private sector savings with respect to the 1965–67 period.

Notwithstanding the fact that external and general government savings increased significantly in relation to GDP during the 1964–74 period, the reasons why private savings dropped so much in relative terms seem somewhat perplexing, since, as was displayed in Table II–1, a substantial increase in

---

[10]The reasons for the increased use of external savings are examined in detail in the following chapter.

financial savings occurred during these years. In fact, a reasonable expectation for this period would be that financial savings (as measured by the growth of financial assets) and economic savings (as measured in the national income accounts) should have at least moved in the same direction (in relation to GDP), even acknowledging that a one-to-one correspondence does not exist between the two forms of savings. Perhaps the most direct explanation to this enigma is that a large proportion of the increase in financial savings appears to have been diverted for consumption outlays rather than investment in productive activities.[11] This hypothesis is supported by the fact that expansive economic policies were followed in the 1964–74 period. Private consumption, although expanding at a less rapid pace than fixed investment, nevertheless rose at a 11.9 average annual rate, or equal to GDP growth over the same period.

Another conclusion that can be drawn from the preceding analysis is that the introduction of indexation procedures in itself did not appear to exert a strongly positive or negative effect on investment and savings, at least through the first oil price shock, and for several different reasons. First, during the 1968–74 period indexation was partial and had not become fully integrated into Brazil's economic fabric; hence, the problem of transferring past inflation to the present via monetary correction (that is, inertial inflation) had yet to become the fully automatic and generalized phenomenon that was later the norm.[12] Second, and of particular importance, inflationary expectations were steadily declining throughout the 1968–74 period, at least until the last year of the period. The primary reason for this decline was the substantial improvement in government finances, which, as indicated, greatly reduced one of the principal sources of disequilibrium that had existed in the Brazilian economy. After 1980, however, this situation changed significantly, and government savings declined.

The reasons for this shift in trend will be examined in detail in subsequent chapters, but it can already be anticipated that, whatever policies the authorities decide to adopt, reduction of general government dissavings from their current levels (−7.4 percent of GDP in the 1982–88 period) must be a central objective for any sustained recovery in investment and for renewed economic growth.

Finally, the hike in the savings ratio was translated into a rapid expansion of productive capacity, as real fixed investment, after rising at an average annual rate of 6.7 percent in the 1961–67 period (to 20.6 percent of GDP), jumped to a 15.5 percent annual growth rate in the 1968–74 period (25.4 percent of GDP). Moreover, fixed investment increasingly occurred in the form of outlays for machinery and equipment; the combined share of these two categories in total investment rose from about 40 percent during the 1960s

---

[11]By definition, some diversion of financial savings to consumption inevitably occurs, and Brazil was no exception. See Paulo de Tarso Medeiros, "Poupança e Poupança Financiera", *Conjuntura Econômica*, Vol. 39, No. 7, julho 1985.

[12]Werner Baer, *The Brazilian Economy: Growth and Development* (New York: Praeger, Third Edition, 1989).

to approximately 60 percent by 1974. These large investment expenditures were directed essentially toward the following: hydroelectric development; basic physical and social infrastructure, including housing and education; and massive private and mixed-government outlays in manufacturing, especially for steel, petrochemicals, and a wide range of consumer durables.

CHAPTER III

THE IMPACT OF THE DEBT CRISIS AND EXTERNAL ADJUSTMENT ON SAVINGS, INVESTMENT, AND GROWTH

The Growth and Structure of the External Debt

Trends in the 1974–81 Period

The tripling of world petroleum prices in the 1973–74 period posed a major challenge for the Brazilian authorities. The shock occurred at the peak of the nation's so-called economic miracle; not only had real GDP growth been averaging about 10 percent annually since 1968 but also inflation had remained remarkably low and stable, following the economic stabilization measures and reforms of the mid-1960s. The problem was that Brazil, prior to the oil shock, had already emerged as one of the largest petroleum-importing nations because of the combined effects of its energy-intensive rapid growth, its declining domestic oil production, and its heavy dependence upon its vast car and truck industry. This panorama was further complicated by the government's perception that economic activity needed to continue at an accelerated pace in view of the large numbers of new entrants into the labor market each year and the growing realization that previous policies, although relatively successful at maintaining overall growth at high levels, had done little to rectify a mounting income distribution problem.

Largely for these reasons, Brazil opted not to implement market-driven responses to the oil shock, such as currency devaluation and major realignments in relative prices, since such measures would have inevitably resulted in real income declines. Instead, the strategy was to transform economic structure in such a way that the dislocations posed by higher real energy costs could be minimized, without interrupting the ongoing growth process. Specifically, the authorities initiated a new phase of government-stimulated import substitution investment, which was to be supported in part by continuing the same types of incentives and tariff policies applied throughout the postwar era (Chapter II). To help finance the proposed investments, Brazil also made a deliberate decision to step up its use of external savings to supplement resources mobilized domestically. This seemed like a prudent strategy, in view of the eagerness of international bankers to recycle part of the vast supplies of funds available in the Eurocurrency markets (at low interest rates), on the one hand, and Brazil's privileged access to such markets, on the other.[13]

In many respects, Brazil's response to the oil price shock was a success. First, the growth of investment, although slowing with respect to the exceptionally rapid pace of the late 1960s and early 1970s, still averaged nearly 6 percent annually in the 1974–78 period. More importantly, fixed investment was increasingly channeled to priority areas consistent with the strategy of modifying economic structure, including the development of the nation's vast hydroelectric potential, the exploration and development of new sources of domestic petroleum, and the undertaking of various large-scale projects in mining and basic industry that not only substituted imports but also contributed to growth of export capacity (discussed later in detail). The surge in investment, coupled with the continuation of other growth-oriented policies, enabled real GDP to rise at a 7.8 percent average annual growth rate in the 1974–78 period, well above the 4.4 percent average recorded for the rest of Latin America over the same period. Moreover, solid gains were achieved in lowering the trade deficit from its unprecedented $4.7 billion level in 1974 to a $1.8 billion average over the 1975–78 period.

The positive results of the government's post-1974 economic strategy, however, were not without their negative consequences. A largely predictable outcome, for instance, was the substantial growth of the total external debt, which soared from $19.4 billion in 1974 (17.7 percent of GDP) to $53.6 billion by year-end 1978 (27 percent of GDP)—nearly a tripling in just five years (Graph III-1). At the same time, the growth in the stock of the debt was accompanied by sharply increased servicing obligations (interest plus amortization), which rose from $3.3 billion (38 percent of exports of goods and nonfactor services) in 1974 to $8.6 billion (62.3 percent of exports of goods and nonfactor services) by 1978. Finally, the government's strategy and the changing international financial markets resulted in a rising proportion of medium- and long-term (M&LT) debt being contracted at variable interest rates. Initially, the increase in variable-rate debt posed no problem for Brazil, because real international interest rates were low and even negative in some

---

[13]Eliana Cardoso, "Debt Cycles in Brazil and Argentina," paper presented at the Conference on "Financing Latin American Growth: Prospects for the 1990s," sponsored by the National Autonomous University of Mexico, Washington University, and Jerome Levy Economics Institute, Annandale on Hudson, New York, October 1988, pp. 19–20. See also Paulo Nogueira Batista, Jr., *Da Crise Internacional à Moratória Brasileira* (Rio de Janeiro: Editóra Paz e Terra S/A, 1988) and Werner Baer, *The Brazilian Economy: Growth and Development*, op. cit.

GROWTH AND STRUCTURE OF DEBT

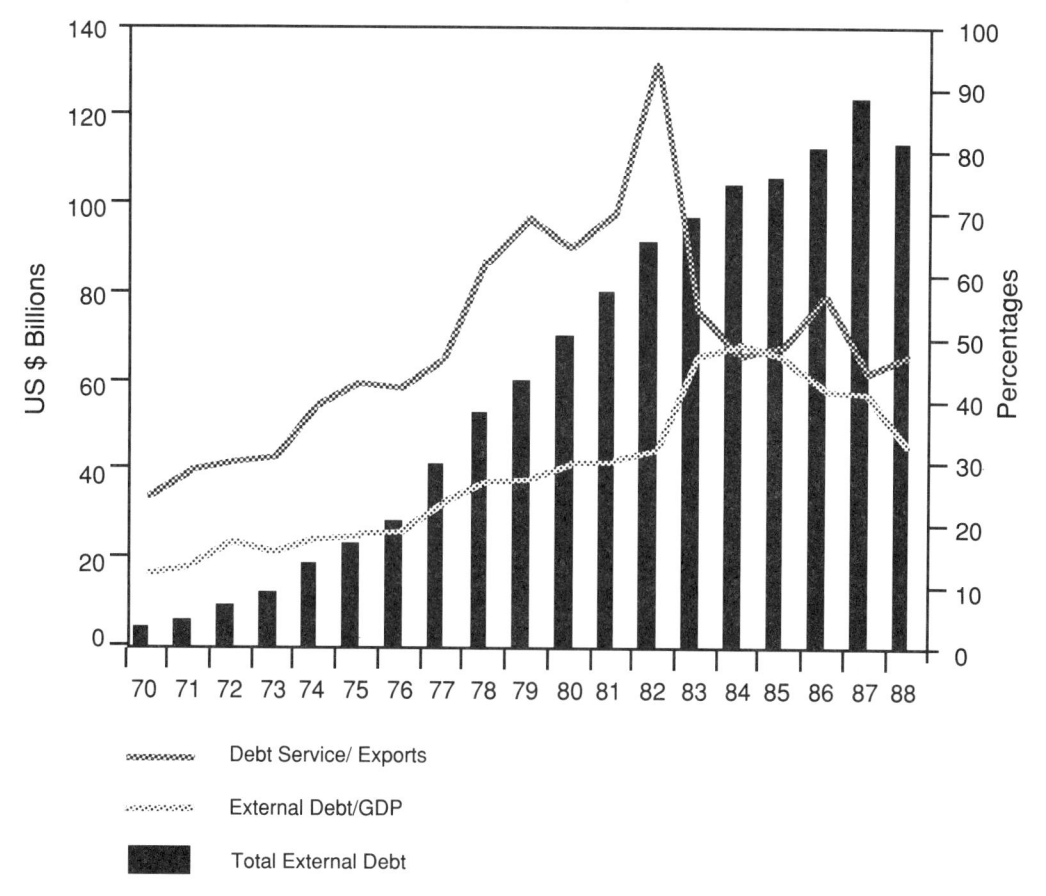

Graph III-1. BRAZIL. Total External Debt, 1970-1988

[Graph showing Total External Debt (bars), Debt Service/Exports and External Debt/GDP (lines) for Brazil from 1970 to 1988. Y-axis left: US $ Billions (0-140); Y-axis right: Percentages (0-100).]

Source: IDB Country Studies Division based on the Statistical Appendix, Table 6

years (Statistical Appendix, Table 5). Despite this, it was clear by 1978 that, given the level of Brazil's debt and the rising share of servicing requirements tied to variable rates, the nation's external accounts were in a potentially vulnerable position.

This vulnerability manifested itself in the 1979–81 period, when Brazil's external debt continued to expand at an accelerated pace, but in the context of a deteriorating economic environment. Confronted with a gradual slowdown in the growth of exports, rising oil prices, and, especially, steep increases in international interest rates, Brazil began to experience increasing difficulties in meeting its debt-servicing requirements. As displayed in Table III-1, the nation's interest and amortization obligations totaled $17.8 billion by 1981,

Table III-1 BRAZIL. External Debt Indicators, 1978–1988

	1978	1979	1980	1981	1982	1983	1984	1985	1986	1987	1988*
I. *Disbursed External Debt* (US$ Millions)	53,614	60,419	70,565	80,373	91,916	97,488	104,708	106,473	112,767	123,962	114,000
A. Long-Term	46,546	51,785	57,039	65,052	73,921	80,636	89,241	90,848	98,991	106,086	—
Public	30,394	35,921	40,434	45,260	50,797	59,124	69,937	73,671	84,349	91,652	—
Private	16,152	15,864	16,605	19,792	23,124	21,512	19,304	17,177	14,641	14,434	—
B. Short-Term	7,068	8,634	13,526	15,321	17,451	14,204	11,500	11,017	9,286	13,868	9,900
II. *Total Debt Service* (US$ Millions)	8,606	11,598	14,118	17,854	20,641	12,872	13,598	13,398	13,754	12,424	18,032
A. Interest	3,334	5,261	7,460	10,359	12,562	10,260	11,463	11,123	10,054	9,319	10,591
B. Amortization	5,272	6,337	6,658	7,495	8,079	2,612	2,135	2,275	3,700	3,105	7,441
III. *Relationships* (Percentages)											
Interest Payments/Exports	24.1	31.4	34.1	40.4	57.1	43.4	39.5	40.3	41.4	33.2	29.5
Total Debt Service/Exports	62.3	69.3	64.5	69.7	98.5	54.4	46.9	49.8	56.2	44.2	49.0
Total Debt Service + Petroleum/Exports	92.7	107.8	109.4	112.6	139.8	88.9	70.4	69.4	68.1	58.3	58.9
Debt/Exports	388.1	361.2	322.2	313.6	417.6	412.1	361.0	385.3	462.9	441.4	317.3
Debt/GDP	26.8	27.2	30.0	30.0	32.3	47.2	49.1	46.7	41.7	40.9	32.2

*Preliminary.
Source: World Bank, Central Bank of Brazil, and IDB Country Studies Division.

a doubling in only four years, while the debt service ratio reached nearly 70 percent. With oil imports absorbing some 43 percent of export earnings, and in the absence of sustained measures to slow the growth of aggregate demand, the result was a rapid increase in the level of the external debt. Thus, Brazil's M&LT external debt reached $65.1 billion by 1981, the largest of any developing nation; moreover, about 95 percent of the net increment in the M&LT debt in the 1979–81 period was at variable interest rates, a fact that exacerbated the debt-servicing problem.

The remaining portion of the increase in Brazil's total outstanding and disbursed debt in the period being analyzed was accounted for by the burgeoning short-term debt. In particular, the nation began to make growing use of short-term financing mobilized in the interbank markets by foreign branches of Brazilian commercial banks, especially the Bank of Brazil. Such resources were traditionally used to finance exports and were therefore quickly self-liquidating, but it is clear that by the early 1980s some of these funds were being re-lent to private and public entities at longer maturities and at significant spreads over the London Interbank Offer Rate (LIBOR). Available estimates indicate that such liabilities had reached $15.1 billion in 1981 and, when added to the nation's M&LT debt, pushed the total disbursed debt to $80.4 billion by year-end 1981.

The 1982 External Debt Crisis

Faced by the increasingly severe external sector constraint and an unacceptable growth in the price level, the authorities adopted restrictive monetary policies in late 1980 and 1981. These measures succeeded in dampening demand, especially in 1982, but they did not improve the current account, largely because the anti-inflationary policies adopted by the United States caused Brazil's net interest payments (and those of most other non-oil LDCs as well) to soar, while precipitating a severe contraction in world trade. Consequently, in the first half of 1982 the current account deficit increased from its 1979–81 average of nearly $12 billion to an annualized rate of $15.5 billion; at the same time, new borrowings from private commercial banks began to diminish and were sufficient to cover only 35 percent of the deficit, despite Brazil's willingness to accept average spreads of around 2.25 points over LIBOR.

Brazil's access to international capital became further restricted during the third quarter of 1982, in the wake of the debt-servicing crisis in Mexico and Argentina. By early December, in the face of the deteriorating financial environment, bankers had cut back sharply on new lending as Brazil edged increasingly close to the need to restructure the servicing of its external debt. In addition to initiating negotiations for an Extended Fund Facility Arrangement with the International Monetary Fund (IMF), the nation resorted to a variety of measures to secure foreign funds, including the following: obtaining short-term bridge loans; making additional drawings on its already meager holdings of international reserves; using nearly all the Bank of Brazil's cash deposits, which were normally used to finance trade operations; and pledging its holdings of monetary gold.

Table III-2. BRAZIL. Balance of Payments, 1978-1988
(millions of dollars)

	1978	1979	1980	1981	1982	1983	1984	1985	1986	1987	1988*
Net External Borrowing	12,217	6,805	10,146	9,808	11,543	5,572	7,220	1,765	6,294	11,195	-9,962
Long-Term	11,140	5,239	5,254	8,013	8,869	6,715	8,605	1,607	8,143	7,096	n.a.
Public and Public Guaranteed	7,994	5,527	4,513	4,826	5,537	8,326	10,813	3,735	10,678	7,303	n.a.
Private	3,146	-288	741	3,867	3,332	-1,611	-2,208	-2,128	-2,535	-207	n.a.
International Monetary Fund (IMF)	(—)	(—)	(—)	(—)	544	2,104	1,319	641	-118	-483	n.a.
Short-Term	1,077	1,566	4,892	1,795	2,130	-3,247	-2,704	-483	-1,731	4,582	-3,968
Direct Investment	1,876	2,220	1,542	2,317	2,550	1,374	1,554	1,282	333	500	2,185
Other Capital Flows	-2,802	-2,691	-2,008	705	-2,639	-1,401	-3,824	-2,736	-4,891	-9,275	5,780
Errors and Omissions	299	1,225	-351	-392	-379	-620	406	-498	-530	289	-722
Net Changes in Foreign Reserves	-4,558	2,907	3,462	-674	5,255	1,873	-5,410	523	3,185	-1,270	-2,100
(Balance on Current Account)	(-7,031)	(-10,465)	(-12,793)	(-11,763)	(-16,332)	(-6,797)	(-53)	(-337)	(-4,391)	(-1,439)	(-4,819)
Transfers (Net)	71	18	168	197	-8	108	171	155	87	100	90
Net Disposable Flows	7,103	10,484	12,960	11,957	16,324	6,905	118	492	4,478	1,539	4,747
Balance of Factor Payments	-4,232	-5,459	-7,032	-10,325	-13,521	-10,997	-11,482	-11,208	-10,970	-10,450	-11,361
(Of Which: Interest Payments on External Debt)	(-3,334)	(-5,261)	(-7,460)	(-10,359)	(-12,562)	(-10,259)	(-11,464)	(-11,124)	(-10,072)	(-9,319)	(-10,591)
Balance of Trade	-2,871	-5,025	-5,928	-1,632	-2,803	4,092	11,364	10,716	6,312	8,911	16,108
Nonfactor Services	-1,715	-2,318	-3,117	-2,877	-3,592	-2,394	-1,750	-1,696	-2,128	-2,250	-2,992
Merchandise (FOB)	-1,156	-2,707	-2,811	1,242	789	6,486	13,114	12,412	8,440	11,161	19,100
Exports of Goods	12,450	15,235	20,140	23,342	20,189	21,923	27,050	25,539	22,451	26,213	33,784
Imports of Goods	13,606	17,942	22,951	22,100	19,400	15,437	13,936	13,127	14,011	15,052	14,684
Memorandum Item: LIBOR	9.2	12.1	14.0	16.6	13.5	9.8	11.2	8.2	6.5	7.2	7.9

*Preliminary.
n.a. Not available.
Source: IMF Balance of Payments Tapes; Central Bank of Brazil; and IDB Country Studies Division.

These extraordinary initiatives did mobilize sufficient resources for financing the 1982 current account deficit, but they also made Brazil's external debt situation untenable, as evidenced in part by the fact that the nation was forced to obtain $3.2 billion of the total $8.9 billion increase in M&LT debt in the form of loans without public guarantee—a substantially higher percentage than in most previous years. This increase, coupled with a $2.1 billion increment in short-term obligations, caused the total foreign debt to reach $91.9 billion. Consequently, the debt service ratio jumped nearly 29 percentage points to 98.5 percent, the highest level in Brazil's history. More importantly, the sudden contraction in the supply of external credit clearly dictated the need for fundamental adjustments in the nation's economy, not only in terms of easing the constraints on the external sector but also in terms of effecting concomitant adjustments in the domestic sectors as well.

The Balance of Payments and the External Adjustment Process through 1985

The Restrictions Imposed on the Balance of Payments by the 1982 Debt Crisis

The mounting restrictions imposed on Brazil's external payments situation after mid-1982 can be conveniently analyzed in the context of a modified balance of payments format such as that presented in Table III-2. This format compares net disposable flows (that is, net foreign borrowing; non-debt-creating flows such as direct foreign investment and unrequited transfers; use of reserves; other capital flows; and errors and omissions) with claims on these flows (such as interest payments and other items in the service accounts). The trade accounts are presented as a residual or balancing item for the following two reasons. First, the trade balance can act either as a claim on disposable resource flows in the event of a deficit or as a financing item in the event of a trade surplus. More fundamentally, however, because interest payments are essentially given, any adjustment to an exogenously induced change in total disposable flows, such as that of 1982, must essentially be accommodated through a change in the trade balance, particularly imports for which the greatest hope for short-term adjustment exists.

With this framework in mind, much useful information can be derived from Table III-2. For instance, 1978 is significant in that it was the last year of low international interest rates, and given the large number of capital-intensive public investments in various stages of completion, net foreign borrowing exceeded $12 billion, the highest level in Brazil's history; this amount not only covered the services deficit of $5.9 billion and trade deficit of $1.2 billion but was also sufficient to permit a $4.6 billion accumulation of net international reserves. By year-end 1978, net reserves totaled a record $11.8 billion, equivalent to more than ten months of imports.

In the 1979–81 period, however, the balance of payments situation changed in a number of significant respects. First, the services deficit more than doubled to $13.2 billion (with respect to 1978) in the aftermath of unparalleled increases in LIBOR and the U.S. prime rate. Second, the trade balance also deteriorated in this period, especially in the 1979–80 period, primarily because of the second oil price shock, which caused the oil bill to rise from only $4.2 billion in 1978 (31 percent of total imports) to $11 billion by 1981 (50 percent of the total), despite intensified efforts at energy conservation. Finally, to meet these increased claims, net disposable flows nearly doubled with respect to 1978 to an annual average of $11.8 billion in the 1979–81 period. To a considerable extent, however, these funds were generated not only by continued disbursements from M&LT debt as had been the pattern during the 1970s but also by large drawdowns of accumulated reserves—$6.4 billion in the 1979–80 period alone—and increased resort to short-term indebtedness.

The adverse tendencies of the 1979–81 period were greatly accentuated in 1982. Again, the principal problem was caused by the service imbalance, which increased by $3.1 billion to a total of $16.3 billion. Much of this growth was accounted for by net interest payments, which reached $12.6 billion and had become—by far—the most important deficit item in the balance of payments and in the growth of the external debt. This development constituted a total departure from the rationale of external borrowing, since the nation's external obligations were increasingly contributing to claims on future output, but without expanding productive capacity. In the same fashion, the onus posed by debt servicing also progressively reduced the scope for economic policy formulation, since a significant portion of the debits in the balance of payments had become essentially a fixed burden and, therefore, independent from the level of economic activity.[14]

At the same time, exports, which had performed remarkably well in the preceding years despite a fall of almost 50 percent in the terms of trade between 1977 and 1981, declined 13.5 percent in 1982 as earnings were affected by plummeting prices for primary commodities, the appreciation of the cruzeiro, the widening international recession, and rising currents of protectionism in both developed and developing nations. Imports also declined more than 12 percent, in response not only to controls and the low level of economic activity but also to lower petroleum prices and rising domestic oil production. As a result of these trends, Brazil was able to achieve a trade surplus of only $789 million, more than a third lower than in 1981 and far below the $3 billion target established in early 1982. More importantly, this surplus was extremely low in relation to the services deficit. Thus, to generate the $16.3 billion in disposable flows required to cover the current account deficit, the nation undertook a number of extraordinary measures: in addition to new net borrowing of $11.5 billion ($2.1 billion of which was short term), the nation experienced a massive $5.3 billion loss of reserves as net foreign reserves fell to only $899 million. At the same time, Brazil was forced to obtain nearly $4.3 billion in short-term bridge financing, including $544 million from the IMF, $500 million from the Bank for International Settlements, $876 million from the U.S. Treasury, and $2.3 billion from the commercial banks.

---

[14]IDB, *External Debt and Economic Development in Latin America* (Washington, D.C., January 1984), p. 59.

The 1983 External Sector Program and the IMF Accord and Their Combined Impact on Balance of Payments Adjustment in the 1983–85 Period

Confronted with the prospect of weak export demand and a probable shortage of loanable funds in international financial markets, the authorities began, in August 1982, to prepare a comprehensive program for 1983—with implications for subsequent years as well—that would greatly accelerate the ongoing process of economic adjustment. Among the principal components of the 1983 program were measures to cut the public sector deficit from an estimated 6 percent of GDP in 1982 to 3.5 percent in 1983, primarily through a sharp decrease in fixed investment by the state enterprises. Second, measures were adopted to eliminate gradually the interest rate subsidies granted to agriculture in recent years and to limit the growth of domestic public debt. Third, exchange rate policy was modified to ensure that the pace of minidevaluation in relation to the dollar would follow the rate of domestic inflation. Fourth, efforts were to be redoubled to increase domestic production of oil and oil substitutes such as alcohol; the authorities also reaffirmed the previous policy of increasing the prices of oil products at a rate above domestic inflation.

Most of the initiatives just summarized constituted part of a comprehensive external sector program designed to adjust the balance of payments in 1983. In particular, the strategy of the authorities was to slash the current account deficit to $6.9 billion, less than half the level of the preceding year, primarily by obtaining an unprecedented $6 billion trade surplus (compared with $789 million in 1982). It was anticipated that this surplus would be achieved primarily by curtailing imports, which were projected to fall by more than 17 percent to $16 billion, their lowest level since 1978. In short, given the anticipated decline in net disposable flows, the need for a large trade surplus can be interpreted as a constraint imposed on Brazil's balance of payments by the rest of the world. The fact can be readily ascertained from the data presented in Table III-2.

To mobilize the projected external financing needed for 1983, the authorities undertook several parallel courses of action. First, an agreement was reached with the IMF in January 1983 that was to provide drawings of up to $5.9 billion through 1985. Of this total, $4.8 billion was to be made available through the Extended Fund Facility (EFF) and $1.1 billion through the Compensatory Financing Facility (CFF). It was projected that about $2.5 billion would be disbursed from both facilities in 1983. Second, fortified by anticipated IMF support of their economic program, the authorities also launched, in December 1982, a four-point initiative for obtaining additional funds and continued support from foreign banks; this was especially important since, as indicated, foreign banks accounted for nearly 80 percent of Brazil's outstanding M&LT debt. The key elements of this initiative were the following: a request for $4.4 billion in new loans; the rolling over of $4 billion in amortization payments due in 1983; the continuation of $8.8 billion in short-term trade-related debt to finance raw material imports and the prefinancing of Brazilian exports; and a request that foreign banks reestablish deposits and short-term lines of credit in foreign branches of Brazilian banks to the $9.2 billion level existing at June 30, 1982.

The tightening of economic policies imposed by the IMF agreement, coupled with strict controls over imports, strongly impacted Brazil's economic performance in 1983. On the one hand, real GDP declined 3.5 percent and, in per capita terms, living standards dropped for the third consecutive year. With respect to the external sector, however, the policies implemented in late 1982 enabled Brazil to make substantial progress in adjusting its balance of payments in 1983. As displayed in Table III-2, the nation achieved an impressive $6.5 billion trade surplus, considerably in excess of the targeted level. In part, this reflected the additional stimulus provided by a 30 percent maxidevaluation in late February, which enabled exports to increase 8.5 percent to $21.9 billion despite weak demand for manufactured goods and depressed prices for most primary commodities; most of the trade surplus, however, was attributable to imports, which plunged over 20 percent, aided by the fall in oil prices and reduced dependence on imported fuels. Moreover, a four percentage point drop in LIBOR to an average of 9.8 percent during 1983 was the principal factor contributing to a $3.4 billion reduction in the services deficit, which fell to $13.4 billion. As a consequence of these trends, the current account deficit was more than halved to $6.8 billion, more than was required to meet the IMF target.

Notwithstanding the substantial improvement in the current account, capital flows did not reach expected levels in 1983 for several reasons. First, many smaller regional banks became increasingly reluctant to renew short-term lines of credit to foreign branches of Brazilian banks. Second, capital flows were also adversely impacted by the fact that Brazil and the IMF were negotiating a revised Letter of Intent from May to November of 1983; during this period, both the IMF and the private banks suspended lending. The suspension was especially important in the case of the private banks, because it caused $3 billion in pending disbursements to be postponed from December 1983 to March 1984. As a result of all these developments, Brazil registered an overall deficit of $3.3 billion in the balance of payments, which was financed partially by an additional drawdown of net reserves and the accumulation of external payment arrears. Nevertheless, despite the sharp contraction in net disposable flows (from $16.3 billion in 1982 to only $6.9 billion in 1983), Brazil's M&LT debt rose an additional $6.7 billion to $80.6 billion, partially because of the conversion of short-term debt into medium- and long-term obligations (Table III-1).

Notwithstanding the problems in the capital account, substantial progress was made in adjusting Brazil's balance of payments during 1983. Moreover, many of the problems that hampered capital inflows in 1983 were largely resolved by year-end, when Brazil successfully negotiated, in conjunction with a revised IMF agreement, a new loan and debt-refinancing package with private banks and major creditor governments to cover the nation's external borrowing requirements for 1984 and to pay off accumulated arrears through the end of 1983. The basic elements of this package—the largest ever negotiated—included a "Paris Club" arrangement to reschedule $3.8 billion in amortization and interest payments of the Brazilian Government due in the period from August 1983 to December 1984 and $12 billion in new credits and refinancing with the private banks. The latter agreement, signed in January, 1984 after protracted negotiations with more than 800 banks, included a $6.5 billion jumbo loan and the rescheduling over a nine-year period of $5.5 billion in loans. In the current account, the principal targets established for 1984 in the revised IMF agreement were a trade surplus of $9.1 billion ($6.5 billion in 1983) and a deficit in the current account of $5.3 billion ($6.2 billion in 1983). With respect to policies, the accord called for continuation of minidevaluations at a rate in line with domestic inflation, as well as new measures to liberalize foreign trade, especially imports.

Brazil's external adjustment process continued at a rapid rate in 1984 and 1985. During 1984, improvement was especially evident in merchandise exports, which, in response to the recovery of the U.S. economy, climbed 23 percent to a record $27 billion. Most of this increase was accounted for by sales of manufactured and semimanufactured goods, which increased by more than 37 percent to about $17.9 billion. At the same time, merchandise imports declined 9.7 percent to $13.9 billion. The bulk of this decrease was attributable to outlays for oil, which dropped 13.9 percent to $6.7 billion, owing not only to the increase in domestic production but also to falling world oil prices and the widespread substitution of fuel oil by hydroelectric energy in the industrial sector.

As a consequence of these trends, Brazil recorded an unprecedented $13.1 billion trade surplus in 1984, significantly above the $9 billion target projected at the beginning of the year and double the $6.5 billion level of 1983. Moreover, the results in the trade accounts were accompanied by a reduction in the service deficit, which fell fractionally to $13.2 billion, and permitted Brazil, when net transfers are taken into account, to achieve a $53 million current account surplus. This outcome constituted a dramatic improvement when compared with the $11.6 billion average deficit of the preceding three years. Moreover, the $12 billion loan and refinancing agreement negotiated with the private banks in January 1984 was of considerable importance in normalizing capital inflows. These achievements enabled Brazil to reduce its short-term debt and substantially increase its holdings of foreign exchange. In 1984, Brazil's net international reserves reached $4.4 billion, up $5.4 billion with respect to December 1983. Finally, the total external debt (including short-term obligations) increased $7.2 billion to $104.7 billion by year-end 1984; in part, however, this increase reflected the large accumulation of reserves.

Results in the balance of payments continued for the most part to be favorable during 1985, since Brazil achieved a $12.4 billion trade surplus, only $702 million less than the previous year's record. The trade surplus was achieved despite a 5.6 percent decline in export receipts, which were adversely affected by slower economic growth and increased protectionism in the industrialized nations and by depressed prices for key primary commodities. To a large extent, however, the fall in export revenue was cushioned by a simultaneous decrease in imports, which fell 5.8 percent to $13.1 billion. Again, most of this import decline was attributable to the continued reduction in outlays for petroleum and its derivatives, which plummeted an additional

16 percent in the wake of tumbling world prices and the steady growth of domestic oil and alcohol production. Even so, the trade surplus was not sufficient to cover interest payments and nonfactor service obligations, both of which grew fractionally during the year. Including net transfers, the result of these trends was a $337 million deficit in the current account. The small size of the deficit did enable Brazil largely to avoid new net external borrowing, but the external debt rose $1.8 billion during 1985 to reach $106.5 billion by year-end. This growth in the debt, however, was exclusively the result of the devaluation of the dollar, which, from an accounting standpoint, increased the dollar equivalents of those debt obligations that had been contracted in other currencies.[15] In fact, had the dollar not fallen, Brazil's external debt would have declined in nominal terms during 1985.

The preceding analysis indicates generally that Brazil achieved impressive progress during the 1982–85 period in adjusting its balance of payments. Again, referring to Table III-2, the nation's satisfactory accommodation to the reduction in net disposable flows, primarily through the extraordinary results in its trade accounts, is clearly evidenced. Moreover, whereas the 1983 trade surplus had been achieved primarily by curtailing imports—and provoking, in the process, a deepening domestic recession—the 1984 and 1985 adjustments were more a consequence of a substantially higher level of exports which, in turn, stimulated a number of industries producing export-related or import substitution goods. In this regard, it should be noted that the cumulative 14.7 percent decline of total imports in the 1984–85 period conceals the fact that non-oil imports, which constitute more than half of the import bill, rose by more than 2 percent during the same period.

Finally, it should be emphasized that Brazil also used the 1983–85 period to good advantage for restructuring the maturity schedule of its M&LT debt. As shown in Table 6 of the Statistical Appendix, for instance, the nation was able to renegotiate 67 percent ($5.2 billion) of a total $7.72 billion in scheduled amortization payments during 1983; moreover, more than 82 percent of this amount was variable-rate debt (both with and without public guarantee) contracted from private banks under the aegis of Central Bank Resolution 63 and Law 4.131. No scheduled payments to international agencies were refinanced. In the 1984–85 period, even greater success was attained; rescheduled amortization payments totaled $14.6 billion or 80 percent of the $18.3 billion in total payments projected for the period, and almost 84 percent of this amount was variable-rate debt.

---

[15]At the end of 1985, about one-fourth of Brazil's external debt was denominated in nondollar currencies; especially important were the yen and deutsche mark, which accounted for 6.8 percent and 5.5 percent of the total, respectively.

Import Substitution Investment and Brazil's Adjustment Process

The Characteristics of Brazil's Import Substitution Policies

Given the urgency of the Latin American nations' need to adjust their balance of payments after the 1982 debt crisis, it was not surprising that most of them, in addition to intensifying efforts to stimulate exports, simultaneously renewed efforts to substitute imports. Brazil was no exception, but its experience with import substitution as part of the adjustment process differs in fundamental ways from that of other nations in the region. In particular, the following analysis suggests that the import substitution investments initiated in the wake of the first oil price shock resulted in the emergence of various industries during the 1980s that were sufficiently large not only to achieve the economies of scale and the sophistication necessary for meeting domestic requirements but large enough also to compete successfully in external markets. This link became especially important in the 1983–84 period, when the shortage of foreign exchange, weak domestic demand, and major capacity expansions presented numerous additional opportunities for substituting imports. The emphasis on substituting imports and simultaneously stimulating export growth was, in fact, essential to the continuance of production for certain manufacturing activities, at least in the short run.

As seen in the preceding chapter, import substitution constituted the cornerstone of Brazil's industrialization policies throughout the era following World War II. Even with the advent of the export boom that began in August 1968, when a policy of periodic minidevaluations was adopted, and even after allowance is made for the nation's large geographic size and population, Brazil remained a relatively closed economy. Table III-3 reveals, for instance, that the nation's import coefficient averaged 13 percent of GDP in the 1970–73 period, compared with 14.9 percent for the rest of Latin America, as many Brazilian industries eschewed competition in export markets for the safer

Table III-3 Brazil, Latin America, and the United States: Indicators of Openness
(percentages of GDP and GNP)

	Average 1970–73	Average 1974–82	1983	1984	1985	1986	1987	1988
Brazil[1]								
Exports of Goods and n.f.s.	8.2	10.1	12.3	14.2	14.1	11.7	11.9	12.9
Imports of Goods and n.f.s.	13.0	14.2	8.2	7.6	7.0	8.3	7.7	7.2
Latin America[1,2]								
Exports of Goods and n.f.s.	20.4	17.6	19.2	19.8	19.8	20.2	20.4	20.6
Imports of Goods and n.f.s.	14.9	15.6	13.2	13.6	13.2	13.3	13.7	14.7
United States[3]								
Exports of Goods and n.f.s.	7.7	10.7	10.6	10.6	10.1	10.2	11.1	12.8
Imports of Goods and n.f.s.	9.2	10.4	11.2	13.0	13.0	13.9	14.5	15.2

[1] Measured in 1988 dollars; percentages of GDP.
[2] Excludes Brazil.
[3] Measured in 1982 dollars; percentages of GNP.
Sources: IDB and U.S. *Economic Report of the President*, January 1989, pp. 310 and 311.

confines of a growing domestic market where high levels of protection were generally available. This anti-export bias is suggested by the low ratio of Brazil's exports of goods and services to GDP; in the early 1970s, this ratio hovered around 8 percent, fractionally above the ratio in the United States but less than half the average for the rest of the Latin American region.

At first glance, this situation changed little in the 1974–82 period, when existing high levels of nominal tariffs were supplemented by numerous direct import controls. At the same time, however—and in contrast to most other non-petroleum-exporting nations of the region—Brazil also initiated massive investments in the energy sector to exploit the nation's vast hydroelectric potential, to initiate a major fuel alcohol production program, and to locate and develop new sources of domestic petroleum.[16] In addition, other priority investments, supported by strong fiscal and credit incentives, were directed toward expanding the production of capital goods and basic inputs. In regard to capital goods, the objective was to substitute rapidly the nation's traditionally heavy net imports of machinery and equipment with domestic production in as many areas as possible. In regard to basic inputs, priority was focused on tapping the nation's large potential in the mining sector, where reserves were deemed sufficient not only for domestic requirements but also for creating new export capacity (Statistical Appendix, Table 7).

The accelerated pace in implementing Brazil's import substitution projects began, however, to slacken notably by late 1981, largely because of the deepening recession, the widening imbalance in the current account, and spiraling inflation, all of which obliged the authorities to cut back on capital outlays in most of the public sector. The principal exceptions were hydroelectric generation projects, especially the massive 12,600 MW Itaipú hydroelectric dam, which was nearly completed by 1981, and petroleum exploration and development, which continued at a frenzied pace (Statistical Appendix, Table 8). Further investment cuts were implemented in 1982, owing to the reductions in export earnings and in capital inflows and to the worsening inflationary environment, which made the curtailment of aggregate demand an urgent policy priority. At the same time, import restrictions were significantly tightened, primarily by means of additional prohibitions incorporated in Central Bank Resolution 851. As a consequence of those measures, the Brazilian economy became more closed than at any point after World War II, as the import ratio plummeted from its already low average of 14.2 percent in the 1974–82 period to 7.6 percent in the 1983–85 period, only 57 percent of the average for the rest of Latin America.

---

[16]The nation's investment strategy in this period was guided by the Second National Development Plan (II PND), which was adopted in late 1974.

An Evaluation of Brazil's Import Substitution Investments and Their Impact on the Balance of Payments Adjustment Process

Although a detailed evaluation of Brazil's import substitution investments transcends the scope of the present study, a brief analysis of their consequences on the balance of payments adjustment process, both in the short term and over the longer term as well, is nevertheless indicated. A useful starting point in this regard is Table III-4, which displays the nation's trade balances for capital goods and basic inputs as they evolved over the 1973–88 period, in both current and constant dollars.

In the case of capital goods, the table reveals that, in current dollar terms, imports of machinery and equipment rose rapidly in the 1973–75 period (averaging 29 percent of total imports), then stagnated through 1979 before recovering to $4.4 billion (20 percent of the total) in 1980; thereafter, they fell rapidly to a rather stable $2.4 billion average in the 1983–85 period and accounted for 16.9 percent of total imports. Although much of the decline in this period—especially in the 1983–84 period—was attributable to recession, the fact remains that previous investments in this area contributed to a significant growth of installed capacity. For instance, in the 1973–87 period, when real GDP expanded by a total of 116.3 percent, capital goods imports, measured in constant dollars (Table III-4), plummeted over 56 percent. The impact of capacity growth was even more dramatic in the case of capital goods exports, as sales of machinery and equipment soared more than sevenfold (in current dollar terms) between the 1974–76 average of $831 million and their $6.8 billion level in 1987; in constant prices, such exports more than quadrupled over the same period. This growth was, to a considerable extent, made possible by the widespread use of fiscal incentives and credit, which, coupled with aggressive pricing and devaluation, made Brazilian capital goods highly attractive and—it might be added—increasingly well known in foreign markets.

A similar trend emerges in the trade accounts for basic inputs. As displayed in Table III-4, such imports increased from a relatively stable $3 billion average in current prices during the 1973–85 period to $4.9 billion in the 1986–87 period, whereas, in constant prices, they declined more than 44 percent in the period after 1974. It must be clarified, however, that the operations of many industries, particularly those supplying the domestic market, were severely constrained by the lack of imported basic inputs and spare parts. Despite this, exports of certain types of basic inputs rose rapidly during the period and, taken together, expanded by a factor of 16 in current terms from a relatively stable $290 million average in the 1973–77 period to an estimated $7 billion in 1988.

Much of the growth in exports of basic inputs resulted from the completion of large investments in the mining sector, where Brazil's strategy was, as mentioned, not only to supply the domestic market but to create new export capacity as well. A case in point is aluminum: despite having the world's third largest bauxite (aluminum ore) reserves and ample energy potential, Brazil had traditionally been a heavy net importer of aluminum. As a con-

Table III-4 BRAZIL. Exports and Imports of Capital Goods and Basic Inputs in the Balance of Payments
(millions of dollars)

Capital Goods

	Millions of Current Dollars			Millions of 1980 Dollars		
Year	Exports	Imports	Balance	Exports[1]	Imports[2]	Balance
1973	303	2,142	−1,839	606	6,900	−6,294
1974	646	3,119	−2,473	1,068	5,550	−4,482
1975	893	3,934	−3,041	1,404	6,366	−4,962
1976	954	3,619	−2,665	1,448	5,508	−4,060
1977	1,382	3,101	−1,719	1,938	4,253	−2,315
1978	1,924	3,553	−1,629	2,408	4,333	−1,925
1979	2,431	3,775	−1,344	2,695	4,121	−1,426
1980	3,360	4,381	−1,021	3,360	4,381	−1,021
1981	4,191	4,023	168	4,242	3,956	286
1982	3,323	3,272	51	3,454	3,152	302
1983	3,014	2,505	509	3,224	2,468	756
1984[a]	4,757	2,151	2,606	5,251	2,186	3,065
1985[a]	5,251	2,480	2,771	5,822	2,267	3,555
1986[a]	3,814	3,464	350	3,732	2,946	786
1987[a]	6,767	3,958	2,809	6,130	3,021	3,109
1988[ab]	8,250	4,350	3,900	—	—	—

Basic Inputs

	Millions of Current Dollars			Millions of 1980 Dollars		
Year	Exports	Imports	Balance	Exports[1]	Imports[2]	Balance
1973	208	1,669	−1,461	416	3,692	−3,376
1974	342	3,941	−3,599	585	7,012	−6,447
1975	279	3,375	−3,096	439	5,461	−5,022
1976	275	2,673	−2,398	417	4,068	−3,651
1977	350	2,732	−2,382	491	3,748	−3,257
1978	878	2,738	−1,860	1,099	1,276	−177
1979	1,376	3,493	−2,117	1,525	3,590	−2,065
1980	1,702	4,311	−2,609	1,702	4,311	−2,609
1981	2,005	3,108	−1,103	2,029	3,056	−1,027
1982	1,740	2,367	−627	1,808	2,280	−452
1983	2,873	3,013	−140	3,073	2,332	741
1984[a]	4,766	3,288	1,478	5,260	3,341	1,919
1985[a]	4,706	3,361	1,345	5,217	3,072	2,145
1986[a]	4,345	4,706	−361	4,251	4,001	250
1987[a]	4,724	5,121	−397	4,279	3,909	370
1988[ab]	7,030	5,180	1,850	—	—	—

[1]Deflated by Wharton's World Price Index for imports of manufactured goods by developed nations.
[2]Deflated by the IDB's trade-weighted price index for imports of manufactured goods by Brazil.
[a]Exports of capital goods in 1984–88 are estimated as the sum of sales of transport equipment; machines and mechanical equipment; electrical and electronic equipment; and one-half of the metallurgical products category. Exports of basic inputs are estimated as the sum of sales of iron ore and other ores; chemical products; and one-half of the metallurgical products category.
[b]Preliminary.
Source: CACEX, CIEF, Central Bank of Brazil, and estimates of the IDB Country Studies Division.

sequence of investments in the sector and related outlays for hydroelectric power development, however, Brazil achieved in 1982, for the first time, a trade surplus of $23.4 million in aluminum products. In 1983, the trade surplus in aluminum products rose tenfold to $236.3 million, as Brazil registered its first overall trade surplus in nonferrous metals ($247.8 million).

The attainment of self-sufficiency in aluminum is of great importance. In 1979, imports of this metal cost Brazil three times more than net earnings from bauxite. Thus, the nation's abundant and expanding reserves bode well for the balance of payments over the medium term.[17] At the same time, as economic recovery proceeds, the new capacity coming onstream will also be sufficient to accommodate rising domestic demand, where much room for expansion exists. Average per capita consumption of aluminum in 1983 was only 3 kilograms, as compared with 27 kilograms in the United States, one of the so-called mature markets for aluminum. In addition to aluminum, various other products originating in the mining sector are just beginning to yield results because of the investments effectuated after 1974. Production of tin, for instance, more than doubled, from 8,000 metric tons in 1980 to 18,000 metric tons by 1984; of this total, some 9,000 metric tons were exported, earning an estimated $115 million in foreign exchange. Also in 1984, Brazil achieved its first trade surplus in petrochemical products (about $200 million) and, in 1985, initiated exports of enriched uranium on a large scale.

Perhaps in no other area, however, are the consequences of Brazil's import substitution outlays as apparent—or as important—as in the energy sector, where the nation made a firm commitment to reducing its extreme vulnerability to increases in oil prices—years before the 1982 foreign exchange crisis came to a head. Despite deficiencies in planning and despite cost overruns in certain areas such as the nuclear program, Brazil's energy substitution efforts have generally yielded excellent results.[18] This fact is especially evidenced by the nation's much improved energy profile. Table III-5 reveals, for instance, that, after accounting for 45 percent of energy consumption in 1973, petroleum's share shrank to 31 percent by 1984 as imported petroleum was replaced by hydroelectric power, alcohol/sugarcane bagasse, and domestic oil.

Brazil achieved 52.8 percent self-sufficiency in oil production by year-end 1987, compared with a low of only 15 percent as recently as 1979. In this area, the nation has also obtained remarkable results; domestic production, after averaging a relatively stable 172,700 barrels per day from 1973 to 1979,

---

[17]In November 1984, the authorities announced the discovery of an estimated 50 million ton deposit of high-grade bauxite ore in the state of Maranhão. It should be noted that this new deposit is not only located within the area comprising the vast Carajás mining project but also in close proximity to the Carajás Railroad and existing ore smelters as well. For those reasons, it is believed that development outlays for the new deposits will be minimal. Besides bauxite, large deposits of iron ore, copper, nickel, gold, tin, and lead have been discovered in the Carajás area. Subsequently, in April 1987, new discoveries of manganese, iron, and other high-grade ores were announced in the state of Pará near the Trombetas River, which is a major tributary of the Amazon; bauxite had already been discovered in the Trombetas area.

[18]The heavy borrowing to support the nuclear program was particularly wasteful, since it has added very little to the nation's total generating capacity to date.

Table III-5 BRAZIL. Selected Indicators of Substitution in the Energy Sector
(Percentages)

	1973	1979	1984	1986
I. *Apparent Energy Consumption*				
Petroleum	45	41	31	32
Hydroelectricity	20	25	32	30
Biomass	32	29	30	30
Charcoal/Wood	(26)	(20)	(18)	(18)
Sugarcane/Bagasse	(6)	(9)	(9)	(12)
Alcohol	(—)	(—)	(3)	n.a.
Coal	3	4	5	6
Others	—	1	2	2
Total	100	100	100	100
Total in petroleum equivalent (millions of m.t.)	77	134	166	177

	1973	1979	1983
II. *Fuel Oil Consumption in Kilos per Ton of Finished Product in Selected Industries*			
Cement	128	100	28
Steel	155	88	40
Paper/Pulp	262	221	96

n.a. Not available. *Source:* ELECTROBRAS, Ministerio de Minas e Energia, and FIBGE.

soared to 592,000 barrels per day in the 1986–87 period. This trend continued in 1988, with self-sufficiency reaching 57 percent, based on 639,000 barrels per day of output. Much of Brazil's impressive energy substitution efforts have been concentrated in industry, a fact that will also have considerable bearing on the nation's ability to continue achieving large trade surpluses over the medium term. For industry as a whole, the use of oil had already dropped from 36 percent of total energy consumption in 1977 to 18 percent by 1983, with additional declines in subsequent years. This drive was spearheaded by some of the largest industrial subsectors, such as cement, steel, and pulp and paper, whose dramatic declines in consumption of fuel oil are documented in Table III-5.

In this context, special mention should also be made of Brazil's ambitious National Alcohol Program (PROALCOOL), which was launched in 1975 with the objective of saving foreign exchange by partially substituting alcohol for gasoline consumption. Initially, this visionary program, which was undoubtedly unparalleled in terms of its scope and objectives in Latin America, was quite successful in reducing imports of petroleum. Brazil had long produced some alcohol as a spin-off from its substantial sugar industry, which was among the ten largest in the world at the time. Consequently, the switch from production of sugar to alcohol was easily accomplished not only because areas already under cultivation could be immediately utilized but also because additional lands could quickly be put into cane in order to expand output at the rate that was required. From the balance of payments viewpoint, the program was also attractive, since, in addition to the relative abundance of available land, virtually all the required equipment and technology could be obtained from domestic suppliers, a fact that held import requirements to a minimum.

As a result of these factors and the wide range of incentives that were provided to producers and consumers alike, alcohol production soared, rising from 580 million liters in 1975 to a decade peak of 7.84 billion in 1985, before declining to 6.69 billion liters in 1986. At first, the emphasis of the program was on the production of anhydrous alcohol, which was mixed with gasoline, usually in a ratio of 20:80. Subsequently, as technological constraints were overcome, production of hydrous alcohol to fuel automobiles also rose; by 1983, about 80 percent of new car sales were accounted for by completely alcohol fueled automobiles.

By the mid-1980s, however, the decline in world oil prices and greater domestic petroleum production made it necessary to reassess the PROALCOOL program, which not only had absorbed about $4 billion in investment, principally for the construction of new distilleries, but also was requiring increasingly large subsidies to cover production costs and maintain consumption at current price levels. In view of this situation, the authorities announced a multiyear freeze on additional investments in March of 1986, while also taking steps to lower subsidies. By the late 1980s the alcohol program continued to present important economic issues, since many observers believed that major subsidies were still being provided. At the same time, other analysts were giving thought to the feasibility of mothballing "autonomous" or non-convertible distilleries, switching production of the convertible distilleries to sugar, and conversion of alcohol-powered automobiles back to gasoline in order to take advantage of lower prices for imported oil.

A convenient means of summarizing the global impact of Brazil's substitution efforts on its economic structure is by examination of the long-term trends in the nation's import propensities. Toward this end, Graph III-2 displays the average import propensities for capital goods (the ratio of capital goods imports to fixed investment), intermediate goods (the ratio of raw material imports to value added in the secondary sector), and consumer goods (the ratio of imports of consumer goods and grains to GDP). As revealed, besides having consistently low propensities for importing consumer goods, Brazil has achieved remarkable progress, especially after 1974, in reducing its dependence on imports of capital and intermediate goods. Moreover, although it is acknowledged that part of the decline in imports during the 1982–83 period was attributable to recession and the downturn in capital formation, the fact remains that average import propensities have remained low, even during the 1984–85 economic recovery and the surge in domestic demand precipitated by the Cruzado Plan in 1986.

Despite these gains, Brazil's import substitution strategy has been subjected to considerable criticism. Critics allege, for instance, that such policies contributed to the nation's borrowing more than it should have during the 1970s, a fact that not only resulted in the rapid accumulation of external debt but that also caused the adjustment process to be postponed and, consequently, to have been more painful than would have been the case if austere expenditure policies had been adopted. It is also alleged that, in their zeal to transform economic structure and reduce dependence on imported oil, the authorities also neglected basic economic criteria for project selection and evaluation.[19] In other cases, it is argued that the heavy use of fiscal and credit subsidies not only did much to set the stage for Brazil's growing inability to control inflation but also resulted in a significant misallocation of resources, especially in the capital goods sector.[20]

Although some of these criticisms may have validity, the preceding analysis has also documented that much of a positive nature was also achieved. Clearly, many of the projects executed in the post-1974 period appear to have been highly successful; after long gestation periods, much new capacity has come onstream, not only to substitute imports in a number of strategic areas—iron and nonferrous ores and metals as well as numerous types of basic inputs and capital goods—but also to supply foreign markets on an increasing scale. These developments augur well for Brazil's longer-term balance of payments prospects.

Further evidence of the success of Brazil's substitution policies is provided in a study by the São Paulo Industrial Federation of Exporters (FIESP), which determined that the share of imported materials per unit of output in the manufacturing sector declined from 15.2 percent in 1980 to 7.7 percent in 1983, and to around 6 percent in the first quarter of 1984. These findings are also supported by the data in Table III-6, which reveal that in major industrial sectors, output declines were accompanied by more than proportional reductions in imported inputs.

Although understandable in the context of Brazil's foreign exchange crisis, the positive results from import substitution were not without their economic costs. Even when allowance is made for the large domestic market, Brazil continues to rank as a relatively closed economy (Table III-3). Moreover, high levels of tariff protection and import restrictions have inexorably biased investment decisions toward production for the domestic market; as indicated, Brazil's heavy use of such policies since World War II has fostered a deeply engrained anti-export bias, despite recent success in stimulating exports.

During the 1980s, in fact, there has been a gradually emerging recognition in Brazil of the antagonistic relationship between the import substitution policies of the past and the need for greater export competitiveness in a world

---

[19]In addition to the nuclear program, much criticism has been leveled at investments such as the "Ferro do Aço" Project, which was initiated without cost-benefit analysis or final designs and subsequently abandoned in July 1984, after an investment of $2.3 billion over an eight-year period. Among other problems, this project, which was intended to provide a railroad link from Minas Gerais to the Santos area for transporting iron and other ores for export, duplicated existing transport alternatives. The economic consequences of poorly chosen investments in Brazil and other developing nations are examined in Jacques J. Polak, *Financial Policies and Development* (Paris: Development Center of the Organization for Economic Co-operation and Development, 1989), especially Chapter 3.

[20]These factors are analyzed in more detail in Chapter IV.

IMPORT SUBSTITUTION INVESTMENT

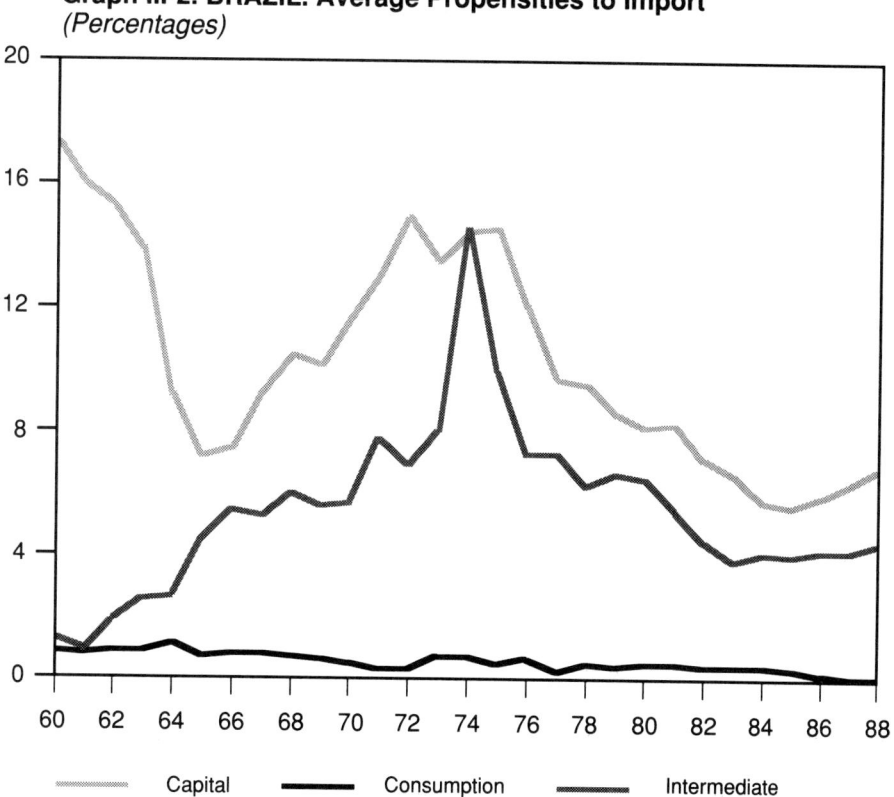

Graph III-2. BRAZIL. Average Propensities to Import
(Percentages)

- Capital Goods
- Consumption Goods
- Intermediate Goods

Source: Estimates of the IDB Country Studies Division.

Table III-6   BRAZIL. Output and Imported Input Declines from 1980 to 1983
(percentages)

Sector	Output	Imported Inputs
Metallurgic	−8.6	−68.1
Mechanical	−24.1	−36.9
Electrical	−2.1	−42.9
Chemical	−1.0	−36.9

Source: FIESP.

that is increasingly interdependent.[21] For instance, in the midst of the 1982–83 foreign exchange crisis, Brazil, with the financial backing of the World Bank and the Inter-American Development Bank, took steps to liberalize its drawback mechanism to facilitate imports of basic inputs for the production of manufactured exports. Subsequently, in September 1984, the authorities adopted additional measures to expedite the import liberalization process, including the elimination of import bans on more than two thousand items from the existing list of four thousand, some of which had been in effect for more than a decade and which at their peak in 1975 comprised more than six thousand items; the gradual reduction and elimination of the 11 percent tax rebate (crédito-premio) for exporters by May 1985; and the simplification of the import procedures administered by the Central Bank of Brazil.

Much of the significant export growth in 1984, 1985, and especially in 1988 admittedly was made possible by "market switching" as producers reacted to depressed domestic demand by increasing foreign sales as much as possible. Conversely, in atypical years, such as 1986, when the Cruzado Plan was implemented, the opposite phenomenon occurred, as export volume contracted because of the combined effects of overheated domestic demand (caused by the recovery in real wages) and the strong appreciation of the cruzado.[22] Whatever the level of domestic demand, however, inefficient firms will tend to be hurt by liberalization; it is equally clear that efficient producers will benefit from having easier access to lower-cost imported inputs and that, overall, productivity could be enhanced by increased competition. The longer-term effect of liberalization, of course, will be to force the nation's economic structure to become more export oriented and open to competition than is presently the case.

In principle, many of the aforementioned concerns were embodied in the government's new industrial policy, announced in June 1988. In broad terms, the policy calls for increased investments to modernize industry, renewed technological development efforts, and continued measures to liberalize foreign trade. By mid-1989 the measures contained in the new policy had been only partially implemented. In selected areas, however, progress was significant. Most notably, tariffs dropped for 11,500 products, in order to lower the cost of imports. The maximum tariff was reduced from 105 percent to 85 percent, with an average duty on all items of about 50 percent.

Although the new industrial policy has been hailed by some segments of the business sector as a necessary, albeit belated, step if a much needed recovery in industrial investment is to occur, the extent of the nation's overall commitment to fuller liberalization remains difficult to evaluate. For instance, critics argue that despite the measures thus far adopted, the extent of gov-

---

[21]William G. Tyler, "The Anti-Export Bias in Commercial Policies and Export Performance: Some Evidence from the Brazilian Experience," *Journal of the Kiel Institute of World Economics*, Vol. 119, No. 1, (1983), pp. 97–108.

[22]The impact of the Cruzado Plan and its effects on savings and investment are analyzed in Chapter V.

ernment intervention and regulation in the economy remains essentially unchanged, in terms of the public sector's continued heavy involvement not only in the productive sectors but also in key policy areas such as the determination of investment priorities and the granting of fiscal benefits and import licenses. At the same time, the concept of "market reserve" for domestic industry as applied to "informatics" (the computer industry), fine chemicals, and other private sector areas of production was in some instances not addressed by the new policies, and in others the market reserve was explicitly protected by the nation's new constitution, approved in October 1988. In fact, the constitution's economic implications (discussed in more detail in subsequent chapters) appear inconsistent in many ways with the specific reforms contemplated by the nation's industrial policies and incompatible, more generally, with a sustained recovery of savings and investment.

CHAPTER IV

ANALYSIS OF THE DOMESTIC ADJUSTMENT AND ITS IMPACT ON SAVINGS, INVESTMENT, AND GROWTH

The Nature of Domestic Adjustment

As examined in Chapter III, the abrupt reduction in Brazil's access to world financial markets after mid-1982 made it imperative to generate increasingly large trade surpluses to cover interest payments on the foreign debt. But the external adjustment measures actually taken —dramatic though they were— were far from optimal in terms of how they were achieved. To offset the increase in net factor payments, for example, the preferred response would clearly have been an incremental growth in exports greater than the increase that actually occurred. For a variety of reasons, however, exports did not respond in the desired way, and therefore, significant cuts in imports were ultimately required to produce the needed trade surpluses.

Domestic adjustment, in turn, was strongly conditioned by the nature of the external adjustment. In this regard, the most satisfactory domestic response would have been a rapid increase in output (fueled by external demand), accompanied by an increased savings effort that as a minimum would offset the fall in external savings and would leave capital formation unchanged from its previous levels. Even at the outset of the debt crisis, however, it seemed unlikely that this objective would be achieved. First, the need to cut imports (as opposed to increasing exports) made it largely inevitable that the investment ratio would fall, at least in the short term. Second, because a rising share of Brazil's overall savings effort (that is, domestic savings) had to be diverted to cover interest payments, the level of national savings available to finance investment declined after 1980.

Graph IV-1. BRAZIL: Relationship Between the Resource Gap and Economic Growth
(Three Year Moving Averages)

$$\frac{\text{Resource Gap}}{\text{GDP}} + 0.34 + .28 \text{ GDP growth rate}$$

$$\frac{\text{Resource Gap}}{\text{GDP}} = -2.3 + .31 \text{ GDP growth rate}$$

RESOURCE GAP AS % OF GDP

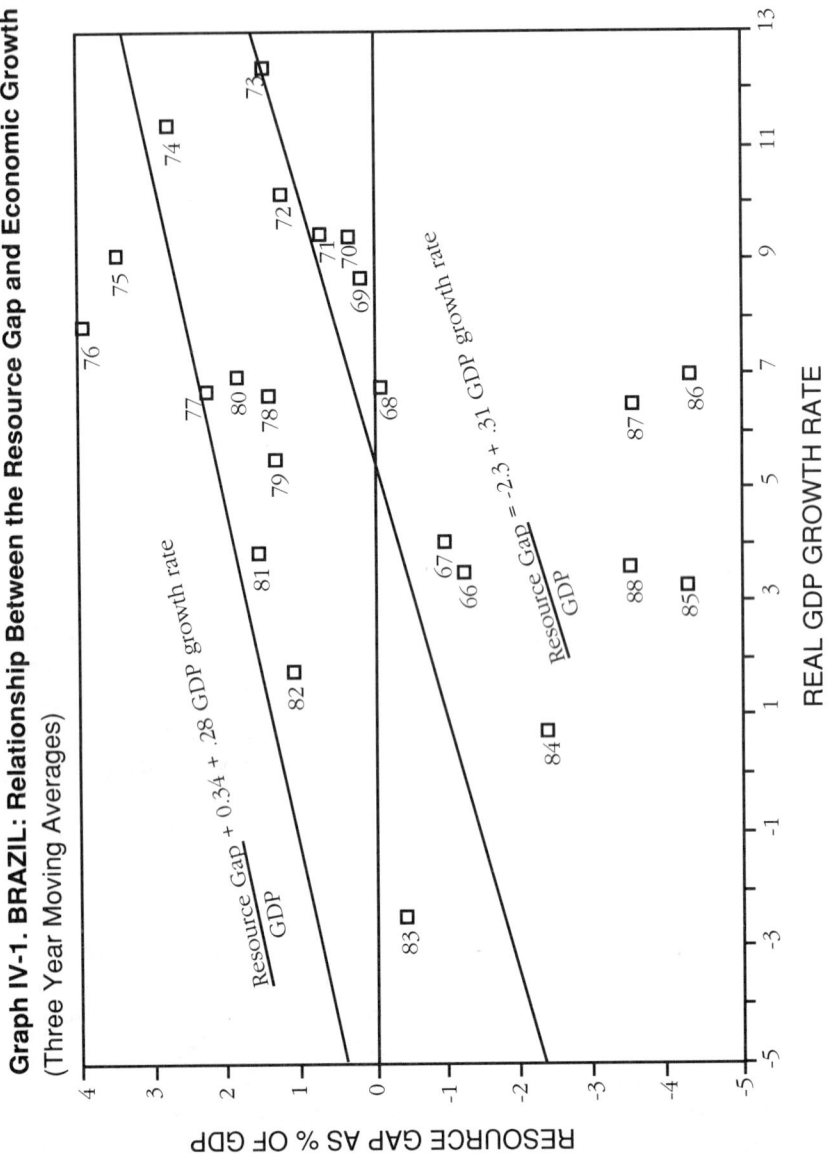

REAL GDP GROWTH RATE

Source: IDB Country Studies Division.

At the same time, the external adjustment process set into motion a wide range of complex and politically sensitive responses that have profoundly affected the domestic economies of not only Brazil but also the other nations of the region. For instance, improvement of trade balances implied the need for austerity across a broad front, as the flow of external resources that had fueled high levels of domestic demand was reversed. To stimulate export growth, substantial modifications in economic policy were needed, such as currency devaluation, to improve the relative profitability of tradable goods and thereby stimulate increases in the capacity to produce them. The challenge, however, was to try to move rapidly toward these long-term and fundamental changes in economic structure without generating unmanageable rates of inflation and unemployment in the short run.

The present chapter focuses on the nature and characteristics of Brazil's domestic adjustment, specifically the responses that occurred in investment and national savings, and analyzes the key factors that conditioned the performance of investment and national savings in the 1980–88 period. The chapter first provides a brief discussion of the savings-investment identity, which is the conceptual tool that underlies the analysis, and it summarizes the results obtained for Brazil. It then examines in more detail the impact of adjustment on the level and composition of investment and savings.

An appropriate starting point of the analysis is to assess the global impact of Brazil's balance of payments adjustment on economic growth, in order to show not only how the balance of payments constraint increasingly affected the country's overall growth process but also how external adjustment has conditioned the nature of the domestic adjustment process. Toward this end, three-year moving averages of the resource gap (that is, trade balance), expressed as percentages of GDP, were regressed on the GDP growth rate, also expressed as three-year averages, for the 1966–73 and 1974–83 periods. The results of this exercise, which are summarized in Graph IV-1, highlight some salient characteristics of Brazil's adjustment process. First, the regression slope is nearly identical in both periods; this result means that for every additional percentage point of GDP growth, the ratio of the resource gap to GDP has tended to widen by about 0.3 percent of GDP. The most striking feature revealed by this analysis, however, is that with the onset of the first oil price shock, the regression line shifted sharply upward by the equivalent of 2.0 percentage points of GDP. This means that, beginning in 1974, the traditional trade-off between growth and the resource gap became far more onerous in that Brazil was forced to accept a much larger trade deficit in its balance of payments if it desired to maintain the same rate of GDP growth.

The annual observations surrounding the regression line also shed considerable light on the actual path of Brazil's adjustment. In the 1975–76 period, for instance, the corresponding observations on the graph confirm that Brazil's expansive economic policies resulted in the maintenance of relatively rapid GDP growth rates, but with large resource gaps as well. Thereafter, as the servicing of the external debt became increasingly unmanageable, efforts were stepped up to contain the growth of aggregate demand and to achieve a larger trade surplus. As a consequence, the observed values move

Table IV-1 BRAZIL. Indicators of External and Domestic Adjustment[a]

	Imports of Goods and n.f.s. (M)	Exports of Goods and n.f.s. (X)	Trade Balance (M−X)		Net Factor Payments Abroad (R)		External Savings (S_E)		Total Investment (I_T)		National Savings[b] (S_N)
I. In Millions of 1980 Cruzados											
1980	1,400	1,121	279	+	333	=	612	=	2,890	−	2,250
1981	1,227	1,360	−133	+	602	=	469	=	2,512	−	1,970
1982	1,153	1,235	−82	+	697	=	615	=	2,297	−	1,587
1983	952	1,412	−460	+	777	=	315	=	1,753	−	1,405
1984	924	1,722	−798	+	758	=	−40	=	1,821	−	1,778
1985	924	1,843	−919	+	878	=	−41	=	2,184	−	2,059
1986	1,189	1,648	−459	+	659	=	200	=	2,550	−	2,319
1987	1,153	1,965	−812	+	828	=	16	=	2,658	−	2,534
1988[c]	1,189	2,241	−1,052	+	1,335	=	283	=	2,590	−	2,307
II. As Percentage of Current GNP											
1980	11.7	9.3	2.3	+	2.8	=	5.1	=	24.1	−	19.0
1981	10.2	9.8	0.4	+	3.7	=	4.1	=	24.0	−	19.8
1982	8.6	7.9	0.7	+	4.7	=	5.4	=	22.1	−	16.7
1983	9.4	11.9	−2.5	+	5.4	=	2.9	=	17.5	−	14.6
1984	8.2	14.1	−5.8	+	5.5	=	−0.3	=	16.2	−	16.6
1985	7.3	12.6	−5.3	+	5.0	=	−0.3	=	17.8	−	18.2
1986	6.6	9.1	−2.5	+	4.0	=	1.5	=	19.1	−	17.6
1987	6.2	9.5	−3.3	+	3.4	=	0.1	=	23.0	−	22.9
1988[c]	5.3	10.5	−5.2	+	3.2	=	−2.0	=	24.4	−	26.4
III. As Percentage of Current GDP											
1980	11.3	9.0	2.2	+	2.7	=	4.9	=	23.3	−	18.4
1981	9.7	9.4	0.4	+	3.6	=	4.0	=	23.0	−	19.0
1982	8.2	7.5	0.7	+	4.5	=	5.2	=	21.0	−	15.9
1983	8.9	11.3	−2.4	+	5.1	=	2.7	=	16.5	−	13.8
1984	7.8	13.3	−5.5	+	5.2	=	−0.3	=	15.3	−	15.7
1985	6.9	12.9	−5.0	+	4.7	=	−0.3	=	16.9	−	17.2
1986	6.3	8.7	−2.4	+	3.8	=	1.4	=	18.3	−	16.8
1987	6.0	9.2	−3.2	+	3.3	=	0.1	=	22.1	−	22.0
1988[3]	5.1	10.1	−5.0	+	3.1	=	−1.9	=	23.5	−	25.5

[a]Details may not add to totals owing to rounding.
[b]Comprises savings of the business sector, households, and general government.
[c]Preliminary.
Source: Fundação Instituto Brasileiro de Geografia e Estatística (IBGE) and estimates of IDB Country Studies Division.

steadily down the regression slope, especially after 1981; this result indicates the slowdown in growth that occurred, on the one hand, and the steady narrowing—and elimination—of the resource gap that was achieved, on the other.

The graph is especially revealing for the 1984–88 period, because the observations corresponding to those years, although excluded from the regression analysis, suggest that the regression line is in the process of shifting sharply downward to a level where the trade-off between the size of the resource gap and GDP growth is even less onerous than the relationship existing in the 1966–73 period, or prior to the first oil shock. This downward shift is clear tribute to the success of Brazil's external adjustment, especially of its export promotion efforts, and to the positive impact of its import substitution programs and the dramatic increases in domestic oil production since 1980.[23]

An Overview of the Domestic Adjustment in Terms of the Savings-Investment Identity

In more disaggregated macroeconomic terms, the domestic adjustment that corresponds by definition to the external adjustment is determined by the ex post identity

$$(M - X) + R = I_T - S_N$$

where

$(M - X)$ = The trade balance[24]
R = Net factor payments (made up principally of interest payments)
I_T = Total investment, including variation in stocks
S_N = National savings.

As was shown in Chapter III, the basic characteristic of external adjustment was that the trade surplus covered a rising share of interest payments during the 1982–88 period. This reality is reflected on the right-hand side of the identity by the fact that national savings (domestic savings less net factor payments) covered an increasing part of total investment, because of the declining levels of external savings. In theory, the investment-savings gap could be closed through an increase in national savings, a reduction in investment, or a combination of the two.

The actual pattern of Brazil's domestic response to the debt crisis is summarized in Table IV-1, which presents the major elements of the savings-

---

[23]The very success of external adjustment, however, has given rise to new problems that are conflicting with simultaneous efforts to foster domestic adjustment. For instance, the expansionary effects of the huge 1988 trade surplus appeared not only to impact the growth of the money supply but also to worsen the fiscal imbalance. The mechanisms through which these problems arise and their implications are examined in Chapter V.

[24]M and X refer to imports and exports of goods and nonfactor services (nfs), respectively.

Graph IV-2. BRAZIL: Savings and Investment Indicators, 1980-1987 *(Percentages of GDP)*

PANEL A: Total Investment = National Savings + External Savings

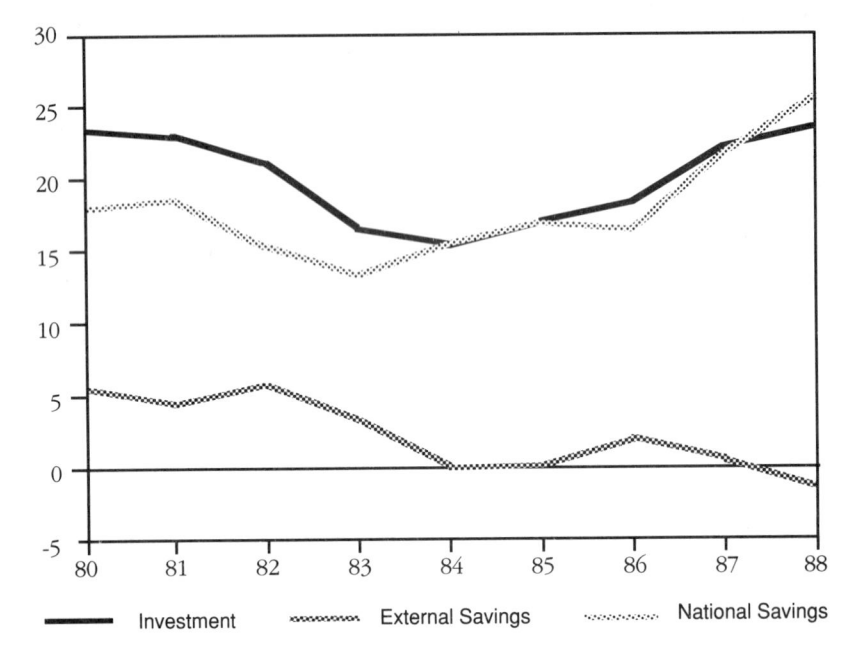

— Investment ⁓⁓ External Savings ⋯⋯ National Savings

PANEL B: National Savings = General Government Savings + Private Savings *(Households + Businesses)*

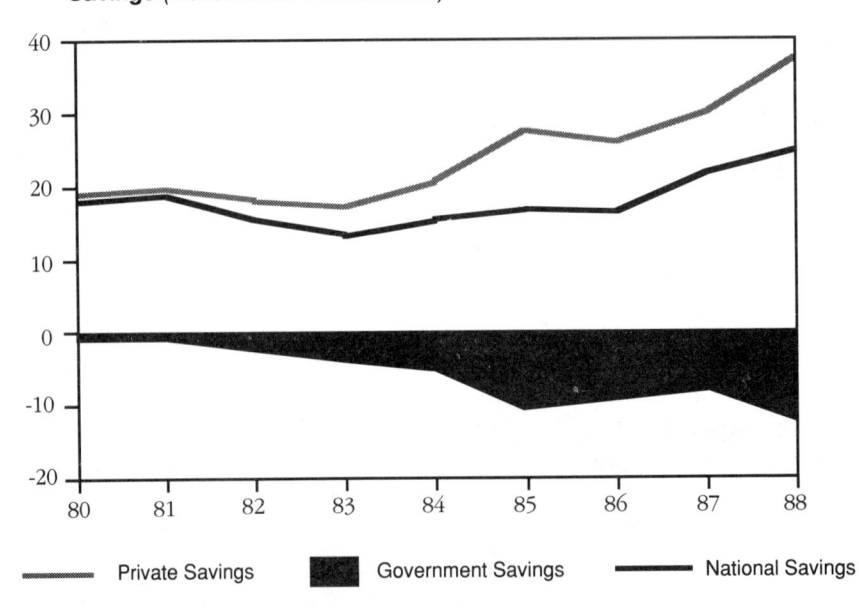

Private Savings   Government Savings   National Savings

Source: IBGE and estimates of the IDB Country Studies Division.

investment identity for the 1980–88 period in constant cruzados and as ratios to current GDP and GNP, and in Graph IV-2, which displays the path of domestic adjustment, expressed as percentages of current GDP.[25] As shown, Brazil was able to maintain a relatively high level of capital formation in the 1980–82 period, since the investment ratio averaged 24.4 percent of GDP, a result facilitated by the significant use of external savings. After 1982, however, external savings plummeted, falling to a negative average of −0.3 of GDP in the 1984–85 period. Thus, since national savings also declined in response to the steady rise in factor payments abroad, the brunt of Brazil's domestic adjustment had to be absorbed by curtailing capital formation. This fact is clearly evidenced by the graph, which reveals a 5.7 percentage point drop in the investment ratio between 1982 and 1984. As a result, domestic investment was effectively limited to availability of national savings. In 1985, however, the investment ratio jumped nearly 2 percentage points to 16.9 percent of GDP, owing to higher levels of national savings made possible by economic recovery, changes in the relative prices of capital goods, and the drop in net factor payments. National savings continued to rise thereafter, pari passu with the continued decline in net factor payments. External savings, in contrast, declined from a 4.2 percent average of GDP in the 1980–83 period to only −0.2 percent in the 1984–88 period.

In short, Brazil's experience does confirm the basic a priori expectation of a narrowing gap between national savings and investment as external savings declined but, it is equally clear that the nature of domestic adjustment was not wholly satisfactory, became a decline in capital formation could not be averted during most of the period under consideration. The investment ratio, in fact, declined by a total of 8 percentage points of GDP between 1980 and 1984. After 1984, nonetheless, the investment ratio recovered rapidly from its period low of 15.3 percent of GDP to reach 22.1 percent by 1987; but, in real terms, capital formation was still 8 percent lower than its level in 1980. The implications of these trends will now be examined in more detail.

The Process of Brazil's Domestic Adjustment

Introduction

To complement the preceding overview of Brazil's domestic adjustment process in the context of the savings-investment identity, this section provides a more detailed analysis of the 1980–88 period and of how the adjustment was actually accomplished. The analysis is presented within the conceptual framework of a social accounts (that is, income-expenditure) matrix, which com-

---

[25]Most of the analysis of this chapter is presented in current values, since changes in relative prices represent a major part of the adjustment process. In some instances, however, references to real changes can supplement and clarify analysis in current prices; consequently, references to real magnitudes are introduced as deemed appropriate.

Table IV-2   BRAZIL. Income-Expenditure Matrix

Receipts from / Payments to	Business Sector	Households	General Government		Rest of the World	Capital Formation	Total
Business Sector	.....	Private Consumption	Government Purchase of Goods and Services		Exports of Goods and Services	Total Capital Formation	Total Final Sales of the Economy
Households	Wages and Rents	.....	Wages	Transfers and Interest on Domestic Debt	Factor Income and Transfers	.....	Household Income
Government	Direct Taxes Plus Indirect Taxes Minus Subsidies	Direct Taxes	Non Tax Revenues		.....	.....	Total Current Receipts of the General Government
Rest of the World	Imports of Goods and Non Factor Services	.....	Profit Remittances and Interest Payments on External Debt	Interest Payments on External Debt	.....	.....	Imports of Goods and Services
Sources of Capital Formation	Business Savings	Household Savings	Government Savings		Trade Deficit		
	Private Savings				Factor Services Deficit Minus Net Unrequited Transfers	Total Savings	
	National Savings				External Savings	Total Capital Formation	
Totals	Total Final Sales of the Economy	Household Income	Total Current Receipts of the General Government		Imports of Goods and Services		Grand Total

bines information from the national accounts, public sector accounts, and the balance of payments. The structure of the income-expenditure matrix is presented in Table IV-2. One of the advantages of this procedure is that it permits the components of national savings to be disaggregated by sector of origin (enterprises, households, and general government) and enables the relative contribution of each to domestic adjustment to be readily examined.[26] The savings variables have all been derived as residuals and are not based on direct observation. The distinction among the three sectors is therefore not very precise. Thus, the savings of the enterprise or business sector and households are for the most part analyzed together as private savings, but because of data constraints that force public enterprises to be included in the business sector, public savings reflect only the current surpluses or deficits of the general government[27]. Nevertheless, the definitions used have been applied consistently over time and therefore give a relatively reliable picture of the trends—if not the actual magnitudes—of the different savings ratios during the adjustment period.

At the outset, it should be noted that several basic features distinguish Brazil's domestic adjustment. First, by late 1980, many of the import substitution investments initiated in the wake of the first oil price shock had been largely completed; hence, the nation had already entered a downswing in the growth cycle. Making a slowdown in growth even more inevitable, however, was the fact that Brazil was also being confronted by increasingly severe inflationary and debt-servicing problems, which, by themselves, foreshadowed the need for adjustment. In response to this situation monetary policy was tightened, and economic activity contracted sharply in 1981.

After taking these factors into account, the fact remains that the bulk of Brazil's domestic adjustment, from the macroeconomic viewpoint, not only began later but also occurred at a somewhat slower pace than that of other Latin American nations. This later start may in part reflect the fact that the urgency for sweeping adjustments in Brazil was mitigated by a different economic structure and a different policy and institutional environment. First, the scope for domestic adjustment would appear to have been constrained—at least through 1983—by the modest share of Brazil's foreign trade in GDP, since large changes in the trade accounts of the balance of payments were not translated into changes of the same order of magnitude in the domestic sectors.[28] Second, rapid adjustment was impeded, at least to some extent, by difficulties in implementing appropriate measures in the context of a largely indexed economy, a situation that is examined in detail in Chapter V.

---

[26]A summary of the methodology used, together with the resulting matrices expressed in current cruzados and as percentages of current GDP, is presented in the Annex.

[27]Because of the efforts of the State Secretariat for State Enterprises (SEST), the data available for public enterprises have improved in recent years, both in terms of quality and coverage. Some of these data are utilized in this report.

[28]As evidenced by the ratio of the average of its imports and exports to GDP, Brazil has traditionally had the most closed economy of the seven largest Latin American nations. In the 1980–88 period, for instance, Brazil's ratio, expressed in 1988 dollars, was 10.3 percent; in ascending order, Brazil was followed by Mexico (11.9 percent), Argentina (14.7 percent), Colombia (16.7 percent), Peru (21.2 percent), Venezuela (23.4 percent), and Chile (24 percent).

Table IV-3 BRAZIL. Income-Expenditure Matrix[1]
(Percentages of GDP)

	Year	Business Sector	Households	Government	Rest of World	Formation Capital	Total
Business Sector	1980	—	69.7	2.9	9.0	23.3	105.0
	1981	—	68.1	2.8	9.4	23.0	103.3
	1982	—	69.7	2.9	7.5	21.0	101.2
	1983	—	71.6	3.0	11.3	16.5	102.4
	1984	—	71.0	2.6	13.3	15.3	102.4
	1985	—	68.4	2.9	12.0	16.9	100.1
	1986	—	68.8	3.3	8.7	18.3	99.1
	1987	—	62.4	4.8	9.2	22.1	98.5
	1988	—	59.4	4.8	10.1	23.5	97.9
Households	1980	79.7	—	9.7	0.9	—	96.6
	1981	78.4	—	10.4	0.8	—	96.1
	1982	77.2	—	11.8	0.8	—	96.7
	1983	77.1	—	12.4	0.6	—	96.6
	1984	79.4	—	13.8	0.8	—	99.5
	1985	78.3	—	18.0	0.9	—	103.9
	1986	76.7	—	18.4	0.5	—	102.9
	1987	78.4	—	17.0	0.4	—	103.2
	1988	79.3	—	20.3	0.4	—	107.1
Government	1980	12.0	-1.0	8.9	—	—	20.0
	1981	12.5	-1.1	9.3	—	—	20.8
	1982	12.5	-1.3	10.1	—	—	21.3
	1983	12.4	-1.5	9.7	—	—	20.6
	1984	10.9	-0.7	8.9	—	—	19.1
	1985	11.1	-0.9	9.4	—	—	19.7
	1986	13.6	-1.6	10.0	—	—	21.9
	1987	12.2	-2.2	8.4	—	—	22.7
	1988	11.4	-2.0	8.1	—	—	21.5
Rest of the World	1980	11.3	1.8	1.8	—	—	15.4
	1981	9.7	2.5	1.9	—	—	14.6
	1982	8.2	3.2	2.1	—	—	14.0
	1983	8.9	3.3	2.4	—	—	15.2
	1984	7.8	3.6	2.4	—	—	14.1
	1985	6.9	3.1	2.5	—	—	13.0
	1986	6.3	2.1	2.2	—	—	11.2
	1987	6.0	2.1	1.6	—	—	10.0
	1988	5.1	1.9	1.5	—	—	9.1

DOMESTIC ADJUSTMENT PROCESS

Sources of Capital Formation	1980	1.1		18.0					19.1		23.3
	1981	1.2		18.6				2.2	19.9	2.7	23.0
	1982	1.4		16.9				0.4	18.3	3.6	21.0
	1983	2.2		15.4				0.7	17.6	4.5	16.5
	1984	1.3		19.6				−2.4	20.9	5.1	15.3
	1985	1.5		26.2				−5.5	27.7	5.2	16.9
	1986	2.0		24.2				−5.0	26.1	4.7	18.3
	1987	−2.3		32.4				−2.4	30.1	3.8	22.1
	1988	−1.8		39.6				−3.2	37.8	3.3	23.5
								−5.0		3.1	
	1980				−0.7		18.4		4.9		
	1981				−0.9		19.0		4.0		
	1982				−2.5		15.9		5.2		
	1983				−3.8		13.8		2.7		
	1984				−5.2		15.7		−0.3		
	1985				−10.4		17.2		−0.3		
	1986				−9.3		16.8		1.4		
	1987				−8.1		22.0		0.1		
	1988				−12.3		25.5		−1.9		
Total	1980	105.0		96.6	20.0			11.3		3.6	259.8
	1981	103.0		96.1	20.8			9.7		4.4	257.4
	1982	101.2		96.7	21.3			8.2		5.3	253.7
	1983	102.4		96.6	20.6			8.9		5.7	250.7
	1984	102.2		99.5	19.1			7.8		6.0	250.0
	1985	100.1		103.9	19.7			6.9		5.6	253.2
	1986	99.1		102.9	21.9			6.3		4.4	252.8
	1987	98.5		103.2	22.7			6.0		3.7	256.3
	1988	97.9		107.1	21.5			5.1		3.4	258.6

[1] Details may not sum due to rounding.
Source: IDB Country Studies Division.

Table IV-4. BRAZIL. Investment Indicators

	1980	1981	1982	1983	1984	1985	1986	1987	1988[a]
I. As Percentage of Current GDP									
Total Investment[b]	23.3	23.0	21.0	16.5	15.3	16.9	18.3	22.1	23.5
Fixed Investment	22.9	22.8	21.4	17.9	16.4	17.0	19.2	22.2	23.2
General Government	2.4	2.6	2.3	1.8	1.9	2.3	3.0	3.4	3.0
Private Sector	20.5	20.2	19.0	16.1	14.6	14.7	16.2	18.8	20.2
State Enterprises[c]	5.4	6.1	5.1	4.2	3.8	3.8	3.3	3.8	n.a.
Other	15.1	14.1	13.9	11.9	10.8	10.9	12.9	15.0	n.a.
II. Real Growth Rates (Percentages)									
Total Investment[b]	12.4	−13.1	−8.5	−22.7	2.6	19.9	16.8	4.2	−2.6
Fixed Investment	9.2	−12.3	−6.2	−16.3	0.2	12.2	22.0	−0.4	−4.4
General Government	4.0	4.5	−10.5	−22.4	11.0	33.5	46.3	−22.4	−20.6
Private Sector	9.8	−13.3	−5.7	−15.5	−1.1	9.5	18.4	−3.9	−2.0
State Enterprises[c]	n.a.	6.9	−13.5	−18.9	0.6	5.9	−1.7	11.9	n.a.
Other	n.a.	−23.1	−1.1	−15.4	4.2	16.1	23.9	−7.4	n.a.
III. Composition of Fixed Investment	100.0	100.0	100.0	100.0	100.0	100.0	100.0	100.0	100.0
Construction	60.5	63.0	65.5	67.1	66.3	69.5	71.9	72.6	n.a.
Machinery and Equipment	35.6	33.4	31.2	30.2	31.2	28.0	25.6	24.9	33.8
National Equipment	30.5	29.6	28.1	26.2	28.0	26.2	22.5	21.8	31.2
Imported Equipment	5.1	3.8	3.1	4.0	3.2	2.8	3.1	3.1	2.6
Other[d]	3.9	3.6	3.3	2.7	2.5	2.5	2.5	2.5	n.a.

[a] Preliminary.
[b] Includes variation in stocks.
[c] Estimated from Ministério da Fazenda, Secretaria de Controle de Empresas Estatais (SEST), *Relatório*, 1988.
[d] Includes reforestation and imports of breeding stock.
n.a. Not available.
Source: Estimates of the IDB Country Studies Division.

Analysis of Investment

By 1983, however, Brazil's domestic adjustment was clearly under way; after averaging a relatively stable 22.4 percent of GDP from 1980 to 1982, investment dropped 4.5 percentage points in 1983 and an additional 1.2 points by 1984, to 15.3 percent of GDP, the lowest level since 1956 (Table IV-3). Although not revealed by the income-expenditure matrix, it is interesting to note that state enterprise capital outlays had already begun to drop in 1982, a year before the generalized decline in Brazil's investment ratio became evident. This decrease reflected a variety of factors, including the acute shortage of foreign exchange, constraints on new foreign borrowing, falling revenues because of weak demand for many types of goods and services produced by state enterprises (for example, steel and electric energy), high real interest rates, and a widening gamut of direct import prohibitions that impacted the public sector. Beyond these factors, a concerted effort was also being made, under the aegis of the State Secretariat for State Enterprises (SEST), to reduce and rationalize public expenditures, with a view toward accelerating the balance of payments adjustment process and easing the steadily intensifying pressures on the price level. As a result of these factors, total state enterprise investment declined 2.8 percentage points of GDP between 1981 and 1986, to only 3.3 percent of current GDP in the latter year (Table IV-4).

Available data suggest that during the early 1980s, the contraction in private sector investment was even more pronounced than was the decline in public outlays. In particular, the private sector investment ratio (that is, excluding state enterprises) plummeted from 15.1 percent of GDP in 1980 to only a 10.9 percent average in the 1984–85 period. By the latter year, however, private investment began to recover, largely in response to the renewed opportunities in export markets precipitated by the real devaluation of the cruzeiro.

Thus, although the phasing of the contraction of capital formation was different for private firms from how it was for state enterprises, through 1985 both groups seem to have been severely impacted by the adjustment process. In some respects, however, it can be argued that the state enterprises were confronted by more constraints than were their private sector counterparts. For instance, some state enterprises were obliged to incur unwanted external debt for balance for payments support, and others were constrained by government policy in implementing desired increases in prices and tariffs (Graph IV-3) and in cutting current expenditures.[29] This is not to say that the situation of private firms was markedly superior. A study of Brazil's 500 largest enterprises in fact detected a severe deterioration in the financial situation of many private firms, particularly in 1984.[30] A major problem was that corporate

---

[29]Graph IV-3 highlights the significant variations in pricing policy that have occurred within the public sector since 1980. In general, the real prices of petroleum derivatives, with the exception of gasoline, have shown sustained increases, while those of other goods and services have tended to fall.

[30]The study was carried out by the Brazilian Institute of Capital Markets (IBMEC) in August, 1985.

Graph IV-3. BRAZIL. Real Price Indexes of Selected Public Enterprises Goods and Services *(1980 = 100)*

PANEL A: Petroleum and Derivatives

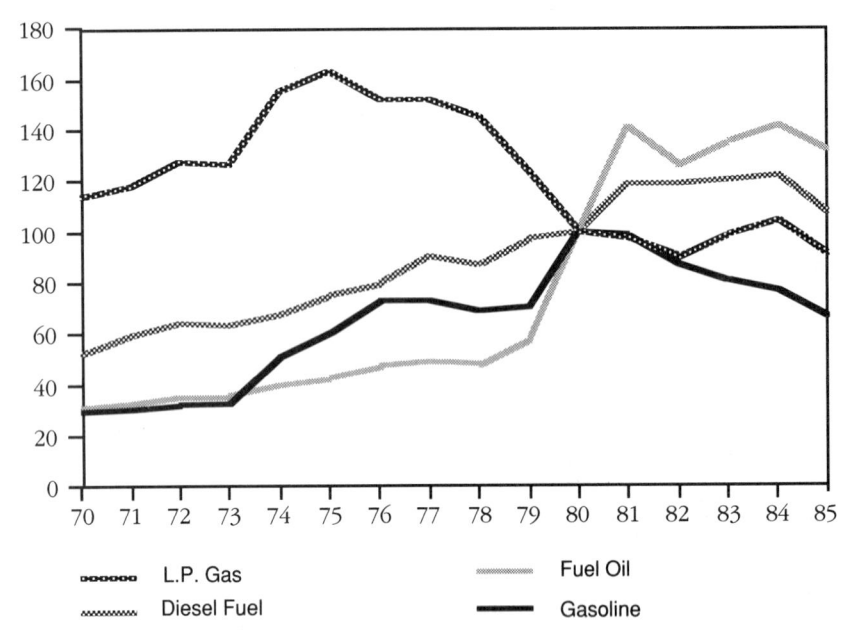

- L.P. Gas
- Diesel Fuel
- Fuel Oil
- Gasoline

PANEL B: Telephone, Steel, Electricity, and Postal Rates

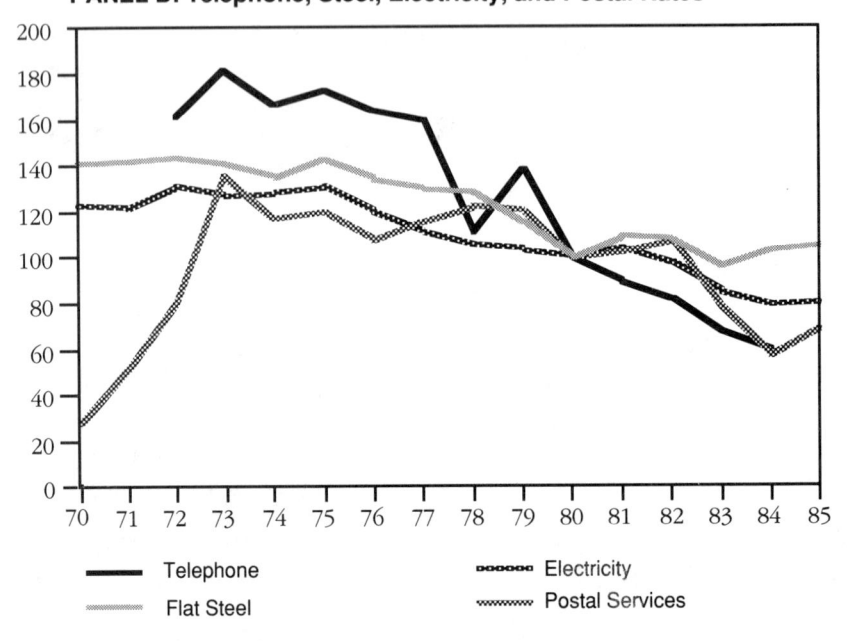

- Telephone
- Flat Steel
- Electricity
- Postal Services

Source: IBGE and estimates of the IDB Country Studies Division

indebtedness, both to the domestic financial system and to external creditors, was at such high levels that further borrowing for capital formation became infeasible, especially in view of the fact that real interest rates continued to escalate. Consequently, to continue operations—even at reduced levels—firms were forced increasingly to generate their own cash requirements; by early 1986, the ratio of internally generated to total financial requirements exceeded 50 percent, dramatically above the 14 percent level of 1983.

Excessive levels of indebtedness also became a progressively acute problem for many of the largest state enterprises, even though numerous state enterprises, after mid-1982, were permitted by Brazilian law to transfer substantial portions of externally contracted debt obligations to the federal government.[31] This indebtedness problem was perhaps nowhere more apparent than in the steel industry. By the end of 1985, for instance, Siderbrás, the holding company for the nation's public steel enterprises, accounted for $15.6 billion of Brazil's $105 billion external debt. Moreover, it was estimated that to meet existing debt-servicing obligations, an additional $11 billion infusion would be required by year-end 1986 to keep these firms from becoming technically bankrupt.[32]

At the same time, efforts to reduce the level of public expenditure after mid-1982 precipitated important changes in the sectoral allocation of investment. Relatively greater attention continued to be given to projects that would strengthen the balance of payments through increasing export capacity or substituting imports, but actual investment priorities became increasingly focused and selective. In the key energy sector, for instance, investment programs were reordered. In the case of the electric subsector, higher priority was given to expansion of transmission lines than to completion of various hydroelectric generation projects, some of which were in advanced stages of construction.[33] The execution of other energy-related investments, especially those included in the nuclear program, was postponed until near the end of the century. The major exception was petroleum exploration and development, where investments were stepped up from a $1.4 billion annual average in the 1978–80 period to $2.6 billion in the 1981–84 period (Statistical Appendix, Table 8).

---

[31]Paulo Oscar França, "Deficit Público: Politica Económica de Ajuste Estructural" (mimeo) (Brasília, novembro 1985) and Rogério L. Furquim Werneck, "Poupança Estatal, Dívida Externa e Crise Financeiro do Sector Público," *Pesquisa e Planajamento Económico* (dezembro 1986), p. 554.

[32]Through year-end 1988, the Siderbrás group continued to experience financial difficulties and to be the subject of considerable debate within Brazil. Some critics argued, for instance, that the nation's public sector steel mills remained overstaffed, despite efforts to rationalize expenditures. Others stressed that the main problem was excessive indebtedness, caused in many instances by government price controls and cost overruns. One study in mid-1985, for example, revealed that a ton of Siderbrás steel cost—excluding financial charges—$271 to produce, compared with $342 for a ton of Japanese steel and $492 for a ton of U.S. steel. Including financial charges, however, all 10 mills in the Siderabrás group registered operating losses in 1985, equivalent to $235, on average, for each ton of steel produced.

[33]A major exception was the $18 billion, 12,600 megawatt Itaipú hydroelectric power plant, which, as indicated in the previous chapter, was near completion by 1981.

Although in most instances government policies served to lower investment and current expenditure, this was not always the case. A recent unpublished study, for example, indicates that spending on social programs (including current outlays) actually rose between 1985 and the end of 1986. At present, such outlays—at all levels of government—account for around 25 percent of GDP, a larger share than in most other middle-income countries. Despite the high level of such expenditures, Brazil's social welfare indicators remain low and appear to have deteriorated during the 1980s. The report identifies two major reasons for these short-comings. First, present programs do not target resources toward the poorest and most disadvantaged groups; indeed, available data suggest that much social expenditure actually subsidizes the higher-income groups. Second, available resources are poorly managed. Aggravating these problems is the fact that many of the types of taxes and financing mechanisms currently used are incompatible with the efficient delivery of social services.

The implications of this study go far beyond the obvious need for improved identification of beneficiaries and for greater efficiency in spending on social programs and on investment in related infrastructure. In the broadest sense, the "mistargeting" of social expenditure is a reflection of the nation's deeply rooted income distribution problem, by dint of which 33 percent of national income is retained by the richest 5 percent of the population as compared with only 16 percent of national income retained by the poorest 50 percent of the population.[34] Reversing this situation will therefore require fundamental political and social-equity adjustments; such changes are difficult in any society, but the fact remains that they must, at some point, be dealt with if Brazil is to realize fully the potential for economic growth suggested by its vast natural resource base and its large domestic market. The need to rationalize social expenditure[35] also epitomizes the magnitude of the effort that is needed to revamp the nation's huge and highly inefficient public sector.[36] As examined in Chapter V, there is an urgent need for visible and sustained progress in lowering the fiscal deficit. Only when such progress becomes evident will the continual escalation of inflationary expectations be reversed and will conditions again become favorable for a sustained recovery in savings and investment.

All things considered, it is difficult to assess accurately the various policies adopted in the 1982–85 period to limit and redirect investment expenditure

---

[34]Hélio Jaguaribe, and others, *Brasil, 2000: Para um Novo Pacto Social* (São Paulo: Editôra Paz e Terra, S.A., 1986) p. 18.

[35]An excellent analysis of Brazil's current social situation and alternative policy paradigms for the future is contained in Hélio Jaguaribe, *Brazil, 2000* (see preceding note).

[36]A clear statement of the types of overall reforms needed is presented in the First National Development Plan of the New Republic for 1986–89 (I PND-NR), which was approved by the Brazilian Congress in December 1985. Although the plan was largely abandoned because of subsequent economic and political developments, the need to implement the recommendations contained in the I PND-NR has grown increasingly urgent.

in terms of their overall impact on the functioning of the economy. It seems clear, nonetheless, that one of the major consequences of such policies as rapid devaluation, credit subsidies, and tax rebates to exporters was to maximize the amount of investment—and output—directed toward export-related activities. Even import prohibitions, which became increasingly commonplace after the mid–1970s and which provided renewed impetus for import substitution, often favored those firms producing inputs needed for exports. As a consequence of this policy orientation, many enterprises producing for the domestic market, including both state-owned and nonpublic entities, fared poorly, at least until 1985, when real wages began to recover in the industrialized Center-South.

Although these results were not surprising in the context of Brazil's immediate external sector constraints, they nevertheless appeared to exacerbate the effect of the recession in many instances. This fact was perhaps most clearly evidenced in the agricultural sector, where a rapidly rising proportion of total output was destined for exports. In some cases, this heightened the tendency for the increase in food prices to outstrip the growth of the general price level. In short, the orientation of investment priorities during the 1982–85 period—which was reinforced by many related policies to benefit exports and selected areas of the energy sector at the relative expense of domestic markets—while understandable, was far from costless.

Largely because of the welfare and distributional consequences of the post-1982 adjustment process, economic policy was substantially modified in February 1986, with the implementation of the Cruzado Plan, which is analyzed in more detail in Chapter V. The Cruzado Plan had various consequences for capital formation. In particular, the immediate effects of the plan were the temporary control of inflation and interest rates, plus an increase in real wages. These developments, coupled with the fact that industrial capacity rapidly rose to near-maximum utilization levels, triggered a partial recovery in investment. This was especially the case of small and medium-sized firms, which responded to the increase in domestic demand. Most of the increase was in the form of construction, which accounted for 71.9 percent of total fixed outlays, up from only 60.5 percent in 1980. In contrast, state enterprise investment outlays stagnated, largely because of continuing debt-servicing constraints, which were aggravated by the fact the tariffs could not be raised. Finally, large domestic and foreign enterprises for the most part postponed new investment, preferring to strengthen their cash balances, while evaluating the longer-term effects of the Cruzado Plan on demand and inflation control.[37] Generally speaking, however, the overall effect of the 1986 measures on capital formation was positive; in real terms total investment rose 16.8 percent, despite a significant drawdown on stocks, and in relation to current GDP, the investment ratio rose 1.4 percentage points over 1985 to 18.3 percent.

---

[37]"Investimentos Físicos na Industria de Transformação," *Conjuntura Econômica* (setembro 1988), p. 124.

In 1987, the ratio of investment to current GDP continued to recover, jumping 3.8 percentage points to 22.1 percent, only fractionally below the 22.4 average of the 1980–82 period (Table IV-3). For the most part, however, this increase appeared to reflect adjustments in relative prices—that is, with the return of rapid inflation, construction costs escalated by rates above the increase in the general price level. Hence, once adjusted for inflation, fixed investment, after rising 22 percent in 1986, dropped about 0.4 percent in 1987. As displayed in Table IV-5, the decline was even greater for fixed investment in the key manufacturing sector, where real outlays decreased in eleven of the twenty-one major industrial subsectors, or by an average of 3.6 percent.[38]

In addition to the generalized failure of the Cruzado Plan and the heightened uncertainty that followed, the contraction in real investment during 1987 reflected various other factors, including the following: lower profit margins for many industries, especially those impacted by the 1986 price freeze; increased indebtedness of small and medium-sized firms, many of which had initiated or expanded capacity during 1986; selected cuts in public investment, which impacted demand for capital goods, electrical equipment, and construction materials; and the virtual stagnation of industrial output. This situation appeared to have worsened in 1988; real fixed investment outlays declined an estimated 4.4 percent as the inflation rate more than doubled to 934 percent, despite a remarkable surge in real exports.[39]

Analysis of Savings

By 1984, and continuing through 1988, Brazil's investment and national savings ratios remained approximately in balance, since external savings, with the exception of a small upturn in 1986, had essentially disappeared. In this regard, the striking feature of Brazil's national savings was that they declined as little as they did during the adjustment period, despite the steady growth of the general government's current dissavings, which, as shown in Table IV-3, widened from −0.7 percent of GDP in 1980 to a −10 percent average

---

[38] As shown, the decline is somewhat less (−1.3 percent) if nominal values are deflated by the wholesale price index for producer goods or slightly positive (3.6 percent) if deflated by the wholesale price index for machines and equipment.

[39] In contrast to the drop when measured in real terms, preliminary data for 1988 suggest that, when expressed in current terms, the investment ratio continued to rise, reaching an estimated 23.5 percent of GDP. If subsequently verified by revised data, this may prove to have been partially a relative price phenomenon, since costs in the construction sector, which accounted for most of the increase in fixed investment, continued to surpass increases in the general price level by a wide margin. It is also possible, however, that the current price measurement of the investment ratio is overstated. This could be the result of several factors. First, some of the increase in savings (which equals investment) may have left the country in the form of capital flight. In support of this hypothesis, evidence exists that overinvoicing of imports and underinvoicing of exports in the current account of the balance of payments increased in 1988. A second factor concerns the reliability of the national income accounts, whose basic accuracy may have been affected in recent years by the growth of a substantial informal sector—a concern expressed by several economists. In any event, the 1988 official estimates are preliminary and subject to revision.

Table IV-5 BRAZIL. Investment in Manufacturing, 1987

	Millions of 1980 Cruzados 1986	1987	Real Growth Rates in 1987 A	B	C
Non metallic Minerals	8,656	9,806	13.3	15.9	21.7
Metallurgical	56,392	42,750	−24.2	−22.4	−18.6
Mechanical	12,705	10,719	−15.6	−13.7	−9.4
Electrical and Communications	14,265	13,754	−3.6	−1.4	3.6
Transport Equipment	36,009	33,602	−6.7	−4.5	0.2
Wood	2,409	1,894	−21.4	−19.5	−15.5
Furniture	552	776	40.6	43.9	51.1
Cellulose, Paper and Pulp	12,191	14,409	18.2	20.9	27.0
Rubber	4,612	3,874	−16.0	−14.0	−9.8
Hides and Skins	547	843	54.1	57.6	65.5
Chemicals	143,683	142,874	−0.6	1.7	6.8
Pharmaceutical Products	2,092	2,532	21.0	23.8	30.0
Perfumes, Soap, etc.	455	752	65.7	69.3	77.7
Plastics	2,586	2,751	6.4	8.9	14.3
Textiles	14,367	14,047	−2.2	0.0	5.0
Clothing, Shoes	5,143	3,323	−35.4	−33.9	−30.6
Food Products	19,742	16,859	−14.6	−12.6	−8.3
Beverages	4,598	10,056	118.7	123.8	134.9
Tobacco	847	3,430	305.0	314.2	334.9
Printing and Graphics	1,295	1,830	41.3	44.5	51.7
Miscellaneous	2,359	2,354	−0.3	2.1	7.2
Total:	345,505	333,237	−3.6	−1.3	3.6

[a] Nominal values deflated by the national account deflator for total investment.
[b] Nominal values deflated by the wholesale price index (domestic supply) for producer goods.
[c] Nominal values deflated by the wholesale price index (domestic supply) for machines and equipment.
Source: Sondagem Conjuntural—CEI/IBRE/FGV (Sept. 1988) and estimates of the IDB Country Studies Division.

in the 1985–88 period. As mentioned earlier, the growth of the deficit was partially attributable to the fact that the General Government was forced to assume responsibility for large amounts of external debt that could no longer be serviced by state enterprises after mid-1982, because of the latters' deteriorating financial situation. At the same time, the growth of the deficit was also impacted by soaring interest and, especially, monetary correction payments on Brazil's mushrooming domestic debt, which escalated from a 2 percent average of GDP in the 1980–81 period to around 6 percent of GDP by 1987.[40] Essentially all of these payments, however, went to the private sector, whose share in national savings rose accordingly (see also Panel B of Graph IV-2).[41]

---

[40] In the present analysis, interest on the domestic debt is measured as the sum of actual cash outlays made by the National Treasury, when domestic debt instruments are redeemed, and accrued monetary correction payments. Excluded in this measure are accrued monetary correction payments on debt instruments yet unredeemed; however, as is examined in Chapter V, not only were such obligations already exceedingly large by the end of 1985 but they also constituted a rising obstacle to reduction of the fiscal deficit.

[41] Silvio Rodrigues Alves, "Por Que o Govêrno é Deficitário?" Artigo preparado para a revista OPÇAO, da Associação dos Funcionarios do Banco Central (novembro 1987), p. 6.

For reasons indicated earlier, a precise breakdown of private savings into household and business savings is extremely difficult. For instance, it could be argued that the level of business savings is understated by the data presented in the income-expenditure matrix. In support of this viewpoint, Table IV-6 reveals that current savings (more precisely, the operating surpluses) of the state enterprises, which comprise part of business savings, were approximately double the average level of overall business savings as shown in Table IV-3 during the 1982–87 period (3.1 percent of GDP for the state enterprises versus 1.2 percent of GDP for the entire business sector). Several important caveats are in order, however. First, state enterprise current revenues (as measured in the Statistical Appendix, Table 9) are substantially overstated according to conventional public finance definitions, since total receipts include large amounts of non-operational revenue, such as transfers from the National Treasury. Second, as was analyzed earlier, most firms supplying the domestic market during the 1980s, which constitute the vast majority of the total, had much lower savings rates, compared with those firms able to export. Besides being unable to benefit from devaluations, such nonexporting firms were heavily affected by the worsening inflationary process, since their incomes, already impacted by high levels of indebtedness, were further squeezed during the 1980s by rising production costs, price controls, and the decline of real purchasing power in the economy.

The difficulties confronting the business sector and its efforts to save are brought out clearly in the income-expenditure matrix (Table IV-3), which reveals that the sector's income has declined steadily in relation to GDP since 1980, or from 105 percent to only 98 percent by 1988. As revealed, this decrease was largely attributable to the contraction in private consumption outlays, which dropped from a 70 percent average of GDP in the 1980–84 period to only 59.4 percent by 1988. The rapid growth of exports was also reversed; after increasing from 8.6 percent of total business income in 1980 to 13 percent in 1984, the share of exports retreated to a 9.5 percent average in the 1986–88 period.

As noted, the income-expenditure matrix also strongly suggests that households have been the primary beneficiaries of the increase in dissavings of the general government. Specifically, Table IV-3 reveals that, after averaging 17.3 percent of GDP in the 1982–84 period, household savings jumped to nearly 40 percent of GDP by 1988. Over the same time period, general government dissavings, propelled by the growth of the domestic debt, rose steadily from a −0.8 percent average of GDP in the 1980–81 period to an estimated −12.3 percent average in 1988. Nevertheless, caveats are again in order. The most obvious is that some of the increase in savings imputed to households may actually be attributable to the business sector. This would be the case if firms with available cash reserves choose to invest in domestic debt instruments, these rates of return on which have become increasingly likely to surpass the rates of return on fixed investments.

The apparent widening divergence in the rates of return to financial and to economic investment points up a major problem facing Brazil. In particular, as long as financial returns continue to exceed probable economic returns,

Table IV-6 BRAZIL. Indicators of State Enterprise Finances, 1980–1987
(percentages of GDP)

	1980	1981	1982	1983	1984	1985	1986	1987
I. Current Revenue	15.0	16.9	15.3	17.1	17.1	16.2	14.7	18.0
II. Current Expenditure	10.2	11.8	12.4	14.3	14.0	13.1	10.9	14.8
Wages and Salaries	2.0	2.2	2.3	2.0	1.7	1.9	1.9	2.5
Financial Charges	0.9	1.3	1.9	2.3	2.5	2.5	1.9	2.8
Other (Net)	7.3	8.3	8.2	10.0	9.8	8.7	7.1	9.5
III. Current Savings (I–II)	4.8	5.1	2.9	2.8	3.1	3.1	3.8	3.2
IV. Capital Expenditure	5.4	6.1	5.2	4.2	3.8	3.8	3.3	3.8
V. Overall Deficit	−0.6	−1.0	−2.3	−1.5	−0.7	−0.7	−0.5	−0.6
VI. Financing	0.6	1.0	2.3	1.5	0.7	0.7	0.5	0.6
Of Which: External (Net)	0.8	1.6	2.3	0.7	0.4	−0.0	−1.0	−1.5

Source: Statistical Appendix, Table 9.

Table IV-7 BRAZIL. Domestic Savings, National Savings, and Net Factor Payments
(percentages of GDP)

Year	National Savings (S_N)	+	Net Factor Payments (R)	=	Domestic Savings (S_D)
1980	18.4	+	2.7	=	21.1
1981	19.0	+	3.6	=	22.6
1982	15.9	+	4.5	=	20.4
1983	13.8	+	5.1	=	18.9
1984	15.7	+	5.2	=	20.9
1985	17.2	+	4.7	=	21.9
1986	16.8	+	3.8	=	20.6
1987	22.0	+	3.3	=	25.3
1988[a]	25.5	+	3.1	=	28.6

[a]Preliminary.
Source: Table IV-1.

any sustained recovery in capital formation, in the absence of basic policy reforms, would seem increasingly remote. Moreover, with the acceleration of inflation, the functioning of Brazil's capital markets has become progressively distorted and biased toward instruments with short maturities, which in turn further complicates the mobilization of longer-term economic savings.

Conclusions

Brazil has responded to the forced reductions in external savings by simultaneously initiating a complex process of domestic adjustment. Ideally, this adjustment would have resulted in a sufficiently large increase in domestic savings not only to maintain investment at earlier levels but also to cover rising net factor payments. During the early years of the adjustment process, an approximation of the incremental savings effort that Brazil would have needed can be derived by relating the change in the average level of net factor payments between the 1980–81 and the 1983–85 periods (when most of the increase occurred) to the average level of domestic savings in the 1980–81 period. The results of this comparison are highly instructive; as shown in Table IV-7, even though domestic savings increased slightly from 21.1 percent of GDP in 1980 to 21.9 percent in 1985, they would have had to have been approximately 11 percent higher than they actually were in the latter year to maintain investment at about the 1980–81 level.

Further inspection of Table IV-7 reveals that after 1984, domestic savings began to recover rapidly from their 1983 nadir of 18.9 percent of GDP, in part because of the ensuing decline in net factor payments. By 1987, domestic savings had reached 25.3 percent of GDP, thereby enabling the investment ratio to recover to 22.1 percent of GDP. As was indicated, however, much of the increase in investment in 1987 reflected a shift in relative prices, since the prices of construction goods rose at rates substantially above the general price level. In real terms, in fact, capital formation appeared to have declined in 1987. The same trend was undoubtedly repeated in 1988, as inflation escalated by unprecedented 934 percent while output stagnated.

Still left unanswered, however, is the fundamental question of why domestic savings did not increase more than they did during the period under consideration. Certainly, a major explanation lies in the severity of the recession that gripped Brazil (and most other countries) during most of the period since 1982, whose effects, in turn, have been exacerbated by extreme inflationary pressures and a largely uncontrollable fiscal deficit. These factors, which are examined in detail in Chapter V, suggest that Brazil has had to make a significant effort merely to achieve modest gains in domestic savings during the last several years.

It should also be noted that the recovery in domestic savings shown in Table IV-7 may be associated with a further deterioration of income distribution. Recent household survey data, for instance, suggest that falling real incomes are increasingly destined toward consumption, not savings, as a consequence of the ongoing erosion of nominal wages because of inflation. At the same time, the extent of the drop in purchasing power in the economy is also indicated by private consumption, whose share in GDP declined from 71.6 percent in 1983 to only 59.4 percent by year-end 1988. Even for wealthy Brazilians, savings and protection of real financial assets in general are becoming increasingly difficult, as indicated in part by the fact that banks, by early 1988, would not accept funds for indexed investments in the "Overnight" and Treasury Bill markets for amounts smaller than the equivalent of $2,000; by definition, such a requirement would exclude the bulk of Brazil's population.

In short, perhaps the major finding stemming from the analysis of Brazil's domestic adjustment process is the inadequacy of the savings effort to date. In particular, what occurred through 1987 (and was undoubtedly repeated in 1988) can be characterized more appropriately as an "accommodation" to the disappearance of external saving rather than as a structural increase in savings capacity. Clearly, a structural increase in savings constitutes a necessary condition for the recovery of investment from its current levels and for the resumption of sustained growth. As detailed in Chapter V, however, unless fundamental changes in economic policy (and public confidence) are forthcoming, such increases will be difficult to achieve.

CHAPTER V

ANALYSIS OF POLICY INSTRUMENTS TO EFFECTUATE ECONOMIC ADJUSTMENT AND THEIR IMPACT ON SAVINGS, INVESTMENT, AND GROWTH

Policy Instruments and the Strategy of Adjustment

The January 1983 Extended Fund Facility Accord between Brazil and the IMF was largely conventional in terms of the policies adopted to restore external equilibrium and reduce inflation. As was examined in Chapter III, the balance of payments problems were attacked along two fronts. First, an agreement was reached with the commercial banks to guarantee an orderly rescheduling of private debt due in the short term, and initiatives were taken to obtain emergency bridge financing from a variety of sources. Second, in the current account, maximum attention was given to achieving a rising trade surplus. Although import restrictions were to play a key role in adjusting the trade accounts in the short run, especially in 1983, the principal focus was upon the need to stimulate export growth. Toward this end, exchange rate policy was modified to ensure that currency devaluation would at least follow domestic inflation. At the same time, to restore internal equilibrium by gradually reducing inflation, domestic absorption was to decline. These objectives were to be pursued through restrictive demand management policies, especially by tightening monetary policy, limiting adjustments in nominal wages, and reducing the fiscal deficit.

By the end of 1984, a number of interesting perceptions began to emerge, which have continued largely to the present, as to the principal successes and failures achieved by Brazil's economic adjustment and stabilization efforts. First, a tendency had surfaced among some analysts to differentiate between external and domestic adjustment, and to regard them as largely separate processes. This interpretation is, of course, erroneous. Rapid devaluation, for instance, certainly contributed to the sharp intensification of inflationary pressures that occurred after 1982. One of the most interesting perceptions, however, has been the tendency of some analysts to regard external adjustment as a great success, while characterizing efforts to achieve domestic adjustment as "halfhearted" and largely unsuccessful. In the first instance, Brazil's success in adjusting its trade accounts was interpreted as supporting the view that the nation has its debt-servicing problems under control; in the second instance, the worsening inflation was viewed as a sign of internal disarray, economic mismanagement, and persistent fiscal disequilibrium.

This characterization of external adjustment as "successful" and domestic adjustment as "unsuccessful" seems both oversimplified and untenable. In an attempt to clarify these issues and put them into a meaningful economic context, this chapter presents a detailed analysis of the principal policy instruments used to effectuate Brazil's adjustment, especially fiscal, wage, and monetary and credit policies. Again, the objective of such an approach is to obtain a deeper understanding of Brazil's savings and investment trends after 1982 and of the problems that must be addressed for a sustained recovery in capital formation to occur. In this context, relatively greater attention is allocated to problems of internal adjustment and inflation control, because the impact of these policies on the balance of payments was for the most part documented in Chapter III. Particular importance is given to the analysis of inflation, which, instead of declining in accord with IMF and government expectations, worsened dramatically in 1983, despite a deepening recession, and which by the end of 1984 had clearly emerged as Brazil's most urgent policy issue.

The Role of Fiscal Policy in the Adjustment Process

The principal thrust of Brazil's domestic adjustment effort was toward reduction of the public sector deficit. This fiscal imbalance, which only gradually became apparent during the 1970s, was the result basically of two factors.

First, current and capital expenditures at all levels of the public sector (including state and municipal governments) were consistently outstripping revenues by widening margins. Most of this increase was accounted for by the state enterprises, whose outlays progressively exceeded federal budget operations and whose external borrowing and import requirements were contributing to the rapid deterioration in the balance of payments, distortions in resource allocation, and pressures on the price level. During 1979–81, for instance, while net federal budgetary expenditure rose three times in current terms to Cr$1.1 trillion, state enterprise outlays rose more than five times to Cr$7.2 trillion. With respect to financing, the contrast between the federal budget and state enterprises was even more striking, since, during the same period, the receipts and outlays of the former, because of the vigorous enforcement of Brazil's budget law, remained in equilibrium, while those of the latter resulted in more than a fourfold increase in their operating deficit, despite being recipients of growing transfers via the federal budget (Statistical Appendix, Table 11).[42]

A second element that contributed to the expansion of the public deficit was the exponential growth of credit subsidies. These were increasingly used as instruments of economic policy to benefit import substitution and export promotion investments initiated after the first oil price shock, as well as priority activities such as agriculture and exports; like the operations of state enterprises, the use of export subsidies had attained macroeconomic proportions on the eve of the 1982 external liquidity crisis. For instance, the sum of subsidized credit (implicit and explicit) and direct subsidies (wheat, oil, soybeans, and sugar) reached the equivalent of 3.3 percent of GDP and 47 percent of federal tax receipts by 1981 (Statistical Appendix, Table 12).

For the foregoing reasons and related factors that are later examined in more detail (such as the associated problems in controlling growth of the money supply, soaring interest rates and distortions in the allocation of credit), reduction of the public sector deficit was indicated as the principal requirement for domestic adjustment. Specifically, the target established in the IMF agreement was to slash the public sector deficit from an estimated 6 percent of GDP in 1982 to 3.5 percent in 1983. This cutback was to be achieved primarily through a 21 percent decrease in real investment by the state enterprises and a significant increase in the current revenue of the federal government that would result primarily from applying indexation to taxes at the moment the obligation was incurred. Measures were also adopted to eliminate gradually the massive interest rate subsidies, especially those granted to the agricultural sector and to exports, and to limit the growth of domestic public debt.

At the outset, however, it should be noted that the IMF and the Brazilian authorities used very different approaches for measuring the fiscal deficit. It is worthwhile explaining these approaches, since not only do they involve different statistical coverage but also—as will be shown later—they provide vitally important insights into the nature of Brazil's inflationary process and the reasons that price stabilization proved to be such an elusive objective. Basically, the IMF's approach is to measure the deficit via the flow involved in its financing rather than via the activities giving rise to the deficit. In part, the IMF's preference for a "financing" or "credit-based" as opposed to an "operational" measurement concept was based on practical considerations; in particular, it was deemed that the financial information needed to monitor the agreement would be available on a more timely (that is, quarterly) basis in the monetary statistics so that the degree of compliance with fiscal targets could be readily determined. The concept of total financial flows used to measure the deficit, then, was defined as the "public sector borrowing requirements" (PSBR); this variable was specified in nominal terms and its growth rate was pegged to the targets for inflation and the monetary aggregates. Of fundamental importance was the IMF's insistence on including in

---

[42]Again, it must be emphasized that many public enterprises were in a precarious state because they were forced to borrow money abroad and were often subjected to price controls by the government in an effort to halt the buildup of inflationary pressures.

the PSBR the financing needs arising from indexation payments (that is, monetary and exchange rate correction) on the domestic debt.

In contrast, the "operational" approach recommended by the Brazilian authorities excluded financial flows for indexation requirements on the domestic debt in the measurement of the public sector deficit, since these were regarded largely as a given parameter over which little control could be exercised in the short run. This distinction thus gave rise to parallel measures of the fiscal deficit, which came to be known respectively as the "nominal deficit" (that is, inclusive of monetary correction payments on the domestic debt) and the "operational deficit" (that is, exclusive of these payments).[43]

The Role of Monetary and Credit Policy in the Adjustment Process

The Brazilian authorities had already begun to tighten monetary and credit policy in the closing months of 1982, prior to the signing of the IMF accord. In September, for instance, reserve requirements on demand deposits of commercial banks were raised from 35 percent to 45 percent, while other financial institutions were obliged to make large compulsory investments in Treasury Bills, in order to offset expansionary pressures on the monetary base. Under the IMF program, inflation was targeted to fall to a 70 percent rate in 1983 (compared with 100 percent in 1982), partially in response to ceilings on the expansion of domestic credit, which would help to limit the growth of the money supply and the monetary base to 60 percent (compared to 71 percent and 85 percent, respectively, in 1982). Success in attaining these targets, in turn, was closely tied to achieving the targets for reduction of the fiscal deficit, via limiting the nominal growth of the PSBR, as just discussed.

The authorities also believed that the various monetary and fiscal measures adopted in late 1982 would enable substantial progress to be made toward achieving a convergence of interest rate levels throughout the economy, principally by reducing the level of subsidies involved. Interest rates on agricultural loans, for example, were to be corrected by 70 percent of the increase in the national consumer price index (INPC), a measure that was expected to reduce the subsidy implicit in such credits by around 15 percentage points in real terms—assuming, of course, that the 70 percent inflation target was met. The anticipated narrowing of interest rate differentials and the resulting move toward a more realistic interest rate structure in the financial markets were in turn linked to the expectation that the need for sizable new issues of domestic debt, which had become increasingly commonplace after 1980, would

---

[43]Despite this apparent distinction, it should be emphasized that the "nominal" deficit is, by definition, a function of inflation and not an independent variable or problem in itself. Stated differently, the nominal deficit is like a nominal interest rate: it depends first on a "real" magnitude (the real interest rate or the "operational" deficit) and second on inflation. An excellent discussion of these approaches, which argues against the use of the "operational" concept due to its lack of congruence with measures of the fiscal deficit in other nations, is presented by Antônio Carlos Lemgruber, "Qual é Déficit Público no Brasil," *Carta Econômica*, Banco Boavista, No. 3 (julho/septembro 1987).

diminish; if achieved, the mounting pressures on interest rates produced by domestic debt operations would also be alleviated.

The Role of Wage Policy in the Adjustment Process

When the agreement with the IMF was signed, wage adjustments were essentially regulated by Law 6.708, which had been approved in November 1979 and which modified previous legislation in a number of ways. The most important modification was to provide semiannual adjustments (as opposed to annual adjustments) equivalent to 110 percent of the increase in the INPC during the previous six months for workers earning three minimum wages or less. In contrast, workers earning from three to ten minimum wages received 100 percent of the increase in the INPC; the percentage received, however, decreased with higher incomes, and workers receiving more than twenty times the minimum wage were free to negotiate salary increases individually with their employers.

Despite the fact that workers receiving less than three minimum wages, who constitute the bulk of the labor force, were receiving adjustments above inflation (at least, as measured by the INPC), the 1979 wage law does not appear to have been a major contributing factor to accelerating inflation, at least in the 1980–82 period.[44] Concern was nevertheless increasing during this period about the feedback effect of full wage indexation on efforts to reduce inflation. Thus, although the 1979 law was not modified when the IMF accord went into effect, measures to de-index wage adjustments from inflation were already being anticipated; these modifications were, in fact, enacted in 1983 and will be analyzed in the ensuing section.

The Implementation and Effects of Policy Instruments on the Domestic Adjustment Process in 1983–85

The tightening of economic policies imposed by the IMF agreement during the 1983–85 period resulted in highly disparate consequences; some surpassed the targets and objectives of the stabilization program and others fell far short of expectations. As indicated above, by the end of 1984 significant progress had been made toward restoring external equilibrium. The improvement in the external accounts, however, was achieved at the cost of rising unemployment and a severe recession, especially in 1983 when GDP dropped 3.5 percent. In 1984, nevertheless, the soaring growth of exports, coupled with a good agricultural harvest, began to ease the effects of the recession on the domestic economy, while unemployment showed signs of stabilizing. Real GDP, in fact, expanded 5.1 percent in 1984, despite continued depressed levels of fixed investment. Although the recession was undoubtedly worse

---

[44] A detailed analysis of the wage law and its economic effects in this period is presented in the World Bank document, *Brazil, Economic Memorandum*, 1984.

Table V-1 BRAZIL. Public Sector Borrowing Requirements as Percentages of GDP[1]

	1982 Year-End Result	1983 IMF Estimate in March	1983 Year-End Result	1984 IMF Estimate in March	1984 Year-End Result	1985 Year-End Result
Operational Surplus or Deficit	−6.8	0.7	−3.0	0.3	−1.6	−4.3
Monetary Correction	−9.8	−9.5	−16.9	−12.3	−20.5	−23.2
Total Deficit	−16.6	−8.8	−19.9	−12.0	−22.1	−27.5

[1] It should be noted that the IMF and the Brazilian authorities incorporated several methodological changes into the calculation of the PSBR in early 1985, which tended to increase their levels by an average of 2 percentage points of GDP for the 1982–84 period. The March estimates for 1983 and 1984 thus are not strictly comparable to the year-end results.
Source: IMF and Central Bank of Brazil.

than had been anticipated, especially in 1983, it had nevertheless been expected as an inevitable consequence of the adjustment process.

Brazil's significant progress in adjusting its balance of payments was tarnished, however, by the singular lack of success in controlling inflation and the monetary aggregates. Inflation, in fact, caused many of the quarterly targets agreed upon with the IMF to be almost consistently missed. For this reason, the assumed rate of inflation in the program had to be frequently revised, a fact partially reflected by Brazil's need to sign seven different Letters of Intent with the Fund during the 1983–84 period.

With this overview in mind, the analysis of this section now turns to a more detailed—but basically qualitative—examination of the effects of economic policies in the 1982–85 period.

The Implementation and Results of Fiscal Policy

As indicated, the reduction of public sector borrowing requirements (PSBR) became a major focus of the IMF accord, since lowering the fiscal deficit was viewed as a principal means to bring about balance of payments adjustment primarily via reduced domestic demand and lower imports, while easing pressures on the price level. As displayed in Table V-1, however, the results obtained through the end of 1985 were mixed.

Clearly, much progress was made in reducing the operational deficit, which declined to a 3 percent average of GDP in the 1983–85 period, a marked improvement when compared with the 6.8 percent deficit registered in 1982. Much of this improvement was the result of sharp real declines in state enterprise outlays, which plummeted by more than one-third between 1981 and 1985. Some components of current expenditures also logged similar declines, especially wages. Despite the reduction in the operational deficit, the authorities were nevertheless forced to mobilize an ever-increasing volume of resources to meet the monetary correction requirements of the burgeoning domestic debt, which soared pari passu with inflation. The magnitude of this problem is clearly displayed in Table V-1, which reveals that instead of stabilizing at their 1982 level of around 9.8 percent of GDP as called for in the

IMF agreement, such payments soared to the equivalent of 16.9 percent of GDP in 1983 and to 23.2 percent by 1985. As a result of these trends, the nominal deficit rose 7.6 percentage points in the 1984–85 period, reaching 27.5 percent of GDP in the latter year.

The results in Table V-1 require further analysis. For instance, the magnitude of the drop in the operational deficit between 1982 and 1984 (5.2 percentage points of GDP) indicates that Brazil did much to eradicate a major source of economic disequilibrium. In this regard, if public outlays can be cut without a concomitant fall in income, then domestic adjustment is relatively painless. This assumes, in other words, that income is determined relatively independently of the level of public expenditure.[45] If, on the other hand, income is a function of government expenditure and outlays are cut, a fall in output and a rise in unemployment are inevitable. The second case summarizes the Brazilian experience: although the "operational" deficit was reduced, this reduction was achieved primarily by heavy declines in investment outlays, which, in turn, resulted in a large drop in output and employment. Moreover, given the huge size of Brazil's public sector and that sector's close economic bonds with the private sector, it becomes politically difficult to maintain government expenditure at reduced levels over time, a fact that already became evident in 1985, when the "operational" deficit jumped more than two and one-half times to 4.3 percent of GDP.[46]

The inability to sustain the reduction in the "operational" deficit was also affected by the trends in Treasury operations, which account for a significant part of general government operations. During 1984, for instance, net Treasury expenditure was limited to a 198 percent increase in nominal terms, well below the rate of inflation and a direct consequence of austerity efforts. At the same time, however, net revenues also rose at the same pace—despite the upturn in economic activity in the last quarter of 1984—as the Treasury accounts closed the year in virtual equilibrium. The resulting 6.4 percent real decline in revenues reflected essentially two factors. First, a substantial part of gross receipts (Cr$3.4 trillion or 22.1 percent of the total) was returned to the private sector in the form of tax credits, primarily as rebates on manufactured exports (crédito-premio) and on the federal value added tax. Second, revenue growth was also impacted by the severity of the 1982–84 recession, the erosion of real receipts because of inflation, and the emergence of a growing underground economy.[47] These factors, coupled with

---

[45]This would be the case, for instance, of an economy with a very small public sector (for example, contemporary Paraguay).

[46]As analyzed later, this problem has persisted to the present and has greatly complicated the initiation of many needed reforms in the public sector.

[47]Based on estimates of tax evasion, the nonreporting of foreign exchange earnings, and wage payments in the informal sector, the size of Brazil's underground economy was conservatively estimated at 10.9 percent of GDP in 1981 and 12.1 percent in 1982. See Beatriz Melo Flôres de Lima, *Criptoeconomia ou Economia Subterrânea*, Estudos Especiais IBRE, No. 5, Instituto Brasileiro de Economia (Editôra de Fundação Getúlio Vargas, 1985), p. 66. The data in this report also suggest the strong possibility that the recovery in the ratio of investment to current GDP may be overstated by the official figures, especially in 1987 and 1988.

the problem that rates were already exceptionally high for some categories of taxes (for example, the corporate income tax and the tax on financial operations), indicated the timeliness of a major tax reform and, more fundamentally, a revision of economic development strategy.

In terms of their implications for economic policy and management, however, the problems posed by the extraordinary growth of monetary correction on the domestic debt as displayed in Table V-1 were in many ways more perplexing and urgent in terms of requiring a solution than were those discussed earlier in relation to the operational component of the public sector deficit. Although various factors contributed to the growth of these payments, a major cause stemmed from the need to generate rising trade surpluses in order to meet interest payments on the foreign debt, whose servicing, as explained in Chapter III, became increasingly the responsibility of the government. The growth of the surplus, however, translated into strong expansionary pressures on the accounts of the central bank. To absorb the resulting increase in liquidity and maintain control over the monetary aggregates (in order to comply with the provisions of the IMF accord), the authorities were forced to rely heavily upon open-market operations. Consequently, the stock of fully indexed domestic debt expanded at an accelerated rate.[48] Moreover, in order to capture the necessary volume of resources in the open market, yields on domestic debt instruments, particularly Readjustable Treasury Bonds (ORTN) and Treasury Bills (LTN), had to be increased. This resulted in rising real interest rates, which in turn were transmitted with increasingly short lags throughout the rest of the financial sector to both deposits and loans. By late 1983, real interest rates on six-month investment bank credits were about 30 percent, a fact that greatly discouraged investment, made overall monetary management increasingly intractable, and heightened expectations for more inflation.

Moreover, as real interest rates rose, additional distortions surfaced. On the one hand, a rising volume of new debt had to be offered just to meet the servicing requirements of existing bonds and bills as they matured or were rolled over; this was in addition to the new issues that were required to conduct normal market operations. Consequently, instead of providing a solution, the rapid growth of the domestic debt itself was becoming a central issue of economic policy; this fact is clearly evidenced in Table V-2, which reveals that the annual increase in value of outstanding federal debt instruments as a percentage of GDP rose from a relatively stable average of 2.5 percent in the 1973–80 period to 6 percent in 1981 and, by 1985, had reached 14.5 percent. At the same time, concern was mounting about the "crowding out" effect of open-market operations on the private sector. In particular, many analysts alleged that the public sector's increasing demand for resources not only raised interest rates but also reduced credit availabilities to private sector

---

[48]Rogério L. Furquim Werneck, "Poupança Estatal, Dívida Externa, e a Crise Financiero do Setor Público" (see note 31) pp. 553–554 and Paulo Nogueira Batista, Jr., "Formação de Capital e Transferência de Recursos ao Exterior", *Revista de Economia Política*, Vol. 7, No. 1 (janeiro-março 1987), p. 19.

Table V-2 BRAZIL. Federal Domestic Debt in Bonds and Treasury Bills[a]
(millions of cruzados)

Year	ORTN/OTN[b] (1)	Stock at Year-End LTN/LFT[c] (2)	LCB[d] (3)	Total (4)	Annual Flows (5)	GDP in Current Prices (6)	Annual Flows/ GDP (%) (7) = (5)/(6)
1972	15.9	8.1	—	24.0	—	346.6	—
1973	20.8	12.6	—	33.4	9.4	511.9	1.8
1974	32.9	14.4	—	47.3	13.9	745.2	1.9
1975	58.4	22.1	—	80.5	33.2	1,049.5	3.2
1976	80.9	64.7	—	145.6	65.1	1,634.7	4.0
1977	97.7	106.2	—	203.9	58.3	2,495.5	2.3
1978	151.8	161.9	—	313.7	109.8	3,618.3	3.0
1979	233.6	163.9	—	397.5	83.8	5,963.7	1.4
1980	439.5	186.1	—	625.6	228.1	12,399.8	1.8
1981	1,357.6	788.3	—	2,145.9	1,520.3	24,662.2	6.2
1982	4,027.3	709.5	—	4,736.8	2,590.9	51,029.4	5.1
1983	8,782.9	360.4	—	9,143.3	4,406.5	118,936.3	3.7
1984	50,867.0	2,214.0	—	53,081.0	43,937.7	393,745.4	11.2
1985	249,596.0	8,893.0	—	258,489.0	205,408.0	1,413,792.4	14.5
1986	148,697.0	8,057.0	202,465.0	359,219.0	100,730.0	3,708,196.0	2.7
1987	617,542.0	41,431.0	1,633,602.0	2,229,575.0	1,870,356.0	11,884,734.0	15.7
1988							
January	674,732.0	250,147.0	1,851,568.0	2,776,439.0		—	—
March	1,011,945.0	693,106.0	1,773,447.0	3,478,498.0		—	—
June	2,606,479.0	3,064,540.0	1,847,478.0	1,847,478.0		—	—
October	5,070,415.0	12,622,392.0	—	17,692,797.0		—	—
December	9,921,852.0	21,605,595.0	—	31,527,447.0	29,297,872.0	92,993,144.0	31.0
1989							
January	124,000.0	36,644,000.0	—	36,768,000.0		—	—
March	876,000.0	57,926,000.0	—	58,882,000.0		—	—
June	1,481,000.0	84,258,000.0	—	85,739,000.0		—	—
October	1,717,000.0	298,080,000.0	—	299,797,000.0		—	—
December	747,000.0	705,877,000.0	—	706,623,000.0	675,095,553.0	1,366,421,000.0	49.4

[a] Includes only debt instruments held by the public.
[b] ORTN (Obrigações Reajustáveis do Tesouro-Readjustable Treasury Bonds) and OTN (Obrigações do Tesouro-Treasury Bonds). During 1986, the OTN were not indexed; by early 1987, they were indexed exactly as the ORTN had been.
[c] LTN (Letras do Tesouro-Treasury Bills) and LFT (Letras Financieras do Tesouro-Financial Treasury Bills).
[d] LBC (Letras do Banco Central-Central Bank Bills).

Source: Central Bank of Brazil and estimates of the IDB Country Studies Division.

Table V-3 BRAZIL. Indicators of Money and Quasi-Money

	M₁			M₂			M₃			M₅			M₁/M₄
	NCzS Thousands[d]	Percentage Growth in the Year	Percentage of Current GDP	NCzS Millions[d]	Percentage Growth in the Year	Percentage of Current GDP	NCzS Millions[d]	Percentage Growth in the Year	Percentage of Current GDP	NCzS Millions[d]	Percentage Growth in the Year	Percentage of Current GDP	Percentage
1980	1,407.0	70.2	8.9	2.1	66.3	12.8	3.1	72.6	19.1	3.7	68.7	23.0	38.0
1981	2,790.0	87.2	8.0	5.0	135.2	13.1	7.4	140.7	19.4	8.8	140.5	23.1	31.7
1982	4,649.0	81.7	7.1	7.5	51.5	12.0	15.2	104.6	20.8	18.6	110.7	25.1	25.0
1983	9,177.0	97.4	5.5	18.7	148.8	10.0	36.2	141.9	19.9	46.5	150.5	24.7	19.7
1984	27,698.0	201.9	4.0	80.8	331.9	9.9	143.3	288.8	18.5	182.5	292.7	23.4	15.2
1985	111,967.0	304.3	3.9	370.5	358.6	12.2	588.1	310.4	20.5	737.3	303.9	25.9	15.2
1986	455,476.0	306.7	6.1	815.0	119.9	14.8	1,145.0	94.6	22.1	1,436.0	94.8	27.7	31.7
1987													
March	424,991.0	−6.7	—	1,010.0	23.9	—	1,754.0	52.4	—	2,191.0	81.9	—	19.4
June	475,166.0	4.3	—	1,621.0	98.9	—	2,702.0	136.0	—	3,246.0	179.1	—	14.6
October	695,783.0	52.8	—	2,087.0	156.1	—	3,582.0	212.8	—	4,204.0	224.6	—	9.7
December	1,035,920.0	127.5	5.8	3,228.0	308.6	13.6	5,539.0	383.9	21.2	6,500.0	352.6	25.7	15.9
1988													
March	1,170,122.0	13.0	—	4,649.0	39.7	—	8,578.0	54.7	—	10,097.0	55.4	—	11.6
June	1,844,030.0	78.0	—	9,443.0	183.7	—	16,818.0	189.1	—	18,533.0	185.3	—	10.0
October	3,711,124.0	258.2	—	17,408.0	423.1	—	29,941.0	569.9	—	43,013.0	561.8	—	8.6
December	6,958,155.0	571.7	2.9	38,486.0	1,056.4	12.9	64,446.0	1,063.5	20.3	74,409.0	1,044.8	23.6	9.4
1989													
March	9,751,000.0	40.1	—	68,553.0	78.0	—	116,577.0	80.9	—	125,495.0	68.7	—	7.8
June	15,988,000.0	129.8	—	101,728.0	164.0	—	167,258.0	159.5	—	187,181.0	151.6	—	8.5
October	38,441,000.0	452.5	—	338,238.0	778.9	—	512,402.0	695.1	—	571,868.0	668.4	—	6.8
December	105,956,000.0	1,422.8	2.0	812,579.0	2,011.4	13.1	1,127,379.0	1,649.3	19.7	1,266,451.0	1,602.0	22.5	8.4

[a]M₁ + domestic debt titles held by the public.
[b]M₂ + savings deposits.
[c]M₃ + time deposits.
[d]December unless otherwise indicated.
Source: Central Bank of Brazil and IDB Country Studies Division.

firms, especially those producing basically for the domestic markets. Some analysts, in fact, pointed to a "double crowding out" effect, since even credit available to the public sector had to be increasingly allocated to servicing of the domestic debt rather than to productive investments.

The Implementation and Results of Monetary and Credit Policy

For reasons largely anticipated in the preceding section, the ceilings established for the expansion of monetary variables such as M_1, the monetary base, and, to a lesser extent, net domestic credit were almost consistently surpassed from the time that the IMF accord began to be implemented. Moreover, this occurred despite the heavy use of open-market operations as indicated earlier. In the case of M_1, for instance, the 1983 target was a 60 percent increase, but the actual increase was 97.4 percent. In 1984, M_1 soared 201.9 percent compared with a target that was adjusted upward from 60 percent at the beginning of the year to 95 percent in September. Most of this increase occurred in December 1984, when both M_1 and the monetary base registered unprecedented 35.8 percent increases. Essentially the same pattern was repeated in 1985, when M_1 rose 304 percent, including a 33 percent expansion in December.

As was indicated, part of the difficulty in complying with the monetary targets stemmed from Brazil's success in adjusting its balance of payments. This problem became evident in 1984, when the monetary impact produced by the higher-than-expected accumulation of net international reserves could not be fully neutralized. To offset—partially, at least—these expansionary pressures, measures were also adopted to increase reserve requirements of state commercial banks as well as the receipts of the social security system. Despite these and numerous other minor measures to contain the money supply, the velocity of currency in circulation rose dramatically to accommodate the increase in reserves and other sources of inflation.[49] This fact is clearly indicated by the decline in the ratio of the money supply to GDP, which plummeted from 15 percent in the mid–1970s, to less than 4 percent by 1985. The growing unwillingness of the public to hold cruzeiros is also indicated in Table V-3, by the relatively more rapid growth of quasi-money, which afforded greater protection against inflation since virtually all forms of time deposits were adjusted by monetary correction.

The Implementation and Results of Wage Policy

As explained earlier, Brazil's existing wage legislation was not modified when the IMF agreement went into effect. Nevertheless, it was clear from the outset

---

[49] The expansionary pressures from Brazil's trade surplus reached especially dramatic proportions in 1988. As will be analyzed in ensuing pages, however, it is somewhat misleading to attribute surging inflation to the monetization of reserves or to any other isolated factor or set of factors. A more satisfactory explanation resides in the increasingly inertial nature of Brazilian inflation, a phenomenon that became more widely understood during 1984 and a subject that is analyzed extensively in the rest of this chapter.

Table V-4 BRAZIL. Trends in Income Distribution of the Economically Active Population

Deciles	Percentage of Total Income 1979	1984	1987	Average Real Monthly Income[a] 1979	1981	1984	1987	Percentages Change in Average Income 1979–1981	1981–1984	1984–1987	1979–1987
1st	1.3	1.0	0.8	15,750	13,049	9,578	9,745	−17.1	−26.6	1.8	−38.1
2nd	1.8	2.0	1.9	22,450	23,883	20,441	23,006	6.4	−14.4	12.6	2.5
3rd	2.8	2.6	2.6	34,139	32,953	26,624	30,790	−3.5	−19.2	15.7	−9.8
4th	4.0	3.6	3.5	50,047	47,986	36,008	41,802	−4.2	−25.0	16.1	−16.6
5th	4.9	4.4	3.9	60,797	57,302	44,702	47,477	−5.7	−22.0	6.2	−21.9
6th	4.9	5.2	5.5	60,547	66,028	51,764	66,988	9.1	−21.6	29.4	10.6
7th	7.4	7.6	7.2	91,598	93,928	76,471	87,218	2.6	−18.6	14.1	−4.8
8th	10.1	10.5	10.1	125,737	126,242	105,527	122,240	0.4	−16.4	15.8	−2.8
9th	15.8	16.5	16.1	196,201	193,491	165,300	193,933	−1.4	−14.6	17.3	−1.2
10th	47.0	46.6	48.4	583,199	547,606	468,296	583,613	−6.1	−14.5	25.1	0.4
Total:	100.0	100.0	100.0	124,049	120,247	100,471	120,881	−3.1	−16.4	20.3	−2.6
Bottom 40%	9.9	9.2	8.7	121,996	117,871	92,651	105,344	−3.4	−21.4	13.7	−13.7
Top 40%	80.3	81.2	81.7	996,717	961,267	815,594	987,007	−3.6	−15.2	21.1	−0.8
Top 5%	34.2	33.3	35.2	843,775	787,106	668,950	850,640	−6.7	−15.0	27.2	0.8
Top 1%	14.3	13.4	16.1	1,660,025	1,558,761	1,343,133	1,944,832	−6.1	−13.8	44.8	17.2
Gini Coefficient	0.590	0.576	0.591								

[a] Measured in 1980 cruzeiros. (Nominal data deflated by the average values of Rio de Janeiro Cost of Living Index).
Source: IDB Country Studies Division, based on Statistical Appendix, Table 14.

that the IMF was pressing for the de-indexing of salary adjustments from past increases in prices as a key policy instrument for reducing inflation. After considerable debate, this modification of wage policy was accomplished by congressional approval of Decree Law 2.065 in November 1983. The new law retained major features of the previous law in that wage adjustments would continue to be made biannually on a sliding scale related to income (expressed as multiples of the monthly minimum wage) and tied to variations in the INPC. Thus, at the bottom end of the income scale, workers earning less than three minimum wages were entitled to 100 percent of the variation in the INPC (as compared with 110 percent under the previous law). At the top end of the scale, workers earning more than the equivalent of fifteen minimum wages were entitled to only 50 percent of the variation in the INPC (as compared with 60 percent under the previous law). Based on the salary structure existing in the private sector, it was estimated that the wage bill of a typical firm would be adjusted by an average of 87 percent of the increase in the INPC.

Although it is difficult to quantify the effects of Law 2.065, available evidence suggests that the implementation of this legislation, coupled with other restrictive demand management measures and persistently high rates of inflation, effectively lowered real wages and negatively impacted income distribution. Estimates through 1984, for example, suggest that the purchasing power of wages was, on average, about 30 percent lower than in 1979. Even the middle and upper income strata were affected by the recession; in this regard, a Getulio Vargas Foundation study showed that 97.7 percent of the 436 items included in the Rio de Janeiro cost of living index registered increases during the 1979–84 period above the nominal salary gains of an average professionally trained technician over the same period.[50]

Still, the brunt of Brazil's domestic adjustment and wage policy revisions appears to have been borne by the lower income groups. Based on the annual samples conducted by the Brazilian Institute of Geography and Statistics (IBGE), for instance, the data in Table V-4 reveal that, while the real income of all groups fell by an average of 16.4 percent during the recession phase of the 1981–84 period, real income of the bottom 40 percent (whose share in total income accounted for only 9.2 percent in 1984) declined even more rapidly, plummeting an estimated 21.4 percent; conversely, workers in the top 40 percent, whose earnings accounted for 81.2 percent of total income in 1984, registered a decline of only 15.2 percent. By the latter year, it was estimated that 66 percent of the economically active population (EAP) had incomes of two minimum wages or less—the cutoff line used by many specialists for measuring absolute poverty in Brazil. Moreover, the average value conceals important regional disparities, especially in the Northeast, where it was estimated that more than 86 percent of the EAP earned less than the equivalent of two minimum wages.[51] Finally, it should be noted that, despite

---

[50]Although this study did not specify the income level of such an "average professionally trained technician," it is assumed to be equivalent to at least ten minimum wages.

[51]Hélio Jaguaribe, *Brasil, 2000* (see note 35), p. 60.

the brief recovery of the 1985–86 period, real income levels for nearly all groups were lower in 1987 than in 1979. Again, the principal exceptions were the wealthy groups, especially the richest 10 percent of the EAP, whose share rose about two percentage points during the period to account for more than 48 percent of the total.

In the case of employment, the effects of recession were also severe. Although numerous deficiencies exist with respect to Brazil's labor force and employment statistics, it is nonetheless clear that unemployment reached unprecedented levels during 1983 and the first half of 1984, especially in the highly industrialized Center-South. Open unemployment, which averaged 6.7 percent in major metropolitan centers during 1983, reached a peak of 8.3 percent in May 1984. Thereafter, however, unemployment stabilized and began declining, largely in response to the substantial growth of exports and the gradual recovery of domestic industry in the closing months of the year. Nevertheless, if comprehensive data were available for underemployment, the effects of the recession could undoubtedly be shown to have been much worse. In partial support of this point, studies carried out by the IBGE indicated that the number of "self-employed" workers (many of whom are employed in low-income, tertiary-type activities) rose 15 to 16 percent during 1984 in Brazil's major metropolitan areas (São Paulo, Belo Horizonte, Rio de Janeiro, Salvador, Fortaleza, Recife, and Porto Alegre); consequently, given the combined economically active population of about 13.5 million persons in these areas, those figures imply that between 1.9 million and 2.2 million persons were only marginally employed at best, a fact consistent with the data on income distribution presented in Table V-4. Finally, an additional cost to the economy resulting from unemployment was the loss of fiscal revenue; if employment had been 2.5 million higher in 1984 (total unemployment was conservatively estimated at 3 million, or 6.4 percent of the economically active population) and if each worker had paid the equivalent of only one minimum wage in taxes, the incremental effect on revenues would have been an estimated one trillion cruzeiros, equivalent to more than 4 percent of total receipts during 1984.[52]

Taken together, the evidence tends to support the hypothesis that wage policy was not a primary source of inflation in the 1983–84 period. In economic and social welfare terms, however, it is equally clear that the costs of de-indexing wage adjustments from inflation after November 1983 were substantial. By late 1984, in fact, pressures mounted to make wage policy less restrictive. Toward this end, wage legislation was modified again in late Oc-

---

[52]At the national level, a study carried out by the Ministry of Labor suggested that the economic cost of unemployment to Brazil was on the order of $27 billion, an amount roughly equal to 1984 exports and nearly two and a half times the interest payments on its foreign debt. This study was based essentially on estimated expenditures either not made or made only in minimal amounts by the unemployed, including, *inter alia*, basic subsistence expenditures (food, clothing, and other basic needs); forgone expenditures for medicines and medical treatment (whose attendant social costs on well-being and productivity were not included); and the loss from investments in education.

tober. At the bottom end of the scale, workers earning from one to three minimum wages continued to receive biannual adjustments equal to 100 percent of the variation in the INPC, whereas workers receiving more than three minimum wages were entitled to a flat 80 percent of the variation (instead of a decreasing share as stipulated in Law 2.065). Moreover, all categories of workers were entitled to negotiate additional increases based on productivity gains. Although the implementation of this law has yet to be evaluated, it nevertheless represented a first step toward recouping the income losses of the 1983–84 period; it is clear, however, that wage adjustments granted in 1985 and 1986 were instrumental to the exceptional recovery of consumption outlays—and economic growth—that occurred in that period.

A Quantitative Analysis of the Impact of Brazil's Economic Adjustment Policies on Output and Inflation

The previous section provided a largely qualitative evaluation of the impact of Brazil's economic policies on the adjustment process. The present section attempts to measure the relative effects of adjustment policies on output and prices, in order not only to identify the causal variables underlying the acute stagflation of the 1982–84 period but also to recognize essential modifications to economic policy that were required by year-end 1985—and which, it might be added, were still necessary in early 1990.

Toward this objective, several regression models were developed in an effort to explain the behavior of GDP and prices in terms of several of the key policy instruments analyzed earlier, especially credit to the private sector, minimum wages, and the exchange rate. The models developed for this purpose are somewhat restricted in that they largely abstract from structural changes, especially those affecting production functions, which, in turn, may impact output and prices in the longer run. Moreover, many short-run factors such as fluctuations in the terms of trade, agricultural output, and capital inflows are introduced implicitly rather than explicitly, through their effects on the explanatory variables. Imports, for instance, are determined essentially outside the model rather than as a function of investment or secondary sector output. In part, this is because, in times of balance of payments crisis such as those that prevailed in the 1982–84 period, prohibitions, effective tariffs, and foreign exchange constraints (as analyzed in Chapter III) have a major impact on the level of purchases abroad. Finally, despite its critical relationship to the level of economic activity, the public sector, largely because of insufficient data, does not enter directly as a producing sector in the models specified, but does clearly influence the results obtained through the policies it pursues.

With the foregoing considerations in mind, the equation specified to measure variation in real GDP over the 1963–85 period is as follows:

$$y = 5.712 + 0.178 r_{-1} + 0.086(c-w) - 8.545d$$

$$(8.305) \quad (2.655) \quad\quad (4.365) \quad\quad\quad (4.347)$$

$$R^2 = 0.61$$

$$\overline{R}^2 = 0.55$$

$$D\text{-}W = 1.60$$

where

y = Real GDP growth rate
c = Nominal growth rate of credit (lagged) to the private sector
w = Nominal growth rate of the minimum wage
r_{-1} = Lagged percentage change in the real effective exchange rate
d = Dummy variable.

As revealed, the above regression, besides possessing relatively good statistical properties and providing a reasonable fit to historical data, also generates useful information about the relationship between growth trends and the impact of economic policy. In broad terms, the regression constant can be regarded as a measure of Brazil's long-term growth trend (that is, 5.7 percent per annum), whereas the other explanatory variables shed light on the fluctuations around that trend. For instance, the variable $(c-w)$, or credit expansion to the private sector, deflated by the growth in nominal wages, can be interpreted as the amount of "working capital" available to the economy for productive activities. For purposes of analyzing the impact of stabilization measures on current output, this formulation is instructive. Specifically, if the difference between the growth of credit and nominal wages is 1 percent, the result in Brazil's case would be stimulus of 0.086 percentage points to the growth rate of output. The interpretation of the real effective exchange rate variable is similar in that a 1 percent real devaluation (that is, an increase) would imply a hike of 0.178 percentage points in the GDP growth rate.

The respective trends of $(c-w)$ and r_{-1} during Brazil's recent adjustment process are displayed in Table V-5. In the first instance, the table reveals that $(c-w)$ turned sharply negative in 1979 and, after nearly stabilizing in 1982, reached a maximum decline of 62.6 percent in 1985. During the 1980–83 period, this result clearly reflected increasing efforts to tighten money and credit policies on the one hand, and the fact that wage increases, although perhaps not primary sources of inflation in this period, were nevertheless fully indexed to past inflation for the bulk of the labor force and, thus, tended to obviate or weaken the effect of other adjustment polices.

Although this interpretation is appropriate for explaining how the reduction in "working capital" contributed to the deepening recession in the 1980–83 period, it is unsatisfactory for reconciling the fact that when $(c-w)$ became even more negative in 1985, economic activity was recovering strongly.

Table V-5 BRAZIL. Trends in Growth Rates of Credit to the Private Sector, Minimum Wages, and the Real Effective Exchange Rate
(Percentage Change)

	Lagged Credit to Private Sector (c)	Minimum Wages (w)	Lagged Credit Minus Minimum Wages (c − w)	Lagged Real Effective Exchange Rate (r_{-1})
1973	51.5	16.1	35.4	4.3
1974	55.6	20.8	34.8	−2.4
1975	55.9	41.4	14.5	3.5
1976	56.1	44.1	12.0	−1.8
1977	58.0	44.1	13.9	1.4
1978	51.1	41.0	10.1	5.1
1979	49.0	88.0	−39.0	10.6
1980	64.9	97.4	−32.5	21.4
1981	73.1	106.1	−33.0	−13.9
1982	91.2	97.6	−6.4	6.0
1983	95.8	142.4	−46.6	32.4
1984	146.4	191.6	−45.2	7.7
1985	203.4	266.0	−62.6	2.8
1986*	248.9	144.0	104.9	4.3
1987*	119.3	140.4	−21.1	−1.9

*Excluded from the regression.
Source: Estimates of the IDB Division of Country Studies.

Several factors could help to explain this seemingly paradoxical result. First, as indicated in the previous chapter, firms were forced by their high levels of indebtedness to rely increasingly on internal cash generation as a source of financing; this fact, coupled with the existence of ample capacity in most sectors, appeared to ameliorate partially the problems caused by continued tight credit policies in the 1984–85 period. Second, for a large number of firms, the shortage of "working capital" was also eased by currency devaluation, which stimulated a dramatic growth of exports (and profits) in the second half of 1984 and led to generalized economic recovery in 1985. In this regard, Table V-5 reveals that, after appreciating in the wake of the ill-fated attempts to pre-fix monetary correction and the exchange rate in 1980, the cruzeiro was depreciated substantially thereafter in real terms, especially in 1983 when a 32.4 percent decline occurred. Finally, it must be emphasized that by 1985, with real wages and employment increasing steadily, the restrictive phase of Brazil's adjustment to the debt crisis was essentially over. Economic growth was now conditioned much more by expansive demand policies than by the restrictive measures that characterized the IMF accord, a trend that also carried over into 1986.

With respect to prices, a similar procedure was followed in order to examine the effects of stabilization policies on Brazil's inflationary process. In this instance, the key explanatory variables identified were lagged inflation and the growth rates of the real effective exchange rate and minimum wages. The resulting regression estimated for the 1964–85 period was as follows:

$$p = 9.76 + 0.41_{p-1} + 0.56w_m + 0.46_{r-1} - 1.06y$$

$$(1.85) \quad (3.87) \qquad (7.40) \qquad (2.44) \qquad (2.26)$$

	Elasticities	Short-Term	Long-Term
$R^2 = 0.982$	Lagged inflation	0.40	—
$\bar{R}^2 = 0.978$			
D-W = 1.995	Minimum wages	0.56	0.95
	Real effective exchange rate (lagged)	0.46	0.78

where

p = Inflation rate in period t
p_{-1} = Inflation rate in period t-1
w_m = Growth rate of minimum wage
r_{-1} = Growth rate of the real effective exchange rate in period t-1
y = Growth rate of real GDP.

As was the case for the output regression, the regression estimated for prices also possesses good statistical properties, provides a reasonable fit to actual data (Table V-6), and, most importantly, permits valuable insights into the nature of Brazil's inflationary process. First of all, the equation indicates that the speed at which inflation can be reduced is greatly constrained by the strong relationship that exists between price increases in current and past periods. Assuming, for instance, that inflation in year t-1 was 100 percent (that is, about equal to Brazil's annual average for the 1980–82 period), then a price increase of 41 percent could be expected—even if all other explanatory variables were perfectly controlled, that is, neutral in terms of their impact on the price level. The interpretation of the other regression coefficients involving policy variables is the same: assuming 100 percent inflation in the previous year and holding the effect of other explanatory variables constant, the predicted increase in prices in year t would be 46 percent in the case of the real effective exchange rate and 56 percent for minimum wages.[53]

The most important insights to be derived from the regression, however, do not stem from the analysis of individual variables (while holding the others constant) but rather from the realization that the indicated variables tended to move together at accelerating rates and, consequently, exercised mutually reinforcing effects on the escalation of prices.[54] For this reason, it becomes

---

[53] It should be noted that even though average real wages were low in the 1982–84 period and contributed directly to the severity of Brazil's recession, the nation's wage legislation nevertheless constituted an increasingly serious barrier to reducing inflation. Specifically, by permitting the real value of wages to be restored twice a year, for workers earning up to three minimum wages, to their peak—as opposed to their average—level during the preceding six months, the laws prevailing through 1984 limited the rate at which inflation could be reduced, even if inflationary expectations from other sources were sharply curtailed. An excellent treatment of this problem is presented in an article by Mario Henrique Simonsen, "Desindexação e Reforma Monetaria," *Conjuntura Economica* (novembro 1984), pp. 101–104.

[54] Statistically, this fact is also confirmed in the larger values obtained for the long-term elasticities of the price regression, which measure the impact of the explanatory variables, if inflation remains at a high or rising rate over a period of several years.

Table V-6 BRAZIL. Actual and Predicted Changes in Output and Prices, 1973-1985
(Percent growth)

	Real Output Growth Actual	Real Output Growth Predicted	Average Growth in the Rio de Janeiro Consumer Price Index Actual	Average Growth in the Rio de Janeiro Consumer Price Index Predicted
1973	14.0	9.6	12.6	12.9
1974	9.0	9.5	27.6	19.0
1975	5.2	6.5	30.5	37.7
1976	9.8	7.3	40.2	38.2
1977	4.6	6.6	43.7	45.2
1978	4.8	6.8	38.7	46.2
1979	7.2	3.2	52.7	69.5
1980	9.1	4.8	82.8	81.2
1981	-3.1	-1.9	105.9	116.4
1982	1.1	2.7	98.0	100.3
1983	-2.8	0.6	142.0	130.1
1984	5.7	7.6	196.7	184.3
1985	8.4	10.2	227.0	234.3

Source: Official data and estimates of the IDB Country Studies Division.

especially important to provide a satisfactory explanation for the tremendous growth in prices since 1982, when monetary and demand management policies were significantly tightened as part of the overall adjustment program agreed to with the IMF. This result is particularly paradoxical in that the analysis of this chapter has already demonstrated that over the same period substantial gains were made in reducing the operational component of the public sector deficit (Table V-1), which was unquestionably a major source of economic disequilibrium (and pressure on the price level) by the late 1970s (see first part of this chapter and Statistical Appendix, Table 11). Undeniable progress had likewise been achieved in reducing direct and indirect subsidies from their extremely high levels of the late 1970s.

Certainly, an important part of the increase in the rate of inflation since 1982 reflected the substantial real devaluation of the cruzeiro, which, while directly stimulating exports and fostering balance of payments adjustment, also strongly impacted the rate of domestic inflation.[55] A more generalized answer, however, must be sought in the increasingly widespread and institutionalized use of indexation procedures throughout the Brazilian economy, which provided nearly automatic mechanisms for restoring nominal values of key economic variables in the current period to their real values in the previous

---

[55]The quantitative analysis of this section has confirmed both the positive impact that currency depreciation had on Brazil's balance of payment adjustment and the recovery of economic activity, on the one hand, as well as its negative impact on the price level, on the other. This conflicting impact of depreciation on the region's adjustment process is also stressed by other analysts. See, for instance, Rudiger Dornbusch and Mario Henrique Simonsen, "Inflation Stabilization with Incomes Policy Support: A Review of the Experience in Argentina, Brazil, and Israel," Paper prepared for the Group of Thirty, New York, October 2-3, 1986, p. 7.

Graph V-1. BRAZIL: Inflation versus Idle Capacity
(Percentages)

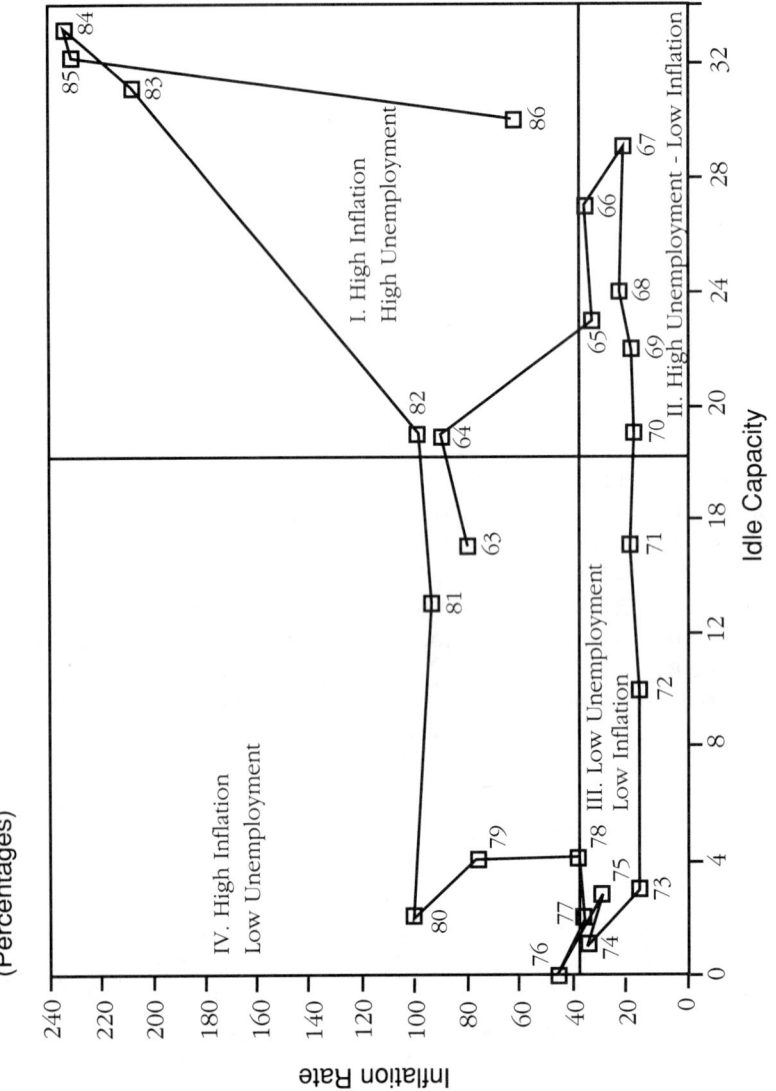

Quadrants:
- I. High Inflation High Unemployment
- II. High Unemployment - Low Inflation
- III. Low Unemployment Low Inflation
- IV. High Inflation Low Unemployment

Axes: Inflation Rate (vertical), Idle Capacity (horizontal)

Source: IDB Country Studies Division.

period.[56] Inflation, under these conditions, becomes *inertial* in nature, and, as will be argued later, nonconventional and imaginative solutions were required if it was to be successfully combated.[57]

Between the Charybdis of Indexation and Continued Inflation and the Scylla of Restrictive Demand Management Policies

In order to understand the intricate relationship between stabilization measures and the acceleration of inflation during the 1980s, it is imperative at this juncture to analyze briefly the evolution and implementation of Brazilian indexation in the broad context of the nation's stabilization programs of the mid-1960s and the early 1980s. Such an approach provides additional insight into the economic policy difficulties that must be resolved in order to achieve sustained increases in savings and investment. An appropriate starting point is 1964, when inflation briefly reached the 100 percent level during the early part of the year, largely because of a growing fiscal deficit and expansionary monetary policies. In response to this situation, the military government, which assumed control in March 1964, adopted a vigorous stabilization program based primarily on austere wage controls and fiscal reforms (Chapter II). As indicated in Graph V-1, inflation plummeted in response to these policies, falling to less than 40 percent in the 1965–66 period and to only 24 percent by 1967. At the same time, idle capacity in the economy (measured by the difference between potential[58] and actual GDP) rose steadily to a peak of about 22 percent in 1967 as unemployment reached serious levels. By the end of 1967, however, the necessary economic adjustment had essentially been accomplished. Inflation remained low (averaging around 20 percent through 1973), and capacity utilization increased steadily. The 1968–73 period, in fact, coincided with Brazil's so-called economic miracle as real GDP registered annual growth rates of around 10 percent.

Of particular interest for the present analysis, however, is the fact that indexation was gradually introduced in this period. As was examined in Chapter II, this process began in the financial markets but subsequently spread to exchange rates and then to public utilities, rents, housing mortgages, and wage contracts. Despite this, no apparent effect of indexation on inflation control was evidenced until 1974, when the growth of prices doubled to 40 percent in the wake of the first oil price shock and remained at that level through 1978.

---

[56]It bears emphasis that the link between price increases in periods t and t-1 is clearly established in the price equation estimated earlier.

[57]Good analyses of inertial inflation are presented in John Williams (ed.), *Inflation and Indexation: Argentina, Brazil and Israel* (Washington, D.C.: Institute for International Economics, March 1985); Luis Bresser Pereira, and Yoshiaki Nakano, *The Theory of Inertial Inflation: The Foundation of Economic Reform in Brazil and Argentina* (Boulder and London: Lynne Rienner Publishers, 1987); and Werner Baer, "The Resurgence of Inflation in Brasil, 1974–86", *World Development*, Volume 15, Number 8 (August 1987).

[58]Potential GDP is calculated to grow at 7 percent with respect to its assumed 1976 base year.

Even though inflation remained relatively constant in the 1974–78 period, it was nevertheless showing increasing signs of downward rigidity, as well as potential vulnerability to future price shocks. This vulnerability manifested itself in 1979 when inflation soared to nearly 80 percent, in part because of the second oil price shock, and then to a 100 percent rate in 1980. Besides higher energy costs and rising interest rates—especially in 1980—this escalation was aggravated by the halving of the indexation interval for wages and rent contracts to only six months and a 30 percent devaluation of the cruzeiro in December 1979, which came on top of regular minidevaluations throughout the year.

In many ways, 1980 was a benchmark year in Brazilian economic history; after more than a decade of expansive growth policies, the authorities began to tighten monetary policy and turned to open-market operations on a massive scale in an effort to stem the increasingly serious inflation problem. As revealed in Graph V-1, however, inflation remained impervious to these policy changes and continued at around the 100 percent level through 1982; in contrast, the growth of output slowed, with idle capacity rising steadily from about 4 percent in 1980 to 19 percent in 1982, when the IMF agreement was signed. Despite the adoption of increasingly restrictive demand management policies, the two indicators displayed in Graph V1 deteriorated at alarming rates, especially inflation, which more than doubled to a 224 percent average in the 1983–84 period. Moreover, even with the return of rapid growth in 1985, idle capacity declined only moderately while inflation remained essentially unchanged.

Taken together, Brazil's 1964–67 and 1982–84 stabilization and adjustment periods suggest some important conclusions, as well as challenges for the future. In both periods, stabilization produced unemployment and falling incomes. In the first period, however, restrictive demand and monetary measures rapidly reduced inflation since the underlying causes of the inflation were eliminated (that is, the fiscal deficit) and mechanisms did not exist that tended to perpetuate the effects of past inflation (that is, indexation). In contrast, during the 1982–84 stabilization period, many of the root causes of inflation were also substantially reduced (that is, the operational component of the public sector deficit), but, facilitated by indexation, the inflation rate actually accelerated. Indeed, a basic conclusion stemming from the analysis of this chapter is that in the absence of fundamental corrective policies, there was every reason to expect inflation to continue its recurring pattern of increasing sensitivity to any adverse supply shocks while remaining less and less responsive to restrictive demand policies.[59]

Inflation control, in short, emerged as the principal barrier to sustaining

---

[59] As examined later, this expectation was confirmed by the economic trends of the 1986–89 period. In 1986, the Cruzado Plan price freeze resulted in a sharp—albeit, short-lived—decline in inflation and a rapid economic expansion (in this regard, Graph V-1 understates the reduction of idle capacity that occurred in 1986). The freeze could not be maintained, however, and in 1987 and especially 1988, inflation exploded, while output languished. In 1989 these results were essentially replicated with the ill-fated Summer Plan.

the fragile economic recovery of 1984. Moreover, it was clear that the *means* for achieving this objective constituted the central policy challenge to the new civilian government that assumed power in March 1985. The dilemma was clear. The austere adjustment policies of the 1982–84 period, although doing much to produce splendid trade surpluses, also fueled expansionary pressures and the more rapid growth of the domestic debt; at the same time, they resulted in heavy economic and welfare costs in terms of higher unemployment, a decrease in the purchasing power of wages, and a worsening income distribution. Not only did little latitude exist for additional restrictive policies but it was also doubtful that such policies would have worked in any event. At the same time, to increase expenditures was also infeasible since, on the one hand, the nation continued to confront a severe constraint on new external borrowing, while on the other hand, unbridled monetary creation would have quickly plunged the nation into a ruinous hyperinflation and, most probably, extreme social unrest.

Thus, given that social demands to resume growth were becoming increasingly difficult to ignore, the principal challenge facing the new government was to try to reduce inflation in such a way that further losses of income and output could be minimized. In this regard, analysts were increasingly in agreement that this could best be accomplished by de-indexing the economy in such a way that the inertial component of the escalating inflationary process was eliminated.

Economic Policy in 1985 and the Cruzado Plan

Following an initial period of ambivalence, the economic policies of the new government came into increasingly sharper focus during the second half of 1985. A principal result of the emerging policy orientation was the strong recovery of domestic demand, which contributed significantly to the 8.3 percent growth in real GDP, the largest increase in six years. Moreover, as indicated in Chapter III, the 1985 recovery was achieved with almost no deterioration in Brazil's favorable external situation, since a decrease in foreign demand was largely offset by lower interest rates and oil prices.

The surge in domestic demand was led by investment, which after declining at a 10.4 percent average annual rate in the 1981–84 period, recovered by 19.9 percent in 1985. Private consumption also jumped by more than 3 percent in real terms for the second consecutive year; this increase was spurred by more liberal wage policies as well as the lagged multiplier effect of the surge in export earnings in 1984. The impact that increasingly generous wage settlements had on demand, in particular, was substantial, since average real wages in manufacturing rose by more than 13 percent, thereby enabling workers to recoup approximately half the estimated loss in purchasing power that occurred in the 1982–84 recession. At the same time, the stepped-up demand for manufactured goods enabled open unemployment in urban centers to decline from 4.8 percent in 1984 to 3.9 percent in 1985.

The 1985 recovery, however, was not costless, since inflation remained at extremely high levels, with pressures on the price level escalating steadily in the closing months of the year. To a considerable extent, the intensification of inflation was a predictable consequence of the economic upturn. For instance, the buoyant demand for consumer durables that resulted from the recovery in real wages rapidly depleted inventories and precipitated price hikes, especially in key industries such as automobiles where capacity constraints were also encountered. At the same time, pressures on the price level were also exacerbated by the increase in the public sector's operational deficit, which, although still well below its 1982 levels of 6.8 percent of GDP (Table V-1), nevertheless rose more than two and one-half times in 1985 to 4.3 percent of GDP. The increase in the fiscal disequilibrium reflected the substantial growth in the public sector wage bill, rising interest charges (especially on the domestic debt), and the hike in subsidies resulting from price and rate controls. Finally, the price level was also impacted by a severe drought in the closing months of the year, which caused food prices to rise substantially. By year-end, inflation, as measured by the expanded consumer price index (ECPI), posted a twelve-month increase of 234 percent, compared with 209 percent in 1984 and 164 percent in 1983. Moreover, in the absence of concerted action, this upward trend was generally expected to escalate, because of the previously discussed problems relating to Brazil's generalized use of indexation mechanisms, coupled with the nation's increasing vulnerability to either supply shocks or demand-pull pressures.

The already highly unstable price environment continued to deteriorate in early 1986 as the effects of generous wage settlements, coupled with rising food prices and growing capacity constraints in a widening number of industries, contributed to a 34.6 percent increase in the ECPI through February and a projected 500 percent increase by year-end. Confronted by this steady drift toward hyperinflation, the authorities declared a bank holiday on February 28, 1986, and announced a sweeping economic program to halt spiraling prices. The principal measures constituting the so called Cruzado Plan are enumerated below:

• A new monetary unit, the cruzado, was introduced to substitute the cruzeiro. The cruzado, which began to circulate on March 3, was equal to 1,000 cruzeiros. The cruzado was traded at an initially fixed rate of 13.8 per dollar, but with the understanding that it could be devalued in the future as deemed necessary by the authorities.[60] Conversion tables were also prepared so that debt previously contracted in cruzeiros could be devalued at a monthly rate of 14.4 percent (equal to the February 1986 inflation rate) against the cruzado; this was intended to enhance the acceptance of the cruzado and enable it to begin as a strong currency.

• Monetary correction on most types of financial assets was abolished

---

[60]Through September, no devaluations occurred, largely because of plummeting oil prices and the decline of the dollar, which enhanced the competitiveness of Brazilian exports in some markets. This situation changed on October 17, however, when the cruzado was devalued 1.8 percent to 14.1 per dollar.

in order to rid the inflationary process of its "inertial" component. The principal exemption was passbook savings accounts (cadernetas de poupança), which are the principal source of savings in Brazil and were to continue to be corrected (that is, the principal) by increases in the cost of living index plus 6 percent interest, the rate currently stipulated by Brazilian law. Similarly, the two most important mandatory government savings accounts for workers (Programa de Integraçao Social or PIS and the Fundo de Guarantia de Tempo de Serviço or FGTS) were also to remain indexed. At the same time, domestic interest rates were allowed to float freely—initially, at least—a measure the authorities were counting on to attract the savings urgently required for new productive investments.

- The Readjustable Treasury Bond (ORTN), undoubtedly the key indexed security in the economy, was abolished and replaced by the nonindexed National Treasury Bond (OTN), whose unit price was frozen, effective March 1, 1986, for one year at 106.4 cruzados. It was expected that this measure alone would immediately—and substantially—lower the borrowing requirements of the public sector, which not only had reached unsustainably high levels but had also resulted in extremely high interest rates, which in turn discouraged investment and caused severe distortions in the allocation of credit.

- Wages and other sources of income were converted into cruzados on the basis of their average—as opposed to "peak"—real value during the preceding six months. This adjustment to the average real wage was necessary to compensate for the fact that workers who received adjustments immediately prior to implementation of the plan would be better off in real terms than those who had received their adjustments six months earlier, especially given the escalation of the inflationary process. At the same time, however, the monthly minimum wage was increased to the equivalent of $57.80, an estimated 8 percent real gain for low-income workers. Rents and mortgage payments were also frozen for the coming year at their average real levels over the past six months; previously these were adjusted every six—and sometimes every three—months, according to the rate of inflation. In the case of wages, a trigger mechanism was also adopted so that if inflation were to rise 20 percent or more within the year, nominal wages would automatically be adjusted by that amount.

- A few prices, including several public utility tariffs, milk, and automobiles, were increased and were to be frozen for an indefinite period, along with prices of all other goods and services, which were to remain at their February 28 prices.

The Cruzado Plan produced highly disparate effects on Brazil's economic performance during 1986—the consequences of which have continued to the present. For instance, although the measures just summarized did facilitate a significant deceleration of inflation during the second and third quarters of the year, they also triggered a boom in consumer expenditures; by year-end, total consumption had risen 10.9 percent in real terms (compared with a 7.6 percent increase in real GDP). This boom occurred principally because the price freeze, coupled with the lower cost of consumer credit and rising real wages, precipitated a dramatic growth in domestic demand. At the same time, fixed investment, despite rising by 22.2 percent, was insufficient to alleviate mounting capacity constraints in the productive sectors; consequently, price pressures once again began to build at a rapid pace by year-end. This situation was aggravated by a 6.2 percent decline in agricultural real value added. For the most part, the drop in agricultural supplies was attributable to the severe drought of late 1985, which reduced harvests of most major crops in 1986; however, it also reflected the fact that the price freeze caused shortages in meat and milk supplies as many producers cut back—and at times suspended—production in order to minimize financial losses.

Most of the intensification of economic activity during 1986 was concentrated in the secondary sectors, whose combined value added rose 14.1 percent in real terms. Construction, for instance, expanded by 19.8 percent, albeit from a depressed base. Owing to its large share of GDP, however, the most important sector was manufacturing, whose real value added jumped 11.3 percent, the largest increase in a decade. Particularly dynamic was the production of capital goods and consumer durables, which increased by rates of 21.6 percent and 20.3 percent, respectively. The intense activity levels in these subsectors also contributed significantly to the estimated 25 percent growth of average real wages in manufacturing as well as to large gains in employment. In the state of São Paulo, for instance, some 330 thousand industrial jobs were created in 1986 alone; it is estimated that the 400 thousand jobs lost during the 1982–83 recession were fully recouped by the end of the 1984–86 period.

In contrast to the buoyant performance in the real sectors, Brazil's balance of payments was adversely affected by the implementation of the Cruzado Plan. This was especially the case of the trade balance, which dropped from its 1984–85 average surplus of nearly $12.8 billion to only $8.3 billion. To a large extent, this decrease reflected the deteriorating performance of exports, which declined by more than 12 percent from their 1985 level to around $22.4 billion. This was attributable not only to weak prices and lower volume for key commodities but also to the increasing diversion of potential exports to the domestic markets to meet soaring demand, a process no doubt encouraged by the maintenance of a fixed exchange rate from March to mid-October. The same factors also stimulated greater demand for imports, which rose 6.7 percent to $14 billion as stepped-up purchases of raw materials, capital goods, and food items more than offset a steep decline in petroleum imports, which plummeted from $5.77 billion in 1985 to $2.8 billion in 1986 in the wake of significantly lower world oil prices and the steady increase in domestic production. At the same time, the service imbalance remained virtually unchanged from the 1985 level at $12.9 billion, despite the continuing drop of international interest rates; in part, this lack of improvement was the result of profit remittances, which reached higher-than-anticipated levels because of uncertainty about exchange rate policy and possible changes in foreign investment legislation. The result of these trends was a $4.39 billion current account deficit, substantially more than the $142 million average in the 1984–85 period (Table III-2).

Brazil's disbursed total external debt also rose by about $6.3 billion to $112.6 billion in 1986. This growth was, however, exclusively the result of the depreciation of the dollar, which, from a valuation standpoint, increased the dollar equivalents of those debt obligations contracted in other currencies. In fact, if the relative exchange rate of the dollar had remained stable, net medium- and long-term capital flows would have actually decreased in 1986. At the same time, net direct foreign investment dropped $949 million to a meager $333 million, largely in response to growing investor uncertainty as to the future course of economic policy. As a result of these negative developments, net international reserves held by the central bank declined $3.2 billion during 1986.

From the standpoint of economic policy, it is clear that the implementation of the Cruzado Plan posed a number of difficult challenges and trade-offs for the authorities. One major preoccupation was the need to establish orderly timetables for phasing out price controls and adjusting public sector prices, without stopping growth and without provoking social pressures. The problem posed by the high levels of demand were already fully in evidence by mid-year, when many goods were in increasingly short supply and numerous firms were circumventing the price freeze by introducing "new products" with higher prices or by charging black-market premiums on top of official prices. At the same time, the fact that public sector prices had been frozen at extremely low levels when the Cruzado Plan was announced made it difficult to lower the fiscal deficit, despite substantially higher revenue collections by the National Treasury and reduced interest payments on the domestic debt.

In an attempt to address these problems, the authorities first implemented a compulsory loan program in July 1986, which was designed not only to dampen demand but also to help finance the government's multiyear investment program. The program consisted essentially of steep surcharges on sales of gasoline, alcohol fuel, and new automobiles, which were to be repayable in three years with interest. Subsequently, in November 1986, a second and more comprehensive set of measures was enacted. Known as "Cruzado II," this package resulted in substantial price adjustments for the public and private sectors, as well as additional tax increases. At the same time, the exchange rate, which remained unaltered until mid-October when a 1.4 percent adjustment occurred, was to be devalued by small amounts on a daily basis. Also, to stimulate exports and savings, a variety of fiscal rebates was introduced, and rates on employer contribution schemes were lowered for firms that exported.

Despite these measures, Brazil's economic situation became increasingly unsettled. Interest rates soared to more than 400 percent by year-end 1986 (compared with an average growth of 142 percent in the general price index, Table V-7) and continued to rise at an even more accelerated pace in early 1987 as the imponderables that surrounded economic policy and the dwindling trade balance set the stage for a new price spiral. Inflationary expectations were especially fueled by the approval of legislation in late 1986 that partially reinstituted monetary correction in the economy and by the additional wage increases granted to industrial workers in early 1987. Consequently, when

Table V-7 BRAZIL. Selected Macroeconomic Indicators, 1986–1990 (percentages)

Year	General Price Index Monthly Increase	General Price Index 12 Month Increase	Consumer Price Index (IPC)[a] Monthly Increase	Consumer Price Index (IPC)[a] 12 Month Increase	Manufacturing Output (Average for 1981 = 100) 12 Month Increase	Industrial Wages in São Paulo (Increase of Last 12 Months) Nominal	Industrial Wages in São Paulo (Increase of Last 12 Months) Real
1985							
December	13.2	235.1	—	—	106.4	270.2	12.8
(Average)	(10.6)	(225.5)			(—)		(—)
1986							
January	17.8	250.4	—	—	108.7	308.2	21.1
March	−1.0	242.5	−0.1	—	104.5	352.6	44.5
June	0.5	175.5	1.3	—	121.3	207.2	18.7
September	1.1	109.6	1.7	—	137.5	166.1	32.1
December	7.6	65.0	7.3	—	114.3	98.5	18.0
(Average)	(5.3)	(142.3)	(—)		(—)	(183.2)	(25.2)
1987							
January	12.0	57.0	16.8	—	116.0	75.3	5.9
February	14.1	55.8	13.9	62.6	116.1	72.5	4.1
March	15.0	69.8	14.4	86.2	120.4	90.7	4.6
April	20.1	105.1	21.0	123.5	119.3	120.5	4.5
May	27.7	160.8	23.2	171.6	120.6	161.1	−0.3
June	25.9	226.5	26.1	238.0	124.0	213.8	−4.5
July	9.3	254.7	3.1	244.3	122.9	202.8	−14.7
August	4.5	265.8	6.4	260.1	123.9	204.0	−16.5
September	8.0	290.9	5.7	274.1	129.8	228.0	−14.3
October	11.2	328.5	9.8	300.9	133.0	251.1	−14.6
November	14.5	378.8	12.8	337.9	123.6	318.2	12.0
December	15.9	415.8	14.1	366.0	109.5	346.7	−3.9
(Average)	(14.9)	(224.8)	(13.9)	(—)	(—)	(253.5)	(−5.0)

ECONOMIC POLICY IN 1985 AND THE CRUZADO PLAN

1988						
January	19.1	448.5	16.5	105.3	371.2	0.1
February	17.6	465.6	18.0	105.0	388.1	1.7
March	18.2	481.1	16.0	119.8	368.9	−8.1
April	20.3	482.4	19.3	109.2	410.5	−3.4
May	19.5	445.5	17.8	113.4	411.3	5.2
June	20.8	423.6	19.5	125.4	398.7	6.9
July	21.5	482.1	24.0	125.3	497.0	4.4
August	22.9	584.6	20.7	133.3	604.3	17.5
September	25.8	697.0	24.0	128.1	673.1	11.3
October	27.6	814.9	27.3	121.9	806.3	11.8
November	28.0	922.8	26.9	114.8	879.5	8.3
December	26.9	1,037.6	28.9	105.0	1,034.5	14.0
(Average)	(22.4)	(684.6)	(21.5)	(—)	(553.6)	(5.8)
1989						
January	36.6	1,203.8	79.3	102.9	1,193.6	14.2
February	11.8	1,139.1	3.6	94.5	1,011.2	−2.3
March	4.2	993.0	6.1	108.7	952.2	3.0
April	5.2	856.3	7.3	106.7	858.5	3.3
May	12.8	801.3	9.9	119.4	834.2	0.3
June	26.8	845.6	24.8	131.2	840.9	−2.0
July	37.9	972.7	28.8	134.7	974.9	7.3
August	36.5	1,091.3	29.3	143.5	1,103.6	9.7
September	38.9	1,215.9	36.0	136.0	1,205.8	8.3
October	39.7	1,340.9	37.6	140.0	1,291.2	16.9
November	44.3	1,524.5	41.4	129.4	1,568.4	23.5
December	49.4	1,782.9	53.6	113.0	—	16.1
(Average)	(28.7)	(1,319.9)	(29.8)	—	—	(8.4)
1990						
January	71.9	2,270.2	56.1	—	—	4.0
February	71.7	3,539.5	72.8	—	—	14.7
March	81.3	6,231.3	84.3	—	—	

[a]The IPC was established as the official measure of consumer prices in March 1986.
n.a. Not available.
Sources: Central Bank of Brazil and *Conjuntura Econômica*.

Brazil's year-old price freeze was largely lifted in February 1987, prices of many goods immediately jumped between 30 and 40 percent. Of greater significance, however, was the fact that inflation was again rising at an annualized rate of around 400 percent—or at approximately the same rate that had existed on the eve of the Cruzado Plan.

The uncertainty that emerged after late 1986 was also accentuated by developments in the external sector. In particular, the drying up of capital flows, coupled with decreasing levels of reserves and the steady deterioration of the trade balance, placed Brazil in an increasingly untenable debt-servicing situation. For these reasons, on February 21, 1987, the government suspended interest payments due on about $68 billion of medium-term and long-term debt with commercial banks. The interest moratorium was regarded as only a temporary expedient, however, until a comprehensive debt-rescheduling accord could be worked out with foreign creditors.

Economic Performance and Policy Formulation in the Post-Cruzado Plan Era: Inflation and Stagnation

In 1987, Brazil's real GDP growth slowed markedly to a 3.6 percent rate. As anticipated in the preceding section, this deceleration reflected the fact that the stimulus to consumer spending provided by the Cruzado Plan in the form of rising real wages and a comprehensive price freeze could not be sustained. Under the best of circumstances, the imposition of a price freeze would have posed problems. For instance, too short a period would not break the link between past inflation with that in the current period, which the analysis of this chapter argues was a major cause of Brazil's difficulties after 1982. Conversely, if the freeze was too long, the resulting distortions would affect investment decisions, the mobilization of savings, and the entire adjustment process in undesirable ways, including the need for complex rationing. In Brazil's case, the failure of the plan to break inflationary expectations was inevitable, since price controls remained in place well beyond the time frame originally envisioned. The Cruzado Plan also greatly aggravated the already serious financial disarray in the public sector, since, as indicated, prices of most public goods and services had been fixed at unrealistically low levels. Coupled with a rising wage bill, this caused a cost-revenue squeeze that led to a significant expansion of public sector borrowing requirements.

Consequently, the process of phasing out the price freeze and adjusting public sector prices that was initiated in early 1987 unleashed a renewed—and virulent—escalation of prices and real interest rates, especially during the first half of the year, when the economy rapidly returned to the fully indexed status that had existed prior to the Cruzado Plan. By year-end, consumer prices (measured by the index for Rio de Janeiro) had risen by an average of 232 percent, the largest increase in Brazil's history. Moreover, with the exception of most of the federal government and major state enterprises, inflation outstripped wage gains by wide margins, despite settlements that were sometimes above those permitted by existing policy. The deteriorating economic environment was also complicated by the uncertainties that surrounded the drafting of Brazil's new constitution, as well as the February 1987 moratorium on interest payments, which further eroded business confidence.

With respect to sectoral performance, the brunt of the slowdown in domestic demand was borne by manufacturing, where not only did fixed investment in industry decline in real terms (Chapter IV) but also the sector's real value added decelerated to a 1.4 percent growth rate. The largest decline occurred in the production of consumer durables, which, following the 20 percent surge in 1986, fell 5 percent in 1987. The buoyant performance of agriculture, however, helped to avert an even greater deceleration of economic activity. Real value added by the sector soared by 14.5 percent, the biggest increase in more than a decade, as good weather and increased plantings in some areas enabled Brazil to recover to a large extent from the effects of the 1985 drought. Of particular importance was the record grain harvest of nearly 65 million tons, which replenished depleted stocks, eased pressures on prices, and reduced the need for food imports.

The strong recovery in agricultural production, coupled with slower growth in internal demand, enabled exports to grow by nearly 17 percent in 1987. Among agricultural goods, this surge was led by orange juice and soya; the bulk of the increase, however, was attributable to manufactured items, whose total export value reached $15.5 billion. Imports rose by more than 7 percent, to $15.1 billion, because of higher outlays for petroleum and derivatives. The $2.8 billion improvement in the trade accounts, combined with a small decline in the services imbalance, resulted in a $3 billion reduction in the current account deficit, to $1.4 billion. Normal channels for external borrowing could not be used because of the debt moratorium, so the financing of the current account imbalance gave rise to a substantial accumulation of payment arrears. Excluding these arrears, Brazil's disbursed total external debt increased an estimated $11.2 billion to $123.96 billion in 1987. This growth in debt, however, was again exclusively the result of the continuing depreciation of the dollar, which increased the dollar equivalents of those debt obligations that had been contracted in other currencies.

With respect to economic policy in 1987, the basic objectives remained unchanged from the previous year; these included price stabilization, maintenance of growth at satisfactory levels, and the stimulation of savings and investment. In an attempt to achieve these objectives, the government announced in mid-year, a "Plan of Macroeconomic Control" (also known as the New Cruzado Plan), whose immediate goal was to halt the escalation of inflationary expectations through another wage-price freeze. In this case, however, the duration of the freeze was to be only three months, in order to minimize the problems posed by shortages and a subsequent inflationary eruption. At the same time, monetary policy was tightened to prevent renewed demand pressures as had occurred in 1986. In general, the new plan placed less emphasis on the need to eliminate inflation completely: the cruzado would continue to depreciate in line with domestic inflation to protect the trade balance, while public sector prices would be subjected to at least moderate adjustments during the freeze.

The primary objective of the plan, in fact, was to mount a frontal attack on the fiscal deficit, which was increasingly recognized as the major source of disequilibrium in the economy. In this regard, a key target was to raise general government savings from their estimated level of zero (excluding monetary correction) in 1987 to more than 5 percent of GDP by 1991; this was to be accomplished through tax reform, revision of fiscal incentives, reduction of subsidies, and rigorous control over other current expenditures. The plan also called for real reductions in capital outlays, especially by state enterprises. These initiatives were intended to limit the operational deficit to 3.5 percent of GDP in 1987, down fractionally from the 3.7 percent level of the previous year.

The New Cruzado Plan, however, achieved few successes and by year-end had been essentially abandoned. Inflation, although dipping to a 5 percent average monthly rate in July-September, reescalated to more than 14 percent by December, and for the year as a whole it registered a 366 percent growth. In part, this reflected the fact that the wage-price freeze garnered only meager public support, especially because large salary awards were granted to the public sector. This fact, added to an increase in public employment, produced substantial growth in the public sector wage bill in real terms. At the same time, inflation combined with collection lags to erode nominal tax receipts, and political resistance held up the approval of new tax measures.

As a result of these trends and the fact that the restrictions on capital expenditure were also exceeded (owing in part to the initiation of economically indefensible projects such as the North-South railway), the operational deficit climbed to 5.5 percent of GDP during 1987, well above the July target. At the same time, in an effort to limit the monetary consequences of the higher deficit, the authorities resorted to open-market operations on a massive scale. Consequently, the value of the domestic debt instruments held by the public rose by more than 530 percent in nominal terms, well above inflation; by year-end, the stock of such instruments surpassed the monetary base by 350 percent. This rapid growth not only produced strong pressure on interest rates during most of the year but also created renewed concern that the servicing of Brazil's domestic debt had become so burdensome that the open market could no longer function as a means of monetary control.

During 1988, highly divergent trends continued to characterize Brazil's economic performance. On the positive side, substantial progress was achieved in normalizing Brazil's relationship with the international financial community; as indicated, this relationship had become strained following Brazil's February 1987 decision to impose a debt-servicing moratorium. Of particular importance was the agreement reached with private banks to refinance $62.1 billion in loans to Brazil that were originally scheduled to fall due by 1993. Negotiated after mid-year and signed in late September, this comprehensive accord lowered interest rates, restructured principal payments over a ten-year period beginning in 1995, and provided $5.2 billion in new loans to finance interest payments.

To a large extent, the agreement with the banks was facilitated by Brazil's successful rapprochement with the IMF, following three years of estrangement from that institution. By mid-year, Brazil had already presented a macroeconomic program to the IMF, which was intended to provide the basis for a new accord. The ensuing negotiations culminated on June 29, 1988, in the approval of a nineteen-month stand-by accord for the equivalent of $1.4 billion. The new agreement was viewed by some analysts as being considerably more flexible (and realistic) than the previous letter of intent signed in January 1983 and subsequently modified five times because of Brazil's inability to meet the different targets. The principal provisions were to reduce the "operational" public sector deficit to 4 percent for 1988 (down from about 6 percent projected early in the year) and to 2 percent in 1989; to limit inflation to 600 percent in 1988, a target applied implicitly in the 1988 federal budget and other public expenditure items; to limit the expansion of the monetary base in 1988 to 375 percent; to achieve a trade surplus of $12.6 billion; to increase net international reserves to $4.2 billion; to roll over 75 percent of the external debt obligations of the states and municipalities; and to limit real growth of the domestic debt to 5 percent.

Renewed negotiations with the IMF were also instrumental in enabling a new agreement to be concluded with the Paris Club during August 1988, which resulted in further reschedulings of medium- and long-term obligations with bilateral creditors. At the same time, the resumption of normalized relations with the IMF and the private banks facilitated the reopening of additional—and vitally important—short-term lines of credit needed to finance trade operations; these had been suspended for the most part since the onset of the moratorium.

These measures provided important relief to Brazil's onerous debt-servicing problems. In addition, the overall balance of payments situation benefited during 1988 from a significant improvement in the trade accounts. In particular, the combined effects of greater external demand, caused in part by the drought in the United States, and depressed levels of economic activity in Brazil resulted in an almost unbroken series of record monthly trade surpluses. By September, Brazil had already achieved the $12.6 billion target required for the IMF accord; by year-end, the trade surplus reached $19.1 billion—by far the largest in the nation's history. At the same time, Brazil more than achieved the IMF's 1988 target for international reserves, while the external debt was reduced by an estimated $10.0 billion through monthly debt-equity conversion auctions.

Despite the exceptionally positive results in its external accounts, Brazil's real GDP declined 0.3 percent in 1988, as economic activity was depressed by widespread uncertainty and the escalation of inflation. By year-end, consumer prices had risen 934 percent—by far the highest inflation in the nation's history (Graph V-2). The explosion in prices was apparently fueled by an extraordinary net transfer of resources abroad, which jumped from zero in 1987 (when the debt moratorium was in effect) to an estimated 7.5 percent of GDP in 1988. This additional claim on real resources, which was simultaneously reflected by the record trade surplus, was offset only partially by a decrease in the operational fiscal deficit, so that there was considerable pressure on private savings to increase through a process of forced savings.

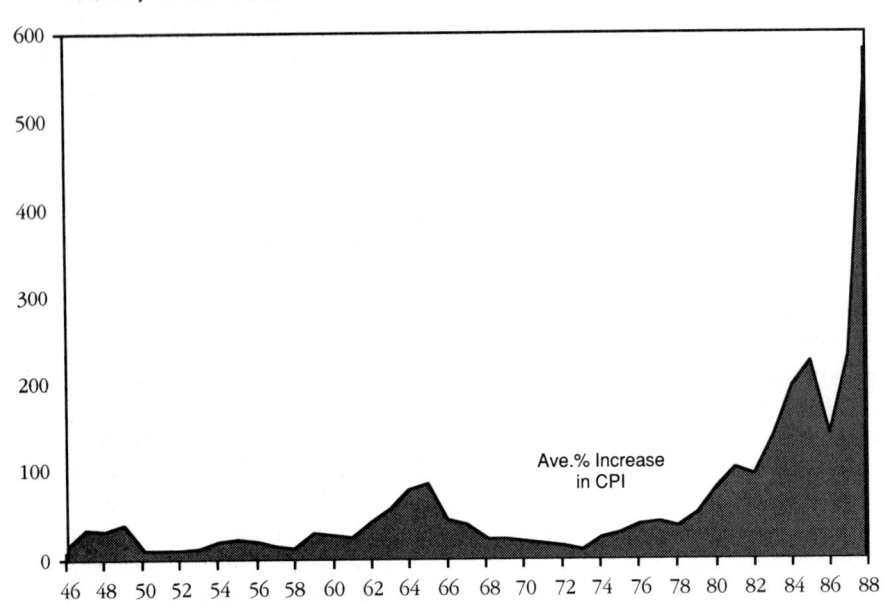

Graph V-2. BRAZIL. Average Percentage Change in Consumer Prices, 1946-1988

Ave.% Increase in CPI

Source: Getúlio Vargas Foundation

Efforts to resist this pressure ignited higher wage demands as well as frequent price markups and pushed inflation up to a new and dangerously high plateau.

Still another set of factors that added fuel to inflationary expectations consisted of the imponderables surrounding the nation's new constitution, which was approved on October 5, after twenty-one months of protracted deliberations. One of the longest such documents in the world, the new constitution contains numerous complex—and often contradictory—provisions whose implementation, according to some analysts, will serve to exacerbate the nation's deteriorating inflationary environment, complicate stabilization efforts, and discourage investment. The following provisions, in particular, have generated widespread controversy:

• The document contains extensive new social and worker welfare provisions (for example, shorter workweeks for workers involved in shiftwork, extended maternity leave, and so forth) without establishing how such benefits will be funded. A concern expressed by entrepreneurs and economists is that such provisions will directly impact production costs as well as the price level and will make more rapid devaluation necessary if exports are to remain competitive.

• The constitution also establishes a real interest rate ceiling of 12 percent for the financial markets. Although this provision had yet to be implemented through appropriate supporting legislation as of early 1990, it is regarded by many economists as being nonviable or, at a minimum, highly damaging to the effective functioning of the nation's capital markets. In fact, widespread concern exists that if efforts are made to enforce such a provision, not only would the risk of hyperinflation increase but also a serious capital flight problem would result; in fact, after mid-1988 a significant widening between the official and black-market rates of exchange was observed, which also continued throughout 1989 and into early 1990.

• In terms of its economic implications, however, one of the potentially most important changes ushered in by the new constitution is the shift in power between the spheres of government. In particular, the executive branch, which had enjoyed highly centralized powers since the promulgation of the 1967 constitution, would be considerably weakened. In part, this weakening is to be accomplished by prohibiting the executive's authority from making arbitrary decisions and from enacting decree-laws without congressional approval. At the same time, the executive is now required to submit for congressional approval complete annual budgets covering the central government, the social security entity (SIMPAS), and the state enterprises.

Perhaps the major expression of the shift in power is through the nation's public finances, since the new constitution stipulates that by 1993 the federal government will have transferred 23 percent of its tax revenues to the states and municipalities. Not only does this constitute a much higher share than required under present revenue-sharing arrangements but it also signals the need for fundamental changes in overall macroeconomic management and policy formulation. For instance, from the standpoint of obtaining financing from the multilateral development banks and other external creditors, the constitution implies that the states and municipalities would assume an increasingly dominant role, while that of the federal government would diminish. In the same fashion, the overall fiscal situation and creditworthiness of the states and municipalities, including their capacity to generate counterpart financing, would also become increasingly important.

In practice, however, the eventual effects of this transfer of tax revenues to lower levels of government remain clouded, for a variety of reasons. First, it must be emphasized that the constituent assembly did not transfer functions from the federal level to the states and municipalities in a way that is commensurate with the latter's greater participation in public revenues. Second, it remains unclear how the transfer of revenue will be apportioned among Brazil's disparate economic regions; in particular, conflict over revenue transfers seems inevitable between the impoverished Northeast and the industrialized Center-South, where most of the nation's population and most of its economic infrastructure are concentrated. In short, many questions concerning the economic implications of the new constitution can be clarified only through time as legislation is enacted to implement the constitution's provisions. And under the best of circumstances, this will be a difficult and arduous process.

The Summer Plan of January 16, 1989

As had been the case on the eve of the Cruzado Plan, price pressures again reached unmanageable proportions by year-end 1988. In December, the money supply soared 50 percent and, with inflation approaching 30 percent a month—or an annualized rate of around 1,900 percent—confidence in the nation's currency had essentially disappeared. Faced with this deepening crisis, the authorities declared bank holidays for January 16 and 17 and announced the so-called Summer Plan. The main elements of the new plan were the following:

• A general price freeze on all goods and services, with the exception of some public sector prices, which are noted later. Although the duration of the freeze was to be "indefinite," it was intended to be shorter than was the case of the Cruzado Plan.
• A new monetary unit, the cruzado novo, was introduced to replace the cruzado which had been created only three years earlier. Equal to 1,000 cruzados, the new cruzado was also devalued by 17 percent; this made one new cruzado equal to $1. The program did not indicate how or when the new cruzado would be devalued in the future.
• The indexed-linked OTN was formally abandoned; as was the case with the OTN's predecessor, the ORTN, which had been abolished when the Cruzado Plan was announced, this abandonment of the OTN was considered to be the key measure for de-indexing the economy. To avoid a flight of capital into assets other than the new cruzado, monetary policy was significantly tightened in order to raise interest rates. The OTN and the fiscal OTN were abolished by the end of January. Passbook savings, beginning in April, would yield inflation plus 0.5 percent in interest.
• If foreign exchange reserves (estimated at $7 billion) fell below an unspecified level, a moratorium would again be instituted on interest payments to foreign banks. Debt-equity auctions were also canceled for the near term.
• In the public sector, three categories of measures were announced. First, a number of prices were increased prior to implementing the general price freeze: air fares (33 percent); alcohol fuel for cars (30.5 percent); gasoline (19.9 percent); electricity (14.9 percent); postal rates (63.5 percent); and telephone charges, with increases of up to 187.5 percent. Second, several ministries (Housing, Science and Technology, Agrarian Reform, and Irrigation) were abolished. Third, an unspecified number of public sector employees were to be dismissed.

Regarded by the authorities as the most stringent set of economic policies ever adopted at one time in Brazil's history, the Summer Plan attempted to correct the errors of the Cruzado Plan and the New Cruzado Plan in several fundamental ways. First, safeguards were incorporated to prevent another eruption in domestic demand, primarily through limiting adjustments in nominal wages and increasing the cost of consumer credit. Moreover, because of the frequent increases implemented during 1988, it was believed that the prices of public sector goods and services were much closer to equilibrium levels than had been the case when the preceding plans had been announced; this was intended to check any surge of "corrective" inflation of the type that occurred when the previous price freeze ended in February 1987. By limiting expenditure to resource availability, reducing redundant employment, introducing institutional streamlining, and offering a privatization program for selected state enterprises, the new measures also adumbrated significant reforms in the public sector.

Only five months after the Summer Plan was initiated, however, popular support for it had collapsed. After being held to low levels through April, inflation jumped to almost 10 percent in May and to 25 percent in June. With prices continuing to accelerate, the authorities were forced to reindex the economy in early July through the creation of a new financial instrument, the National Treasury Bill (BTN), to replace the OTN. The return to rapid inflation was fueled by a large adjustment in the minimum wage (70 percent), the informal reindexation of key economic variables (including most wage contracts) even before the creation of the BTN in July, and, especially, the lack of resolve in lowering the fiscal deficit, which, instead of decreasing to around 2 percent of GDP as had been intended, was projected to reach as high as 7 percent of GDP by year-end. As a result of these factors, inflation spiraled increasingly out of control: by December, 1989 the growth in prices (measured by the government's official cost of living index) reached an estimated 53.6 percent, or more than the rate usually regarded as the threshold of hyperinflation, and for the year as a whole the increase was 1,765 percent. Despite the surge in prices, real GDP is estimated to have expanded between 3 percent and 4 percent. The recovery in output was due primarily to higher consumption outlays, which in turn were fueled by an inflation-induced flight into goods (despite high real interest rates) and also by mounting concerns about the health of the financial markets. The trade surplus declined $3 billion from the previous year's record to $16.1 billion, but was still sufficient to generate a current account surplus of around $380 million, notwithstanding increased interest payments and record profit remittances. At the same time, the capital account deteriorated because of reduced capital flows, a sharp drop in direct foreign investment, and soaring capital flight. By mid-year, these factors were again giving rise to strong pressures on the nation's reserves as Brazil was forced to delay scheduled payments to its creditors.

The Effects of Economic Policies on Savings and Investment: A Synthesis

With regard to domestic adjustment in general and the implementation of economic policy in particular, Brazil's most fundamental problem since the onset of the debt crisis has been the failure to reduce its fiscal deficit. Even before the dislocations of 1982, the nation had an increasingly serious imbalance in its public finances—a legacy of many years of deficit spending by all levels of government and by state enterprises. By the end of 1986, it was clear that neither an approach of "gradualism" to achieve reduction of the deficit nor "heterodox" experiments such as the Cruzado Plan, which attempted over a period of several months to eliminate the memory of past inflation from the economy, would produce the desired results. For these reasons, technicians were increasingly in agreement that future stabilization efforts must take into account, and indeed emphasize, some form of traditional (or "orthodox") fiscal adjustment program, comparable to those carried out in Jamaica and Chile during the 1980s, in order to restore fiscal equilibrium and reverse the unacceptable growth of inflationary expectations. Among other features, the Jamaican and Chilean adjustment programs had highlighted sweeping tax reforms, deep cuts in expenditure (including reduction of redundant personnel), privatization, reduction of subsidies, and comprehensive administrative reform. Although initially painful and requiring time to implement, such programs have had success in restoring the basis for improved economic growth, as borne out in both countries in recent years.

The analysis of Brazilian economic policy also reveals that efforts to reduce the fiscal imbalance have been constrained by the increasingly inertial nature of the inflationary process created by indexation of the economy. In the context of efforts to achieve public sector adjustment, a major problem has been that expenditures and financial charges are adjusted almost instantaneously to reflect inflation, while revenues, for a variety of reasons, have lagged. These problems are compounded by massive sales of indexed domestic debt instruments through the open market in an increasingly futile attempt to finance the deficit and to neutralize other sources of expansionary pressure in the economy, especially those resulting from Brazil's huge trade surpluses.

As a result, not only has fiscal management become progressively intractable but it is also clear that from the standpoint of implementing economic policy, Brazil's external adjustment process has become increasingly incompatible with concomitant attempts to foster domestic adjustment. The magnitude of the latter problem is indicated by the fact that Brazil's nominal fiscal deficit, as measured by the public sector borrowing requirements to cover the operational deficit plus monetary correction on the domestic debt, expanded steadily from 16.6 percent of GDP in 1982 to an estimated 48.5 percent in 1988.

In view of the problems just summarized, a number of important conclusions can be drawn with respect to savings and investment. First, given the present heightened state of inflationary expectations and assuming no fundamental changes are forthcoming in economic policy, there is little basis for expecting a sustained recovery in fixed capital formation in the short term. Investor uncertainty has simply become too pronounced.

Perhaps the most important consequence of the sharp intensification of the inflationary process, however, has been the further erosion of the nation's already weakened savings capacity. Several critical problems can be identified. First, as was the case in the early 1960s, long-term sources of financial savings have again virtually dried up. By late 1988 and continuing into early 1990,

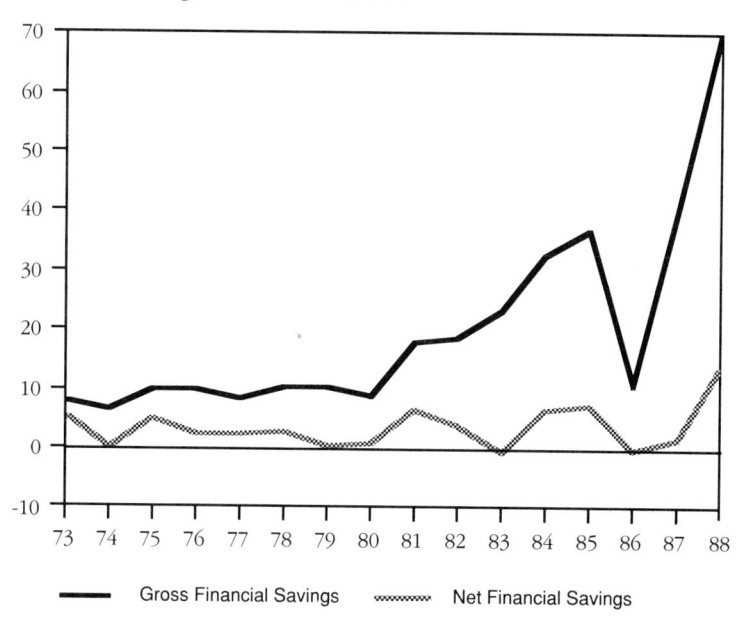

Graph V-3. Brazil. Gross and Net Financial Savings as Percentages of Current GDP

Source: IDB Country Studies Division, based on Statistical Appendix, Table 13.

most government-backed savings instruments, especially Treasury Bonds (OTNs, fiscal OTNs, and so forth) had de facto maturities of around one day. Economic agents, including some of Brazil's best minds, in fact, were utilizing increasing amounts of time and energy in an ongoing effort to protect the real value of financial assets (or in speculative activities of a distinctly nonproductive nature), as willingness to undertake new productive investment steadily waned. It was unclear, however, if these efforts to protect real financial wealth were successful. For instance, Graph V-3 reveals that, with the exception of 1986, the ratio of gross financial savings to GDP increased dramatically throughout the 1980s. When the portion of the increase that is attributable exclusively to monetary correction is netted out, however, the remainder, or the ratio of net financial savings to GDP, is shown to be substantially lower and even negative in some years[61] Clearly, this result indicates that the real capacity of the financial system to mobilize savings is at present extremely limited.

The main reasons for high interest rates, inflation, and capital flight, with their negative implications for savings and investment, may well lie in

---

[61] The author acknowledges the assistance of Dr. David Garlow or the WEFA Group in analyzing the interrelations between monetary correction and financial savings.

fundamental political problems: Brazil has thus far failed to decide how to distribute the costs of adjustment and make the decision stick. Any viable solution to this impasse would be greatly facilitated by a distribution of the adjustment costs that is perceived to be equitable by all segments of society; such a solution would also, of course, necessitate building a strong consensus on medium-term goals, as well as reaching agreement as to the means for achieving these goals and providing for the more equitable distribution of the fruits of future growth than heretofore has been the case.

At the same time, these results also constitute a major indictment of the long-term effects of indexation on the mobilization of savings. In the first instance, the results suggest that an important consequence of such procedures is simply to enhance the economy's capacity to tolerate inflation rather than to contribute to the expansion of the nation's real savings capacity, even though increasing savings capacity was its original intention and has been a fundamental objective of economic policy since the early 1960s. Indexation has also tended to make overall economic management increasingly difficult; in particular, the preceding analysis demonstrates that stabilization programs as they have been applied in the 1980s have essentially served to depress economic activity and worsen income distribution, while inflation, in the absence of a frontal attack on the underlying causes of the fiscal deficit and driven by inertia, has continued its inexorable march to successively higher levels.

On the whole, it is clear that to establish a suitable environment for a sustainable upturn in savings and investment, Brazil continues to require a fundamental correction of its fiscal imbalance as well as the de-indexation of the economy. Besides restoring confidence, these measures are also imperative for reversing the government's negative contribution to national savings. In principle, the ill-fated Summer Plan contained important elements of fiscal reform as well as measures for de-indexation; as indicated, however, these provisions were not implemented. In this regard, it should also be noted that the ultimate success or failure of future stabilization efforts will depend not only upon the resolve of the president but also upon the Brazilian Congress, which, under the nation's new constitution, is now required to approve the federal budget, establish expenditure priorities, and adopt legislation in politically sensitive areas such as wage policy and privatization.

The prospects for success of future reform initiatives could be greatly enhanced if external and domestic interest payments could be lowered from their present levels. The problems posed by large interest payments are not limited to their adverse consequences on the balance of payments, capital markets, and investment: they also concern basic credibility in the implementation of economic policy. It becomes extremely difficult, for instance, to generate widespread support for unpopular fiscal reforms such as the dismissal of public employees when it recognized that the payment of financial charges constitutes an exceptionally high percentage of total public outlays and moreover that selected economic minorities have benefited considerably from the purchase of domestic debt instruments, especially during periods of high real interest rates such as existed in early 1989.

For these reasons, the credibility of fiscal reforms could be improved by a lowering of interest payments. In the case of the domestic debt, this lowering could perhaps be accomplished through a restructuring of the present maturity profile of existing obligations over a substantially longer time horizon. At the same time, if external creditors were convinced that a thorough revamping of the public sector was under way and that all segments of society were participating in the adjustment, these creditors might be willing to provide additional debt relief to Brazil, perhaps in the form of reductions in interest rates or capitalization of interest. In this regard, a principal objective of the failed Summer Plan was precisely to set the stage for a new round of negotiations with external creditors.

Although such measures as the restructuring of domestic debt maturities and capitalization of interest would be politically difficult to achieve and would simply defer and not solve the problems of repayment to creditors, important benefits could nevertheless result. In the case of the external sector, for instance, significantly lower net factor payments would permit Brazil to maintain a smaller trade surplus and would enable imports to rise. This would provide an important stimulus to capital formation and economic growth, which would be beneficial to Brazil and, ultimately, to the banks whose likelihood of recovering past loans would improve. The reduced need for a large trade surplus would also reduce pressure on the open market and, hence, on the need to expand the growth of the domestic debt at such a rapid rate. Such a result would do much, in turn, to eliminate the current fundamental incompatibility between external and domestic adjustment, to free up additional resources for productive purposes at lower cost to borrowers, and to facilitate the implementation of more consistent, growth-oriented economic policies.

STATISTICAL APPENDIX

Table
1	Savings and Investment, 1947–1988	116
2	Total Savings and Its Components, 1947–1988	120
3	Expenditures on Real GDP: 1960, 1973, 1979–1988	121
4	Expenditures on Real GDP: 1961–1973, 1974–1979 and 1980–1988	121
5	Indicators of Oil Prices and Interest Rates, 1973–1989	122
6	Medium- and Long-Term Debt Profile, 1982–1985	123
7	Reserves and Production of Principal Mineral Substances: Comparison Brazil/World, 1985	124
8	Indicators of Oil Exploration, Production, and Reserves, 1960–1989	125
9	Economic Classification of State Enterprises' Budgetary Execution, 1980–1987	126
10	Real Output Price Indexes of Selected State Enterprises, 1970–1985	127
11	Consolidated Accounts of the Federal Public Sector, 1979–1982	128
12	Principal Federal Subsidies and Incentives, 1973–1981	129
13	Indicators of Financial Savings, 1972–1988	130
14	Nominal Monthly Income Distribution of the Economically Active Population, 1979, 1981, 1983–1987	132

Table 1. BRAZIL. Savings and Investment, 1947–1988
(1947–1979: Thousands of Cruzados; 1980–1988: Millions of Cruzados and Percentages)

	1947	1948	1949	1950	1951	1952	1953	1954	1955	1956	1957
I. *Gross Capital Formation*	26.3	26.2	29.8	34.7	51.8	62.3	71.4	111.9	124.0	148.5	216.8
A. *Fixed Investment*	26.6	26.4	31.5	36.0	53.9	60.8	73.7	105.8	109.9	148.8	187.9
1. Construction	15.5	15.8	20.0	22.5	32.9	38.1	49.9	61.0	65.6	94.6	117.3
a. General Government	—	—	—	—	—	—	—	—	—	—	—
b. Private Sector	—	—	—	—	—	—	—	—	—	—	—
2. Machinery and Equipment	10.5	9.9	10.7	12.4	19.7	21.1	22.1	42.4	41.4	50.9	66.7
a. General Government	—	—	—	—	—	—	—	—	—	—	—
b. Private Sector	—	—	—	—	—	—	—	—	—	—	—
3. Other[1]	0.6	0.7	0.8	1.1	1.3	1.6	1.7	2.4	2.9	3.3	3.9
B. *Variation in Stocks*	−0.3	−0.2	−1.7	−1.3	−2.1	1.5	−2.3	6.1	14.1	−0.3	28.9
II. *Total Savings*	26.3	26.2	29.8	34.7	51.8	62.3	71.4	111.9	124.0	148.5	216.8
A. External Savings	2.8	0.0	1.5	−2.6	7.5	12.2	−1.1	5.4	−0.1	−2.5	12.0
B. General Government	6.1	7.0	7.5	5.6	13.0	11.5	4.1	20.2	−12.9	5.6	13.1
C. Private Sector	17.4	19.2	20.8	31.7	31.3	38.6	68.4	86.3	111.2	145.4	191.7
III. *Percentage Composition*											
A. *Gross Capital Formation*	100.0	100.0	100.0	100.0	100.0	100.0	100.0	100.0	100.0	100.0	100.0
1. Fixed Investment	101.1	100.8	105.7	103.7	104.1	97.6	103.2	94.5	88.6	100.2	86.7
a. Construction	58.9	60.3	67.1	64.8	63.5	61.2	69.9	54.5	52.9	63.7	54.1
b. Machinery and Equipment	39.9	37.8	35.9	35.7	38.0	33.9	31.0	37.9	33.4	34.3	30.8
c. Other[1]	2.3	2.7	2.7	3.2	2.5	2.6	2.4	2.1	2.3	2.2	1.8
B. Variation in Stocks	−1.1	−0.8	−5.7	−3.7	−4.1	2.4	−3.2	5.5	11.4	−0.2	13.3
C. *Total Savings*	100.0	100.0	100.0	100.0	100.0	100.0	100.0	100.0	100.0	100.0	100.0
1. External Savings	10.6	0.0	5.0	−7.5	14.5	19.5	−1.5	4.8	−0.1	−1.7	5.5
2. General Government	23.2	26.7	25.2	16.1	25.1	18.5	5.7	18.1	10.4	3.8	6.0
3. Private Sector	66.2	73.3	69.8	91.4	60.4	62.0	95.8	77.1	89.7	97.9	88.5

[1] Includes reforestation and imported breeding stock.
Sources: IBGE, *Estatísticas Históricas do Brasil*, 1987; FGV, *Contas Nacionais do Brasil*, Vol. II, 1972; FGV, *Conjuntura Econômica*, Dez. 1979. Savings estimates after 1970 are those of the IDB Country Studies Division.

(continued)

STATISTICAL APPENDIX

Table 1. BRAZIL. Savings and Investment (continuation)
(Thousands of Cruzados)

	1958	1959	1960	1961	1962	1963	1964	1965	1966	1967	1968
I. *Gross Capital Formation*	282.4	476.7	541.2	700.8	1,318.6	2,412.6	4,418.7	7,859.5	11,575.9	13,461.7	21,853.1
A. *Fixed Investment*	264.1	417.2	500.3	609.8	1,156.2	2,279.1	3,928.9	6,276.8	9,994.3	13,408.4	21,519.2
1. Construction	165.1	246.2	311.2	357.3	719.8	1,402.6	2,487.7	4,089.5	6,116.8	8,804.2	13,835.2
a. General Government	—	—	—	—	—	—	—	—	—	—	—
b. Private Sector	—	—	—	—	—	—	—	—	—	—	—
2. Machinery and Equipment	94.8	165.2	180.6	240.0	415.3	840.0	1,370.3	2,074.4	3,729.3	4,408.5	7,449.1
a. General Government	—	—	—	—	—	—	—	—	—	—	—
b. Private Sector	—	—	—	—	—	—	—	—	—	—	—
3. Other[1]	4.2	5.8	8.5	12.5	21.1	36.5	70.9	112.9	148.2	195.7	234.9
B. *Variation in Stocks*	18.3	59.5	40.9	91.0	162.4	133.5	489.8	1,582.7	1,581.6	53.3	333.9
II. *Total Savings*	282.4	476.7	541.2	700.8	1,318.6	2,412.6	4,418.7	7,859.5	11,575.9	13,461.7	21,853.1
A. External Savings	16.0	30.2	55.9	39.3	149.0	88.4	−156.8	−689.6	−118.8	628.6	1,714.0
B. General Government	56.2	83.7	95.4	54.6	−16.4	36.6	−43.4	836.6	3,169.9	1,892.6	5,947.0
C. Private Sector	210.2	362.8	389.9	606.9	1,186.0	2,287.6	4,618.9	7,712.5	8,524.8	10,940.5	14,192.1
III. *Percentage Composition*											
A. *Gross Capital Formation*	100.0	100.0	100.0	100.0	100.0	100.0	100.0	100.0	100.0	100.0	100.0
1. Fixed Investment	93.5	87.5	92.4	87.0	87.7	94.5	88.9	79.9	86.3	99.6	98.5
a. Construction	58.5	51.6	57.5	51.0	54.6	58.1	56.3	52.0	52.8	65.4	63.3
b. Machinery and Equipment	33.6	34.7	33.4	34.2	31.5	34.8	31.0	26.4	32.2	32.7	34.1
c. Other[1]	1.5	1.2	1.6	1.8	1.6	1.5	1.6	1.4	1.3	1.5	1.1
B. Variation in Stocks	6.5	12.5	7.6	13.0	12.3	5.5	11.1	20.1	13.7	0.4	1.5
C. *Total Savings*	100.0	100.0	100.0	100.0	100.0	100.0	100.0	100.0	100.0	100.0	100.0
1. External Savings	5.7	6.3	10.3	5.6	11.3	3.7	−3.5	−8.8	−1.0	4.7	7.8
2. General Government	19.9	17.6	17.6	7.8	−1.2	1.5	−1.0	10.6	27.4	14.1	27.3
3. Private Sector	74.4	76.1	72.1	86.6	89.9	94.8	104.5	98.1	73.6	81.3	64.9

[1] Includes reforestation and imported breeding stock.
Sources: IBGE, *Estatísticas Históricas do Brasil*, 1987; FGV, *Contas Nacionais do Brasil*, Vol. II, 1972; FGV, *Conjuntura Econômica*, Dez. 1979. Savings estimates after 1970 are those of the IDB Country Studies Division.

(continued)

Table 1. BRAZIL. Savings and Investment (continuation)
(Thousands of Cruzados)

	1969	1970	1971	1972	1973	1974	1975	1976	1977	1978
I. Gross Capital Formation	33,328.2	39,918.0	54,920.0	73,506.0	112,834.0	181,152.0	269,700.0	376,501.0	549,640.0	833,165.0
A. Fixed Investment	28,925.3	36,598.0	51,421.0	70,467.0	104,253.0	162,777.0	244,840.0	366,303.0	532,138.0	805,385.0
1. Construction	18,340.5	21,216.0	29,102.0	40,253.0	61,790.0	95,764.0	140,714.0	215,760.0	325,094.0	480,287.0
a. General Government	—	6,918.0	9,495.0	10,925.0	15,264.0	24,147.0	35,475.0	56,407.0	69,930.0	96,246.0
b. Private Sector	—	14,298.0	9,607.0	29,328.0	46,526.0	71,617.0	105,239.0	159,353.0	255,164.0	384,041.0
2. Machinery and Equipment	10,283.8	14,971.0	21,780.0	29,436.0	41,308.0	64,962.0	100,830.0	144,119.0	196,334.0	296,789.0
a. General Government	—	1,670.0	1,571.0	2,539.0	3,724.0	4,581.0	5,949.0	9,486.0	12,265.0	17,635.0
b. Private Sector	—	13,301.0	20,209.0	26,897.0	37,584.0	60,381.0	94,881.0	134,633.0	184,069.0	279,154.0
3. Other[1]	301.0	411.0	539.0	778.0	1,155.0	2,052.0	3,296.0	6,424.0	10,710.0	28,309.0
B. Variation in Stocks	4,402.9	3,320.0	3,499.0	3,039.0	8,581.0	18,375.0	24,860.0	10,198.0	17,502.0	27,780.0
II. Total Savings	33,328.2	39,918.0	54,920.0	73,506.0	112,834.0	181,152.0	269,700.0	376,501.0	549,640.0	833,165.0
A. External Savings	1,133.6	2,504.0	6,831.0	8,768.0	10,232.0	48,092.0	54,080.0	63,751.0	56,800.0	125,710.0
B. General Government	9,785.2	10,024.0	14,615.0	18,832.0	28,484.0	28,199.0	31,635.0	59,398.0	80,868.0	45,855.0
C. Private Sector	22,409.4	27,390.0	33,474.0	45,906.0	74,118.0	104,861.0	183,985.0	253,352.0	411,932.0	661,600.0
III. Percentage Composition										
A. Gross Capital Formation	100.0	100.0	100.0	100.0	100.0	100.0	100.0	100.0	100.0	100.0
1. Fixed Investment	86.8	91.7	93.6	95.9	92.4	89.9	90.8	97.3	96.6	96.6
a. Construction	55.0	53.2	53.0	54.8	54.8	52.9	52.2	57.3	59.1	57.6
b. Machinery and Equipment	30.9	37.5	39.7	40.0	36.6	35.9	37.4	38.3	35.7	35.6
c. Other[1]	0.9	1.0	1.0	1.1	1.0	1.1	1.2	1.7	1.9	3.4
B. Variation in Stocks	13.2	8.3	6.4	4.1	7.6	10.1	9.2	2.7	3.1	3.3
C. Total Savings	100.0	100.0	100.0	100.0	100.0	100.0	100.0	100.0	100.0	100.0
1. External Savings	3.4	6.3	12.4	11.9	9.1	26.5	20.1	16.9	10.3	15.1
2. General Government	29.4	25.1	26.6	25.6	25.2	15.6	11.7	15.8	14.7	5.5
3. Private Sector	67.2	68.6	61.0	62.5	65.7	57.9	68.2	67.3	75.0	79.4

[1]Includes reforestation and imported breeding stock.
Sources: IBGE, Estatísticas Históricas do Brasil, 1987; FGV, Contas Nacionais do Brasil, Vol. II, 1972; FGV, Conjuntura Econômica, Dez. 1979. Savings estimates after 1970 are those of the IDB Country Studies Division.

(continued)

Table 1. BRAZIL. Savings and Investment (continuation)
(Thousands of Cruzados)

	1979	1980*	1981*	1982*	1983*	1984*	1985*	1986*	1987*	1988*
I. *Gross Capital Formation*	1,379,301.0	2,889.8	5,665.9	10,722.2	19,635.1	60,339.7	238,946.4	676,762.9	2,631,521.8	21,871,209.3
A. *Fixed Investment*	1,392,588.0	2,835.3	5,630.1	10,894.8	21,332.8	64,763.5	240,031.4	713,041.9	2,644,069.8	21,558,789.3
1. Construction	870,207.0	1,714.6	3,559.1	7,157.8	14,371.0	43,094.0	164,560.9	512,693.2	1,922,966.2	13,761,649.9
a. General Government	126,210.0	255.8	n.a.	n.a.	n.a.	n.a.	n.a.	n.a.	n.a.	n.a.
b. Private Sector	743,997.0	1,458.8	n.a.	n.a.	n.a.	n.a.	n.a.	n.a.	n.a.	n.a.
2. Machinery and Equipment	480,140.0	1,011.4	1,884.1	3,408.6	6,441.0	20,205.7	69,674.3	182,740.9	658,058.5	7,283,178.3
a. General Government	21,209.0	37.4	n.a.	n.a.	n.a.	n.a.	n.a.	n.a.	n.a.	n.a.
b. Private Sector	458,931.0	913.6	n.a.	n.a.	n.a.	n.a.	n.a.	n.a.	n.a.	n.a.
3. Other[1]	42,241.0	109.7	186.3	328.4	520.8	1,463.8	5,796.2	17,607.8	63,045.1	513,961.5
B. *Variation in Stocks*	−13,287.0	54.5	35.8	−172.6	−1,697.1	−4,423.8	−1,085.0	−36,279.0	−12,548.0	312,420.0
II. *Total Savings*	1,379,301.0	2,889.8	5,665.9	10,722.2	19,635.1	60,339.7	238,946.4	676,762.9	2,631,521.8	21,871,209.3
A. External Savings	286,514.0	612.0	977.0	2,632.0	3,250.0	−1,282.0	−4,417.0	52,571.0	13,359.0	−1,803,695.0
B. General Government	48,820.0	−83.0	−210.0	−1,255.0	−4,488.0	−20,436.0	−147,583.0	−343,407.0	−964,793.0	−11,551,626.0
C. Private Sector	1,043,966.0	2,360.8	4,898.9	9,345.0	20,873.1	82,057.7	390,946.4	967,598.9	3,582,955.8	35,226,530.3
III. *Percentage Composition*										
A. *Gross Capital Formation*	100.0	100.0	100.0	100.0	100.0	100.0	100.0	100.0	100.0	100.0
1. Fixed Investment	101.0	98.1	99.4	101.6	108.6	107.3	100.5	105.4	100.5	98.6
a. Construction	63.1	59.3	62.8	66.8	73.2	71.4	68.9	75.8	73.1	62.9
b. Machinery and Equipment	34.8	35.0	33.3	31.8	32.8	33.5	29.2	27.0	25.0	33.3
c. Other[1]	3.1	3.8	3.3	3.0	2.6	2.4	2.4	2.6	2.4	2.4
B. Variation in Stocks	−1.0	1.9	0.6	−1.6	−8.6	−7.3	−0.5	−5.4	−0.5	1.4
C. *Total Savings*	100.0	100.0	100.0	100.0	100.0	100.0	100.0	100.0	100.0	100.0
1. External Savings	20.8	21.1	17.2	24.5	16.6	−2.1	−1.8	7.8	0.5	−8.2
2. General Government	3.5	−2.8	−3.7	−11.7	−22.9	−33.9	−61.8	−50.7	−36.7	−52.8
3. Private Sector	75.7	81.7	86.5	87.2	106.3	136.0	163.6	142.9	136.2	161.0

*Millions of cruzados.
[1] Includes reforestation and imported breeding stock.
Sources: IBGE, *Estatísticas Históricas do Brasil*, 1987; FGV, *Contas Nacionais do Brasil*, Vol. II, 1972; FGV, *Conjuntura Econômica*, Dez. 1979. Savings estimates after 1970 are those of the IDB Country Studies Division.

Table 2. BRAZIL. Total Savings and Its Components, 1947–1988
(Percentages of Current GDP)

Year	Total Investment/ Savings	=	External Savings	+	National Savings	=	National Savings — Government Savings	+	National Savings — Private Sector Savings
1947	14.7	=	1.6	+	13.1	=	3.4	+	9.7
1948	12.6	=	0.0	+	12.6	=	3.4	+	9.3
1949	12.3	=	0.6	+	11.7	=	3.1	+	8.6
1950	12.3	=	−0.9	+	13.2	=	2.0	+	11.3
1951	14.9	=	2.2	+	12.7	=	3.7	+	9.0
1952	15.2	=	3.0	+	12.2	=	2.8	+	9.4
1953	14.6	=	−0.2	+	14.8	=	0.8	+	14.0
1954	16.7	=	0.8	+	15.8	=	3.0	+	12.9
1955	15.2	=	−0.0	+	15.2	=	1.6	+	13.6
1956	14.4	=	−0.2	+	14.7	=	0.5	+	14.1
1957	17.4	=	1.0	+	16.4	=	1.0	+	15.3
1958	18.2	=	1.0	+	17.1	=	3.6	+	13.5
1959	20.6	=	1.3	+	19.2	=	3.6	+	15.6
1960	18.9	=	2.7	+	16.2	=	2.6	+	13.6
1961	20.0	=	1.9	+	18.1	=	1.1	+	17.0
1962	24.0	=	2.5	+	21.5	=	0.2	+	21.3
1963	23.0	=	0.6	+	22.4	=	0.3	+	22.1
1964	22.7	=	−0.3	+	23.0	=	0.2	+	22.8
1965	23.4	=	−1.3	+	24.7	=	2.0	+	22.7
1966	23.5	=	−0.1	+	23.6	=	5.3	+	18.3
1967	20.6	=	0.7	+	19.9	=	2.3	+	17.6
1968	22.8	=	1.5	+	21.4	=	6.1	+	15.3
1969	26.4	=	0.8	+	25.6	=	6.4	+	19.2
1970	20.5	=	1.3	+	19.2	=	5.2	+	14.0
1971	21.3	=	2.6	+	18.6	=	5.7	+	13.0
1972	21.2	=	2.5	+	18.7	=	5.4	+	13.2
1973	22.0	=	2.0	+	20.0	=	5.6	+	14.5
1974	24.3	=	6.0	+	17.9	=	3.8	+	14.1
1975	25.7	=	5.2	+	20.5	=	3.0	+	17.5
1976	23.0	=	3.9	+	19.1	=	3.6	+	15.5
1977	22.0	=	8.3	+	19.7	=	3.2	+	16.5
1978	23.0	=	3.5	+	19.6	=	1.3	+	18.3
1979	23.1	=	4.8	+	18.3	=	0.8	+	17.5
1980	23.3	=	4.9	+	18.4	=	−0.7	+	19.1
1981	23.0	=	4.0	+	19.0	=	−0.9	+	19.9
1982	21.0	=	5.2	+	15.9	=	−2.5	+	18.3
1983	16.5	=	2.7	+	13.8	=	−3.8	+	17.6
1984	15.3	=	−0.3	+	15.7	=	−5.2	+	20.9
1985	16.9	=	−0.3	+	17.2	=	−10.4	+	27.7
1986	18.3	=	1.4	+	16.8	=	−9.3	+	26.1
1987	22.1	=	0.1	+	22.0	=	−8.1	+	30.1
1988	23.5	=	−1.9	+	25.5	=	−12.3	+	37.8

Source: IBGE, *Estatísticas Históricas do Brasil*, 1987. FGV, *Contas Nacionais do Brasil*, Vol. II, 1972. FGV, *Conjuntura Econômica*, Dezembro 1979; and estimates of the IDB Country Studies Division.

Table 3. BRAZIL. Expenditures on Real GDP, 1960, 1973, 1979–1988
(Millions of 1980 Cruzados)

	1960	1973	1979	1980	1981	1982	1983	1984	1985	1986	1987	1988*
Total Consumption	2,630.3	6,221.5	9,254.1	9,788.2	9,208.2	9,549.7	9,281.6	9,485.5	10,011.7	11,098.5	11,147.5	10,935.4
Private	2,206.1	5,374.1	8,095.0	8,648.8	8,105.9	8,361.6	8,191.8	8,512.1	8,771.4	9,605.2	9,308.7	9,104.0
Public	424.2	847.4	1,159.1	1,139.4	1,102.3	1,188.1	1,089.8	973.4	1,240.3	1,493.3	1,838.8	1,831.4
Total Investment	509.7	1,924.9	2,570.6	2,889.8	2,511.6	2,296.9	1,774.7	1,820.5	2,183.6	2,550.4	2,658.4	2,590.2
Fixed Investment	474.9	1,815.5	2,597.1	2,835.3	2,485.3	2,330.2	1,950.8	1,954.6	2,190.3	2,681.0	2,670.5	2,553.2
Private	407.1	1,532.0	2,304.0	2,530.4	2,194.2	2,069.6	1,748.5	1,730.1	1,893.6	2,242.6	2,330.5	2,283.2
Public	67.8	283.5	393.1	304.9	291.1	260.6	202.3	224.5	299.7	438.4	340.0	270.0
Variation in Stocks	34.8	109.4	−26.5	54.5	26.3	−33.3	−176.1	−134.1	−9.7	−130.6	−12.1	37.0
Exports of Goods and n.f.s.	246.6	651.3	914.2	1,121.4	1,360.4	1,235.3	1,411.6	1,721.9	1,843.2	1,648.3	1,965.4	2,240.6
Imports of Goods and n.f.s.	355.4	1,097.4	1,390.6	1,399.6	1,226.8	1,152.8	952.2	923.5	924.0	1,188.5	1,153.5	1,188.6
GDP (At Market Prices)	3,031.2	7,700.3	11,348.3	12,399.8	11,853.4	11,929.1	11,515.7	12,104.4	13,114.5	14,108.7	14,617.8	14,577.6

*Estimates. *Source:* Fundação Instituto Brasileiro de Geografia e Estatística (IBGE) and estimates of the IDB Country Studies Division.

Table 4. BRAZIL. Expenditures on Real GDP: 1961–1973, 1974–1979 and 1980–1988
(Percentage Change)

	Average 1961–73	Average 1974–79	1980	1981	1982	1983	1984	1985	1986	1987	1988*
Total Consumption	6.8	6.8	5.8	−5.9	3.7	−2.8	2.2	5.5	10.9	0.4	−1.9
Private	7.1	7.1	6.8	−6.3	3.2	−2.0	3.9	3.0	9.5	−3.1	−2.2
Public	5.5	5.4	−1.7	3.3	7.8	−8.3	−10.7	27.4	20.1	23.1	−0.4
Total Investment[1]	10.8	4.9	12.4	−13.1	−8.5	−22.7	2.6	19.1	16.8	4.2	−2.6
Fixed Investment	10.9	6.1	9.2	−12.3	−6.2	−16.3	0.2	12.2	22.2	0.4	−4.4
Private	10.7	7.0	9.8	−13.3	−5.7	−15.5	−1.1	9.4	18.4	3.9	−2.0
Public	11.6	0.6	4.0	−4.5	−10.5	−22.4	11.0	33.5	46.3	−22.4	−20.6
Exports of Goods and n.f.s.	7.8	5.8	22.7	21.3	−9.2	14.3	22.0	7.0	−10.6	19.2	14.0
Imports of Goods and n.f.s.	9.1	4.0	0.6	−12.3	−6.0	−17.4	−3.0	0.1	28.6	−2.9	3.0
GDP (At Market Prices)	7.4	6.7	9.3	−4.4	0.6	−3.5	5.1	8.3	7.6	3.6	−0.3

[1] Includes variation in stocks. *Estimates. *Source:* IDB Country Studies Division based on Statistical Appendix. Table 3.

Table 5. BRAZIL. Indicators of Oil Prices and Interest Rates, 1973–1988

Year	Average Price of Oil (US$/Barrel)[1]	Increase in Nominal Terms	Percentage Annual Variation	Increase in Real Terms[2]	Percentage Annual Variation	Nominal[1]	Real[3]
1973	2.74	100.0	—	100.0	—	9.3	2.8
1974	11.22	409.5	309.5	312.6	212.6	11.2	2.1
1975	10.97	400.4	−2.2	386.7	23.7	7.8	−2.0
1976	12.01	438.3	9.4	374.6	−3.1	6.2	−0.2
1977	12.81	467.5	6.7	324.7	−13.3	6.4	−0.3
1978	12.80	467.2	0.0	338.3	4.2	9.2	1.9
1979	17.63	643.4	37.7	395.3	16.8	12.2	3.3
1980	30.10	1,098.5	70.7	631.7	59.8	14.0	5.0
1981	35.85	1,308.5	19.1	887.7	40.5	17.4	7.7
1982	34.96	1,275.9	−2.5	987.5	11.2	16.0	9.6
1983	30.87	1,126.6	−11.7	756.6	−23.4	10.7	6.8
1984	28.44	1,037.9	−7.8	682.8	−9.8	11.2	7.5
1985	27.30	996.5	−3.7	754.9	10.6	8.7	5.7
1986	12.70	463.5	−53.5	364.7	48.3	7.9	5.2
1987	16.90	616.8	33.1	446.6	22.5	6.5	3.2
1988	13.70	500.0	−18.9	—	—	7.6	2.9
1989[a]	16.6	—	—	—	—	—	—

[1] Derived from data provided by the Central Bank of Brazil.
[2] Deflated by the Price Index for "All Commodities" (excluding oil), IMF.
[3] Nominal rate deflated by subtracting the percentage increase in the GNP deflator for the United States, *Economic Report of the President*, January 1989, p. 313.
[a] Preliminary.
Source: IDB Country Studies Division based on the sources indicated.

Table 6. BRAZIL. Medium-Term and Long-Term Debt Profile
(Millions of Dollars)

Type of Creditor	Total Outstanding December 31 1982	1983	1984	1983 Total	1983 Refinanced	Amortization 1984 Total	1984 Refinanced	1985 Total	1985 Refinanced
IMF Loans	544	2,648	3,967	—	—	—	—	63	—
Import Financing	13,520	16,242	18,379	2,561	901	2,606	1,489	3,614	1,680
International Agencies	3,847	4,324	5,714	448	—	466	—	654	—
(Of Which: IDB)	(1,202)	(1,367)	(1,397)	(137)	(—)	(110)	(—)	(177)	(—)
Government Agencies	3,690	4,406	6,174	592	161	803	763	1,086	684
Other	5,983	5,713	6,492	1,521	740	1,337	726	1,874	1,034
Currency Loans	52,908	59,626	66,467	4,844	4,305	5,093	4,934	6,655	6,445
Resolution N° 63	16,145	15,115	13,630	2,068	2,068	2,441	2,441	2,475	2,475
Law N° 4131	36,763	44,511	52,837	2,775	2,239	2,652	2,493	4,180	3,970
Other	3,226	2,804	2,277	317	—	352	19	264	14
Total	**70,198**	**81,319**	**91,091**	**7,722**	**5,206**	**8,051**	**6,442**	**10,596**	**8,139**

Source: IDB Country Studies Division, based on data provided by the Central Bank of Brazil.

Table 7. BRAZIL. Reserves and Production of Principal Mineral Substances: Comparison Brazil/World, 1985
(Thousands of m.t. and Percentages)

Mineral Substances	Brazil	World	Percentage Share	Brazil	World	Percentage Share
Aluminum (Bauxite)	2,522,000	22,862,000	11.0	6,251	75,516	8.2
Asbestos[1]	3,653	104,000	3.5	172	4,600	3.7
Barite	132,000	580,400	22.7	112	5,763	1.9
Bentonite	31,365	(...)	—	222	(...)	—
Coal[2]	23,000,000	13,609,000,000	0.2	7,000	2,913,000	0.2
Kaolin[3]	1,237,879	12,000,000	10.6	486	24,298	2.0
Copper[4]	11,000	525,000	2.1	41	7,805	0.5
Chromium[5]	3,400	2,967,100	0.1	130	4,355	3.0
Diatomite	3,065	460,286	0.7	17	1,524	1.1
Tin[4]	250	3,260	7.8	26	210	12.6
Feldspar	15,000	820,000	1.8	83	3,918	2.2
Iron	17,600,000	209,200,000	8.4	123,000	822,500	14.9
Prosphate (P$_2$O$_5$)	258,000	33,963,000	0.8	1,475	159,075	0.9
Gypsum	688,396	(...)	—	560	83,144	0.7
Graphite	27,000	(...)	—	2	3	51.5
Magnesite[7]	177,000	2,568,000	6.7	182	3,286	5.5
Manganese	147,118	11,212,958	1.3	2,428	23,669	10.3
Niobium[4]	4,522	5,030	89.9	14	17	85.3
Nickel[4]	5,450	102,175	5.3	20	755	2.7
Gold[7]	1,270	46,369	2.7	30	1,463	2.0
Quartz	22,300	(...)	—	2,730	172,130	1.6
Talc	108,000	1,259,800	8.6	495	8,088	6.1
Tantalum[8]	0.319	33	1.0	0.057	0.310	18.3
Tungsten[4]	9	3,460	0.3	1	45	2.4
Vermiculite	16,000	181,440	9.0	9	490	2.0
Zinc[4]	2,890	302,890	1.0	152	6,712	2.3
Zirconium[9]	1,129	47,400	2.4	13	723	1.8

[1]Production expressed in fibers.
[2]Includes measured, indicated and inferred reserves of all classes of coal. In Brazil, lignite is not included
[3]Brazil: measured, indicated and inferred reserves. [4]Data in contained metal. [5]Data in CR$_2$O$_3$. [6]Data contained manganese (Mg).
[7]Unit expressed in 1,000 troy ounces. Data in contained metal. [8]Unit expressed in 1,000 pounds. Data in contained metal. [9]Data expressed with average of 65 percent of contained Zro$_2$.
(...)Not available.
Source: Ministry of Mines and Energy. Sumário Mineral. 1986, p. 12.

Table 8. BRAZIL. Indicators of Oil Exploration, Production and Reserves

Year	A National Production (000 bbls per Day)	B Cumulative Total (Millions of Dollars)	C Annual Flow	D Reserve of Oil & Gas at Year End (Millions of bbls)	E = D/A × 365 Years of Reserves at Annual Production	F = B/D Investment per Barrel of Reserves (US$ per Barrel)
1960	80.9	328.0	95.9	604	20.5	0.54
1961	95.4	435.6	107.6	684	19.6	0.64
1962	91.7	556.4	120.8	705	20.4	0.79
1963	99.4	711.3	154.9	699	20.2	1.02
1964	93.3	871.8	160.5	744	21.8	1.17
1965	96.7	1,060.4	188.6	788	22.3	1.35
1966	118.5	1,249.1	188.7	849	24.1	1.47
1967	148.5	1,441.7	192.6	945	17.4	1.53
1968	163.4	1,630.9	189.2	985	16.5	1.65
1969	175.3	1,839.9	209.0	1,005	15.7	1.83
1970	166.9	2,081.2	241.3	1,019	16.7	2.04
1971	174.3	2,288.4	207.2	1,014	15.9	2.25
1972	171.0	2,537.2	248.8	956	15.3	2.65
1973	174.1	2,829.0	291.8	931	14.7	3.04
1974	182.1	3,202.3	514.0	939	14.1	3.41
1975	177.3	3,716.3	589.8	940	14.1	3.95
1976	172.0	4,306.1	757.8	1,084	16.8	3.97
1977	166.4	5,063.9	856.2	1,295	21.3	3.91
1978	166.1	5,920.1	1,013.8	1,325	21.9	4.47
1979	171.0	6,935.9	1,262.9	1,471	23.6	4.71
1980	187.1	8,196.8	1,986.1	1,690	24.7	4.85
1981	220.1	10,182.9	2,761.3	1,880	23.4	5.42
1982	267.6	12,744.3	2,761.4	2,189	22.4	5.82
1983	339.0	15,317.6	2,373.3	2,363	19.1	6.48
1984	473.9	17,002.6	1,685.0	2,543	14.7	6.69
1985	563.9	18,682.6	1,680.0	2,757	13.4	6.78
1986	593.4	20,776.6	2,094.0	2,943	13.6	7.06
1987	590.2	22,938.6	2,162.0	3,181	14.8	7.21
1988	576.0	24,317.6	1,379.0	5,940	28.2	—
1989*	640.0	—	—	—	—	—

*Projection.
Source: Petrobrás and estimates of the IDB Country Studies Division.

Table 9. BRAZIL. Economic Classification of State Enterprises Budgetary Execution, 1980–1987
(CzS Millions)

	1980	1981	1982	1983	1984	1985	1986	1987
I. *Current Revenues*	1,861.6	4,177.2	7,808.9	20,291.3	67,492.9	229,594.6	546,603.5	2,138,752
Operational Revenues	1,459.5	3,106.2	6,036.1	15,327.1	53,547.1	177,926.5	418,521.7	1,847,712
Non-Operational Revenue	189.5	475.5	428.7	1,525.5	4,782.5	17,461.0	19,037.4	35,788
Revenue from Treasury	149.5	394.4	663.7	1,225.5	4,145.7	15,864.9	56,910.8	76,752
Other Resources	63.1	201.2	680.4	2,213.2	5,017.6	18,342.2	52,133.6	178,500
II. *Current Expenditure (Net)*	1,270.8	2,916.2	6,304.0	17,004.2	55,111.5	185,379.0	405,274.5	1,754,520
Wages and Salaries	251.7	550.7	1,173.5	2,413.2	6,829.0	26,421.9	71,745.9	293,634
Financial Charges	106.8	324.7	952.8	2,710.1	9,998.7	36,020.0	69,829.2	328,493
On Domestic Obligations	24.6	137.2	262.6	674.7	1,857.5	7,676.8	17,172.4	178,379
On External Obligations	82.2	187.5	690.2	2,035.4	8,141.2	28,343.2	52,656.8	150,114
Other Current Expenditure (Net)	912.3	2,040.8	4,177.7	11,880.9	38,283.7	122,936.9	263,699.4	1,132,393
III. *Current Savings (I–II)*	590.8	1,261.1	1,504.9	3,287.1	12,381.4	44,215.6	141,329.0	384,232
IV. *Capital Expenditure*	669.7	1,494.5	2,641.5	5,021.1	15,098.7	54,383.6	123,515.3	457,573
Investments	566.0	1,300.1	2,457.2	4,389.8	12,903.9	43,326.5	103,581.7	398,059
Other Capital Outlays (Net)	103.7	194.4	84.3	631.3	2,194.8	11,057.1	19,933.6	59,514
VI. *Overall Deficit*	−78.9	−233.4	−1,136.6	−1,734.0	−2,717.3	−10,168.0	−17,813.7	−73,341
V. *Financing*	78.9	233.4	1,136.6	1,734.0	2,717.3	10,168.0	17,813.7	73,341
Net External Financing	104.4	401.4	972.4	843.5	1,595.0	−272.5	−36,167.8	−179,299
Disbursement	179.7	549.4	1,285.7	1,897.9	12,239.8	22,244.6	28,336.3	100,093
Less Amortization	−75.3	−148.0	−313.3	−1,054.4	−4,644.8	−22,517.1	64,504.1	279,392
Net Domestic Financing	150.2	200.9	434.6	217.3	638.3	2,884.2	−5,903.8	21,051
Disbursement	201.7	285.2	565.5	915.4	2,830.4	9,106.5	22,574.5	149,023
Less Amortization	−51.5	−84.3	−130.9	−698.1	−2,192.1	6,222.3	28,478.3	127,972
Other (Net)	−175.7	−368.9	−270.4	673.2	−5,520.0	7,556.3	59,885.3	231,589

Source: IDB Country Studies Division, based on Ministerio da Fazenda, Secretaria de Controle de Empresas Estatais (SEST), *Relatorio Anual. 1987*, p. 38 and *Relatorio Anual. 1988*, p. 87.

Table 10. BRAZIL. Real Output Price Indexes of Selected State Enterprises[1]
(1980 = 100)

Year	Electricity[2]	Telephone	Flat Steel[3]	Postal Services[4]	Gasoline	Diesel Oil	Fuel Oil	L.P. Gas
1970	123.6	n.a.	141.4	27.7	30.0	53.1	31.5	114.2
1971	121.9	n.a.	142.5	51.7	30.9	59.6	33.1	118.9
1972	131.4	161.8	144.4	80.5	32.8	64.4	35.6	127.9
1973	127.5	181.9	141.4	136.1	33.3	63.7	35.8	127.0
1974	128.8	166.7	135.4	116.1	51.3	68.1	40.1	155.2
1975	131.3	173.3	143.3	120.2	60.0	75.6	43.2	163.4
1976	120.0	164.5	134.6	107.9	72.5	80.2	47.9	152.0
1977	111.6	159.8	130.2	115.9	73.3	90.9	49.6	152.2
1978	105.7	111.4	129.3	122.5	69.0	87.6	48.3	145.1
1979	103.3	139.1	115.9	120.6	70.7	97.4	57.9	123.6
1980	100.0	100.0	100.0	100.0	100.0	100.0	100.0	100.0
1981	104.5	89.6	109.3	102.8	98.9	119.2	141.3	97.6
1982	98.1	82.5	107.8	107.8	87.6	118.9	126.5	90.2
1983	85.2	68.2	95.9	78.2	81.2	120.7	135.7	99.4
1984	79.2	59.4	103.0	57.5	76.5	122.1	142.3	105.1
1985	80.3	n.a.	105.0	69.5	66.9	107.6	132.3	91.2

[1]All prices and tariffs deflated by the General Price Index (IGP-DI).
[2]Average tariff per Kw.
[3]Unplated flat steel
[4]Postage rate for simple letters.
n.a. Not available.
Source: Rogério L. Furquim Werneck, *Texto Para Discussão No. 163, Public Sector Adjustment to External Shocks and Domestic Pressures in Brazil, 1970–85.* Pontifica Universidade Católica de Rio de Janeiro. 1986.

Table 11. BRAZIL. Consolidated Accounts of the Federal Public Sector

Billions of Cruzados

	1979	1980	1981*	1982*
A. *Federal Budget*				
1. Budgetary Revenue	509.8	1,209.4	2,391.2	4,002
2. Transfers	153.2	695.1	1,209.0	1,896.8
Monetary Budget	(14.3)	(287.7)	(255.0)	(386.1)
Charges on the Public Debt	(3.7)	(36.2)	(37.5)	(54.1)
State Enterprises	(135.2)	(380.2)	(916.5)	(1,456.6)
3. Net Federal Expenditure (1 − 2)	356.2	524.3	1,110.2	2,103.4
B. *Monetary Budget*				
1. Revenues	−60.7	284.5	584.2	546.1
Transfers from Federal Government	(14.3)	(278.7)	(214.5)	(386.1)
Net Balance on Public Debt	(−74.9)	(5.8)	(369.7)	(160.0)
2. Expenditures (Subsidies)	181.9	896.4	1,303.2	837.6
3. Deficit (2 − 1)	242.6	611.9	719.0	291.5
C. *Budget of State Enterprises (Excluding Banks)*				
1. Revenue	1,191.5	2,768.9	6,281.3	11,744.9
Generated by the Enterprises	(1,056.3)	(2,388.7)	(5,364.8)	(10,288.3)
Received from the Federal Budget	(135.2)	(380.2)	(916.5)	(1,456.6)
2. Expenditures (Excluding Amortizations)	1,397.8	3,354.9	7,204.5	13,390.2
3. Deficit (2 − 1)	206.3	586.0	923.2	1,645.3
D. *Global Deficit (B.3 + C.3)*	448.9	1,197.9	1,642.2	1,936.8
E. *Ratios to Current GDP*				
1. Budgetary Revenue	8.8	9.7	8.3	7.4
2. Global Deficit	8.1	7.3	5.9	3.6
3. Net Federal Expenditure (Excluding Transfers)	6.2	4.2	3.5	3.9
4. State Enterprise Expenditure	25.6	28.3	27.7	26.4
5. Monetary Budget Expenditure	3.2	7.2	4.7	1.6
6. Total Public Sector Expenditure (3 + 4 + 5)	34.9	39.7	35.9	31.7

*Estimates.
Source: Getulio Vargas Foundation, *Conjuntura Economica*, February 1982.

Table 12. BRAZIL. Principal Federal Subsidies and Incentives, 1973–1981

	1973	1974	1975	1976	1977	1978	1979	1980	1981
A. Subsidies (Billions of Cruzados)									
Total	1.8	9.1	17.6	37.0	57.9	67.8	181.9	745.0	906.1
Implicit in Credit[1]	0.8	4.3	11.0	24.0	44.3	49.3	156.8	479.9	700.4
Direct[2]	0.7	4.1	5.1	6.0	6.5	11.4	18.8	236.4	140.4
Explicit in Credit[3]	0.3	0.7	1.5	7.0	7.1	7.0	6.3	14.9	44.8
Purchase and Sale of Agricultural Products[4]	—	—	—	—	—	—	—	13.8	20.5
B. Ratios									
Subsidies/GDP	0.4	1.3	1.7	2.4	2.5	1.9	3.1	6.0	3.3
Subsidies/Tax Revenue	3.8	13.1	19.8	24.8	27.4	21.9	40.9	77.8	47.3

[1]Agriculture exports.
[2]Wheat, oil, soya and sugar.
[3]Crop insurance (PROAGRO), regional development program (PROTERRA), etc.
[4]Minimum prices and buffer stocks.

Source: Carlos Geraldo Langoni, "Bases Institucionais da Economia Brasileira," Banco Central do Brazil, 1981.

Table 13. BRAZIL. Indicators of Financial Savings
(CzS Millions and Percentages)

December of Each Year	Passbook Savings[1] (1)	Time Deposits[2] (2)	Treasury Bonds (ORTN/OTN)[3] (3)	Treasury Bills LTN[4] (4)	Treasury Bills LFT[5] (5)	Central Bank LBC[6] (6)	Subtotal (7)=(3)+(4)+(5)+(6)	Bills of Exchange and Housing Bonds[7] (8)	State and Municipal Debt[8] (9)	Stock of Financial Savings (10)=(1)+(2)+(7)+(8)+(9)	Annual Flow (11)	Annual Flow as % of GDP (12)
1972	7.7	17.0	15.9	8.1	—	—	24.0	26.0	1.7	76.4	—	—
1973	14.1	25.8	20.8	12.6	—	—	33.4	41.3	3.2	117.8	41.4	8.1
1974	28.9	33.5	32.9	14.4	—	—	47.3	50.7	5.4	165.8	48.0	6.4
1975	55.2	54.6	58.4	22.1	—	—	80.5	64.7	13.8	268.8	103.0	9.8
1976	107.5	73.1	80.9	64.7	—	—	145.6	78.2	23.2	427.6	158.8	9.7
1977	177.3	133.0	97.7	106.2	—	—	203.9	92.4	31.1	637.7	210.1	8.4
1978	288.7	226.5	151.8	161.9	—	—	313.7	139.2	46.7	1,014.8	377.1	10.4
1979	523.5	409.7	233.6	163.9	—	—	397.5	199.9	84.3	1,614.9	600.1	10.1
1980	984.8	639.2	439.5	186.1	—	—	625.6	290.8	150.5	2,690.9	1,076.0	8.7
1981	2,484.9	1,560.2	1,357.6	788.3	—	—	2,145.9	520.2	413.1	7,124.3	4,433.4	18.0
1982	5,671.4	3,360.4	4,027.3	709.5	—	—	4,736.8	1,814.9	1,033.8	16,617.3	9,493.0	18.6
1983	18,153.5	9,646.7	8,782.9	360.4	—	—	9,143.3	4,756.1	2,674.9	44,374.5	27,757.2	23.3
1984	62,510.0	39,256.0	50,867.0	2,214.0	—	—	53,081.0	9,951.0	8,507.2	173,305.2	128,930.7	32.7
1985	217,920.0	149,146.0	249,596.0	8,893.0	—	—	258,489.0	32,960.0	33,474.0	691,989.0	518,683.8	36.7
1986	329,841.0	291,450.0	148,697.0	8,057.0	—	202,465.0	359,219.0	46,721.0	61,406.0	1,088,637.0	396,648.0	10.7
1987	2,210,265.0	961,084.0	617,542.0	41,431.0	—	1,633,602.0	2,229,575.0	72,879.0	398,946.0	5,872,749.0	4,784,112.0	40.3
1988												
March	3,680,240.0	1,527,002.0	1,011,945.0	—	693,106.0	1,773,447.0	3,478,487.0	88,660.0	640,841.0	9,415,241.0	—	—
June	6,255,537.0	2,536,845.0	2,606,479.0	—	3,064,540.0	1,847,478.0	7,590,505.0	130,202.0	1,076,810.0	17,589,899.0	—	—
September	11,712,322.0	4,394,611.0	5,102,905.0	—	9,411,322.0	—	14,514,227.0	188,007.0	1,906,883.0	32,716,050.0	—	—
December	24,976,248.0	9,310,350.0	9,921,852.0	—	21,605,595.0	—	31,527,447.0	365,372.0	3,834,179.0	70,013,596.0	64,140,847.0	69.0

[1] Cardeneta de Poupanca.
[2] Depósitos a prazo fixo.
[3] Obrigações Reajustáveis do Tesouro (ORTN) and Obrigações do Tesouro (OTN-after February 1986).
[4] Letras do Tesouro.
[5] Letras Federais do Tesouro.
[6] Letras do Banco Central.
[7] Letras de Câmbio e Imobiliárias.
[8] Dívida Estadual e Municipal.

Source: Central Bank of Brazil; FGV, *Conjuntura Economica*; and estimates of the IDB Country Studies Division.

Table 13. BRAZIL. Indicators of Financial Savings (continuation)
(CzS Millions)

December of Each Year	Nominal Value of ORTN/OTN in December of Each Year in CzS (13)	Percentage Change in (13)*100 (14)	Adjusted Percentage Change in (14)*100[a] (15)	Lagged Stock of Financial Savings (16)	Adjusted Stock of Financial Savings[1] (17)=[(15/100)*(16)	Actual Stock of Financial Savings[2] (18)	Difference (19)=(18)−(17)	Difference as Percentage of Current GDP (20)
1972	70.07	115.3	122.2	—	—	76.7	—	—
1973	79.07	112.8	119.6	76.4	91.4	117.8	26.4	5.2
1974	105.41	133.3	141.3	117.8	166.5	165.8	−0.7	−0.0
1975	130.94	124.2	131.7	165.8	218.4	268.8	50.4	4.8
1976	119.68	137.2	145.4	268.8	390.8	427.6	36.8	2.2
1977	233.91	130.2	138.0	427.6	590.1	637.7	47.6	1.9
1978	318.44	136.2	144.4	637.7	920.8	1,014.8	94.0	2.6
1979	468.71	147.2	156.0	1,014.8	1,583.1	1,614.9	31.8	0.5
1980	706.70	150.8	159.8	1,614.9	2,580.6	2,690.9	110.3	0.9
1981	1,382.09	195.6	207.3	2,690.9	5,578.2	7,124.3	1,546.1	3.3
1982	2,733.27	197.8	109.7	7,124.3	14,939.7	16,617.3	1,677.6	3.4
1983	7,012.99	256.6	272.0	16,617.3	45,199.1	44,374.5	−824.6	−0.7
1984	22,110.46	315.3	334.2	44,374.5	148,299.6	173,305.2	25,505.6	6.4
1985	70,613.67	319.4	338.6	173,305.2	586,811.4	691,989.0	105,177.6	7.4
1986[b]	106.40	150.7	159.7	691,989.0	1,105,106.4	1,088,637.0	−16,469.4	−0.4
1987	522.99	491.5	521.0	1,088,637.0	5,671,798.8	5,872,749.0	200,950.2	1.7
1988	4,790.00	916.0	971.0	5,872,749.0	57,024,392.8	70,013,596.0	12,289,203.2	14.0

[a]Multiplied by 1.06 to reflect the 6 percent interest rate on passbook savings accounts, which, together with monetary correction, establishes a floor for interest rates in Brazil.
[b]As part of the monetary reform introduced with the Cruzado Plan of February 1986, one cruzado was set equal to 1,000 cruzeiros. Also, by Decree-Law, the Readjustable Treasury Bond (ORTN) was replaced by the non-indexed (for one year) Treasury Bond (OTN). After March 1987, however, the OTN was corrected as the ORTN had been.
[1]Values correspond to the increase in financial savings that is attributable only to the percentage growth of monetary correction and interest paid on passbook savings
[2]Column 10.
Source: IDB Country Studies Division based on Central Bank of Brazil data.

Table 14. BRAZIL. Nominal Monthly Income Distribution of the Economically Active Population, 1979, 1981, 1983–1987

Deciles	1979 Percentage of Monthly Income In Each Decile	1979 Percentage of Monthly Income Cumulative	1979 Average Income[2] In Each Decile	1979 Average Income[2] Cumulative	1981 Percentage of Monthly Income In Each Decile	1981 Percentage of Monthly Income Cumulative	1981 Average Income[2] In Each Decile	1981 Average Income[2] Cumulative	1983 Percentage of Monthly Income In Each Decile	1983 Percentage of Monthly Income Cumulative	1983 Average Income[2] In Each Decile	1983 Average Income[2] Cumulative	1984 Percentage of Monthly Income In Each Decile	1984 Percentage of Monthly Income Cumulative	1984 Average Income[2] In Each Decile	1984 Average Income[2] Cumulative
1st (−)	1.3	1.3	86.15	86.15	1.1	1.1	268.28	268.28	1.1	1.1	1,107.95	1,107.95	1.0	1.0	2,798.74	2,798.74
2nd	1.8	3.1	122.80	104.48	2.0	3.1	491.04	379.66	1.9	3.0	1,905.33	1,506.65	2.0	3.0	5,973.11	4,385.93
3rd	2.8	5.8	186.74	131.90	2.7	5.8	677.51	478.94	2.7	5.6	2,732.43	1,915.24	2.6	5.6	7,779.80	5,517.22
4th	4.0	9.9	274.03	167.43	4.0	9.8	986.59	605.85	3.4	9.0	3,485.94	2,307.92	3.6	9.2	10,521.91	6,768.39
5th	4.9	14.8	332.56	200.46	4.8	14.6	1,178.12	720.31	4.5	13.5	4,582.14	2,762.76	4.4	13.7	13,062.25	8,029.16
6th	4.9	19.6	331.19	222.25	5.5	20.1	1,357.53	826.51	5.2	18.7	5,301.42	3,185.87	5.2	18.8	15,125.84	9,210.27
7th	7.4	27.0	500.94	262.06	7.8	27.9	1,931.15	984.31	7.3	26.1	7,512.29	3,803.93	7.6	26.4	22,345.66	11,086.76
8th	10.1	37.2	687.78	315.27	10.5	38.4	2,595.54	1,185.72	10.3	36.4	10,499.04	4,640.82	10.5	36.9	30,836.09	13,555.43
9th	15.8	53.0	1,073.22	399.49	16.1	54.5	3,978.19	1,495.99	16.5	52.9	16,894.32	6,002.32	16.5	53.4	48,302.34	17,416.20
10th (+)	47.0	100.0	3,190.10	678.55	45.5	100.0	11,258.77	2,472.27	47.1	100.0	48,038.28	10,205.92	46.6	100.0	136,840.86	29,359.67
Average			678.55				2,472.27				10,205.95				29,358.67	
Bottom 40%			667.32	—	9.8	—	2,423.42	—	9.0	—	9,231.65	—	9.2	—	27,073.56	—
Top 5%			4,615.45	—	32.7	—	16,182.89	—	33.8	—	68,953.01	—	33.3	—	195,473.83	—
Top 1%			n.a.	—	13.0	—	32,048.12	—	13.9	—	141,516.91	—	13.4	—	392,476.97	—
Gini Coefficient			0.590				0.561				0.580				0.576	

[1]Excludes the rural areas of Brazil's Northern Region (Rondônia, Acre, Amazonas, Roraima, Pará, Amapá).
[2]Current Cruzeiros.
Source: IBGE, Directoria de Pesquisas, Departamento de Emprego e Rendimento—Pesquisa Nacional por Amostra de Domicilios; and IDB Country Studies Division.

(continues)

STATISTICAL APPENDIX 133

Table 14. BRAZIL. Nominal Monthly Income Distribution of the Economically Active Population, 1979, 1981, 1983–1987 (continuation)

		1985				1986				1987	
	Percentage of Monthly Income		Average Income[2]		Percentage of Monthly Income		Average Income[2]		Percentage of Monthly Income		Average Income[2]	
Deciles	In Each Decile	Cumu-lative	In Each Decile	Cumu-lative	In Each Decile	Cumu-lative	In Each Decile	Cumu-lative	In Each Decile	Cumu-lative	In Each Decile	Cumu-lative
1st (−)	0.9	0.9	9,534.58	9,354.58	1.0	1.0	31,697.0	31,697.0	0.8	0.8	75,271.0	75,271.0
2nd	1.9	2.7	20,149.29	14,841.95	2.2	3.2	67,060.0	49,379.0	1.9	2.7	177,691.0	126,481.0
3rd	2.5	5.3	27,346.88	19,010.26	2.6	5.7	80,134.0	59,631.0	2.6	5.3	237,816.0	163,593.0
4th	3.5	8.8	37,669.48	23,675.06	3.6	9.4	112,607.0	72,875.0	3.5	8.7	322,874.0	203,413.0
5th	4.3	13.0	46,206.66	28,181.38	4.1	13.5	127,620.0	83,824.0	3.9	12.6	366,700.0	236,071.0
6th	5.0	18.1	54,261.95	32,528.13	5.5	19.0	172,657.0	98,629.0	5.5	18.2	517,411.0	282,961.0
7th	7.3	25.4	79,228.81	39,199.67	7.4	26.4	230,950.0	117,532.0	7.2	25.4	673,655.0	338,774.0
8th	10.5	35.9	113,239.25	48,454.62	10.2	36.6	315,851.0	142,322.0	10.1	35.5	944,159.0	414,447.0
9th	16.4	52.3	117,862.13	62,833.26	15.9	52.5	419,832.0	181,600.0	16.1	51.6	1,497,900.0	534,831.0
10th (+)	42.7	100.0	515,044.13	108,054.35	47.5	100.0	1,478,374.0	311,278.0	48.4	100.0	4,523,155.0	933,664.0
Average	—	—	108,054.35	—	—	—	311,278	—	—	—	933,664	—
Bottom 40%	8.8	—	94,700.23	—	9.4	—	291,498	—	8.7	—	813,652	—
Top 5%	34.2	—	739,595.97	—	34.3	—	2,134,777	—	35.2	—	6,570,141	—
Top 1%	14.3	—	1,550,065.03	—	15.2	—	4,728,614	—	16.1	—	15,021,477	—
Gini Coefficient		0.588				0.577				0.591		

[1]Excludes the rural areas of Brazil's Northern Region (Rondônia, Acre, Amazonas, Roraima, Pará, Amapá).
[2]Current Cruzeiros.
Source: IBGE, Directoria de Pesquisas, Departamento de Emprego e Rendimento—Pesquisa Nacional por Amostra de Domicílios; and IDB Country Studies Division.

ANNEX

THE MATRIX METHOD OF NATIONAL ACCOUNTS[1]

Introduction

Of the four forms of presentation of national accounts described by the United Nations,[2] the Matrix method is used here. This form of presentation permits each transaction to be represented by a single entry and the nature of the transaction to be inferred by its position. Each account is represented by a row (horizontal) for revenues and by a column (vertical) for expenditures.

The matrix used appears in Table 1. It consists of accounts for (a) the business sector, (b) the household sector, (c) the general government, (d) the rest of the world; and (e) capital formation.

The first row in the matrix, for example, shows sales of goods and services by the business sector to households (private consumption), to the general government (government consumption), to the rest of the world (exports of goods and nonfactor services), and capital formation (gross total investment). The last column at the far right shows the total revenue of each sector. Thus, the sum of the components in the first row is the market price value received by the business sector for its final sales of goods and services.

Expenditure entries for the business sector, for the general government, and for the rest of the world are split into two separate columns. For the business sector, payments to the government are divided into tax and nontax payments. Similarly, payments to the rest of the world distinguish imports of goods and nonfactor services, on the one hand, from profit remittances and

---

[1] Prepared by A. Rufatt, *Papers on Macroeconomic Analysis*, No. 2, 1985, Methodology Unit, IDB Country Studies Division.

[2] United Nations, Statistical Office, *A System of National Accounts*, Series F, No. 2, Rev. 3 (New York, 1968).

Annex Table 1 Income-Expenditure Matrix

Receipts from / Payments to	Business Sector	Households	General Government		Rest of the World		Capital Formation	Total
Business Sector	- - - - -	Private Consumption	Government Purchase of Goods and Services		Exports of Goods and Services	- - - - -	Total Capital Formation	Total Final Sales of the Economy
Households	Wages and Rents	- - - - -	Wages	Transfers and Interest on Domestic Debt	- - - - -	Factor Income and Transfers	- - - - -	Household Income
Government	Direct Taxes Plus Indirect Taxes Minus Subsidies	Direct Taxes	- - - - -	- - - - -	- - - - -	- - - - -	- - - - -	Total Current Receipts of the General Government
Rest of the World	Imports of Goods and Nonfactor Services	- - - - -	- - - - -	Interest Payments on External Debt	- - - - -	- - - - -	- - - - -	Imports of Goods and Services
Sources of Capital Formation	Business Savings	Household Savings	Government Savings		Trade Deficit	Factor Services Deficit Minus Net Unrequited Transfers		
	Private Savings				External Savings			
Totals	Total Final Sales of the Economy	Household Income	Total Current Receipts of the General Government		Imports of Goods and Services		Total Capital Formation	Grand Total
							Total Savings	

(National Savings shown under Sources of Capital Formation row spanning Business Sector and Households columns)

interest payments on external debt, on the other. For the general government and the rest of the world, purchases of goods and services are shown separately from payments of financial services and net transfers. This arrangement allows a clear identification of two related phenomena: first, the increasing importance of interest payments on external debt and, second, the drastic change in the structure of the current account of the balance of payments, namely, the improvement in the trade accounts, which offsets the deterioration in net factor payments.

Finally, the totals of each column appear in the bottom row. These are total revenues and are transferred from the corresponding cell in the far-right column. Expenditures in each column are subtracted from total revenues to obtain the current savings of each sector.

Since the matrix method is one of several alternative forms of presentation of national accounts, the same standard definitions, accounting conventions, exceptions, etc., that are valid for the other methods, are equally valid for it. Hence, national accounts provide the conceptual and quantitative framework for the matrix. There are, however, some problems with data availability or with the disaggregation required in the matrix. In particular, no reliable data are available for disposable income or for undistributed profits. Thus, to estimate the income of the household sector in the matrix, transfer payments and interest payments on domestic debt by the government are added to national income. Other things being equal, the result is an overestimation of unknown magnitude in business sector payments to the household sector and consequently in the latter's income and savings. Similarly, there is a comparable underestimation of the savings of the business sector. A compromise solution to this problem is to regard the savings of the household and business sectors as private savings. Despite this limitation, the definitions have been applied consistently over time and, for this reason, give a relatively reliable picture of the trends—if not the actual magnitudes—of the savings ratios in these two sectors.

Likewise, national accounts do not provide reliable and up-to-date information on interest payments on external debt by sector; to estimate them, the relative composition of interest payments provided by balance of payments and external debt data has been used.

The Savings-Investment Identity

The matrix method is used to estimate both national savings and, less often, domestic savings and thus to assess the magnitude and the allocation of the savings effort in the economies of the region. Gross domestic savings are measured as savings out of the gross domestic product, that is, savings that come out of the value of production, regardless of whether the factors of production (labor and capital) are provided by residents or foreigners. Gross national savings are measured as savings out of income after they have been adjusted for net factor income and net transfers from abroad.

However, since total savings are by definition identical with total investment, each of these concepts of savings is associated with a different measurement of external savings. The concept of gross domestic savings is consistent with external savings defined as the trade gap or the balance of goods and nonfactor services; the concept of gross national savings is consistent with external savings defined as the deficit on current account with the rest of the world.

The GDP identity is

$$GDP = C + I + X - M$$

where

C = Total consumption
I = Gross investment
X = Exports of goods and nonfactor services
M = Imports of goods and nonfactor services.

Then

$$I = GDP - C + M - X$$
$$I = Sd + (M - X)$$

where

$GDP - C$ = Gross domestic savings (Sd)
$M - X$ = External savings ("trade gap").

If net factor payments abroad (most of which represent interest payments on external debt) are subtracted,

Then:

$$I = GDP - R - C + R + M - X$$
$$I = Sn + (R + M - X)$$

where

$GDP - R$ = Gross national product[3]
$GDP - R - C$ = Gross national savings (Sn)
$R + M - X$ = External savings (deficit on current account).

Thus, the conceptual and quantitative framework for the estimates in the matrix in general and for the estimate of savings in particular is provided by the concept of national disposable income. This income concept is equal to GNP (GDP plus net factor income from abroad) plus net current unrequited transfers. The matrix is used to estimate the magnitude and sectoral composition of national savings. As shown in Table 1, the sum of the savings by sector in the row for sources of capital formation equals total capital formation

---

[3]For simplicity current unrequited transfers are ignored. If they are included in R, the result is national disposable income. See Host-Madsen, Paul, "Macroeconomic Accounts: An Overview," International Monetary Fund Pamphlet Series No. 29 (Washington, D.C., 1979).

or gross investment. Sources of capital formation comprise national savings and external savings. National savings is equal to the sum of business savings, household savings, and general government savings. External savings is the deficit on current account with the rest of the world, and is equal to the sum of the deficit on the balance of goods and services and net transfer payments.

The income-expenditure matrix in millions of current cruzados is presented in Table 2 below and is expressed as percentages of current GDP and current GNP in Tables 3 and 4, respectively.

Annex Table 2 BRAZIL. Income-Expenditure Matrix[1]
(millions of current cruzados)

	Year	Business Sector	Households	Government	Rest of World	Capital Formation	Total
Business Sector	1980	—	8,649	359	1,121	2,890	13,019
	1981	—	16,804	702	2,311	5,666	25,483
	1982	—	35,586	1,494	3,846	10,722	51,648
	1983	—	85,143	3,576	13,393	19,635	121,747
	1984	—	279,708	10,154	52,306	60,340	402,508
	1985	—	967,019	40,616	169,331	238,946	1,415,912
	1986	—	2,550,411	123,528	322,848	676,763	3,673,550
	1987	—	7,414,195	574,715	1,091,348	2,631,522	11,711,779
	1988	—	55,284,418	4,463,671	9,422,891	21,781,208	91,042,188
Households	1980	9,888	—	781	112	—	11,982
	1981	19,344	—	1,583	208	—	23,705
	1982	39,373	—	3,563	402	—	49,339
	1983	91,742	—	7,752	685	—	114,939
	1984	312,742	—	21,833	3,119	—	391,918
	1985	1,106,918	—	95,975	12,852	—	1,469,579
	1986	2,845,180	—	253,835	19,332	—	3,815,275
	1987	9,314,677	—	683,424	44,245	—	12,266,674
	1988	73,698,576	—	2,060,397	335,277	—	99,631,437
Government	1980	1,491	267,339	—	—	—	2,478
	1981	3,087	−265	—	—	—	5,125
	1982	6,385	−647	—	—	—	10,871
	1983	14,792	−1,810	—	—	—	24,478
	1984	42,909	−2,822	—	—	—	75,278
	1985	157,507	−12,020	—	—	—	277,967
	1986	505,251	−60,673	—	—	—	813,759
	1987	1,444,612	257,651	—	—	—	2,702,451
	1988	10,647,715	1,859,863	—	—	—	19,993,526
Rest of the World	1980	1,400	223	221	—	—	1,907
	1981	2,404	608	480	—	—	3,611
	1982	4,182	1,622	1,068	—	—	7,138
	1983	10,563	3,869	2,879	—	—	18,063
	1984	30,595	13,999	9,503	—	—	55,616
	1985	98,094	44,324	35,124	—	—	184,455
	1986	232,693	78,538	82,875	—	—	414,675
	1987	714,420	249,755	184,777	—	—	1,189,619
	1988	4,768,999	1,876,093	1,482,917	—	—	8,483,482

ANNEX 141

	1980		137					
	1981		304	2,227				
	1982		733	4,599				
	1983		2,592	8,620				
	1984		5,082	18,299				
	1985		21,089	77,018				
	1986		72,562	370,080				
	1987		−269,336	895,682				
	1988		−1,809,078	3,852,291				
				36,861,071				
Sources of Capital Formation	1980		2,363			278	334	
	1981		4,903		−83	93	884	
	1982		9,353		−210	335	2,297	
	1983		20,891		−1,255	−2,830	6,080	
	1984		82,103		−4,488	−21,710	20,422	
	1985		391,169		−20,436	−71,236	66,820	
	1986		968,244		−147,583	−90,155	142,726	
	1987		3,582,955		−343,407	−376,928	390,287	
	1988		35,051,993		−964,793	−4,653,892	3,024,733	
					−11,551,626			
	1980			2,277			612	2,890
	1981			4,689			977	5,666
	1982			8,090			2,632	10,722
	1983			16,385			3,250	16,635
	1984			61,628			−1,288	60,340
	1985			243,363			−4,417	238,946
	1986			624,192			52,571	676,763
	1987			2,618,162			13,359	2,631,522
	1988			23,500,367			−1,629,159	21,871,208
Total	1980		13,019	11,982	2,478	1,400	446	2,890	32,215
	1981		25,483	23,705	5,125	2,404	1,092	5,660	63,473
	1982		51,648	49,339	10,871	4,182	2,698	10,722	129,460
	1983		121,747	114,933	24,478	10,563	6,765	19,635	298,126
	1984		402,508	391,918	75,278	30,595	23,542	60,340	984,181
	1985		1,415,912	1,469,579	277,967	98,094	79,672	238,946	3,580,171
	1986		3,673,550	3,815,275	813,759	232,693	162,059	676,763	9,374,099
	1987		11,711,779	12,266,674	2,702,451	714,420	434,532	2,631,522	30,461,377
	1988		91,042,188	99,631,437	19,993,526	4,768,999	3,360,010	21,871,208	240,667,368

¹Details may not sum due to rounding.
Source: IDB Country Studies Division.

Annex Table 3 BRAZIL. Income-Expenditure Matrix[1]
(Percentages of GDP)

	Year	Business Sector		Households	Government		Rest of World		Formation Capital	Total
Business Sector	1980	—	—	69.7	2.9	—	9.0	—	23.3	105.0
	1981	—	—	68.1	2.8	—	9.4	—	23.0	103.3
	1982	—	—	69.7	2.9	—	7.5	—	21.0	101.2
	1983	—	—	71.6	3.0	—	11.3	—	16.5	102.4
	1984	—	—	71.0	2.6	—	13.3	—	15.3	102.4
	1985	—	—	68.4	2.9	—	12.0	—	16.9	100.1
	1986	—	—	68.8	3.3	—	8.7	—	18.3	99.1
	1987	—	—	62.4	4.8	—	9.2	—	22.1	98.5
	1988	—	—	59.4	4.8	—	10.1	—	23.5	97.9
Households	1980	79.7	—	—	6.3	9.7	—	0.9	—	96.6
	1981	78.4	—	—	6.4	10.4	—	0.8	—	96.1
	1982	77.2	—	—	7.0	11.8	—	0.8	—	96.7
	1983	77.1	—	—	6.5	12.4	—	0.6	—	96.6
	1984	79.4	—	—	5.5	13.8	—	0.8	—	99.5
	1985	78.3	—	—	6.8	18.0	—	0.9	—	103.9
	1986	76.7	—	—	7.2	18.4	—	0.5	—	102.9
	1987	78.4	—	—	7.5	17.0	—	0.4	—	103.2
	1988	79.3	—	—	7.2	20.3	—	0.4	—	107.1
Government	1980	12.0	−1.0	8.9	—	—	—	—	—	20.0
	1981	12.5	−1.1	9.3	—	—	—	—	—	20.8
	1982	12.5	−1.3	10.1	—	—	—	—	—	21.3
	1983	12.4	−1.5	9.7	—	—	—	—	—	20.6
	1984	10.9	−0.7	8.9	—	—	—	—	—	19.1
	1985	11.1	−0.9	9.4	—	—	—	—	—	19.7
	1986	13.6	−1.6	10.0	—	—	—	—	—	21.9
	1987	12.2	2.2	8.4	—	—	—	—	—	22.7
	1988	11.4	2.0	8.1	—	—	—	—	—	21.5
Rest of the World	1980	11.3	1.8	—	—	1.8	—	—	—	15.4
	1981	9.7	2.5	—	—	1.9	—	—	—	14.6
	1982	8.2	3.2	—	—	2.1	—	—	—	14.0
	1983	8.9	3.3	—	—	2.4	—	—	—	15.2
	1984	7.8	3.6	—	—	2.4	—	—	—	14.1
	1985	6.9	3.1	—	—	2.5	—	—	—	13.0
	1986	6.3	2.1	—	—	2.2	—	—	—	11.2
	1987	6.0	2.1	—	—	1.6	—	—	—	10.0
	1988	5.1	1.9	—	—	1.5	—	—	—	9.1

ANNEX 143

Sources of Capital Formation	1980	1.1	19.1	18.0	—	—	—	—
	1981	1.2	19.9	18.6	—	—	—	—
	1982	1.4	18.3	16.9	—	—	—	—
	1983	2.2	17.6	15.4	—	—	—	—
	1984	1.3	20.9	19.6	—	—	—	—
	1985	1.5	27.7	26.2	—	—	—	—
	1986	2.0	26.1	24.2	—	—	—	—
	1987	−2.3	30.1	32.4	—	—	—	—
	1988	−1.8	37.8	39.6	—	—	—	—
	1980				−0.7	2.2	2.7	—
	1981				−0.9	0.4	3.6	—
	1982				−2.5	0.7	4.5	—
	1983				3.8	−2.4	5.1	—
	1984				−5.2	−5.5	5.2	—
	1985				−10.4	−5.0	4.7	—
	1986				−9.3	−2.4	3.8	—
	1987				−8.1	−3.2	3.3	—
	1988				−12.3	−5.0	3.1	—
	1980			18.4		4.9		
	1981			19.0		4.0		
	1982			15.9		5.2		
	1983			13.8		2.7		
	1984			15.7		−0.3		
	1985			17.2		−0.3		
	1986			16.8		1.4		
	1987			22.0		0.1		
	1988			25.5		−1.9		
Total	1980	105.0		96.6	20.0	11.3	3.6	23.3	259.8
	1981	103.0		96.1	20.8	9.7	4.4	23.0	257.4
	1982	101.2		96.7	21.3	8.2	5.3	21.0	253.7
	1983	102.4		96.6	20.6	8.9	5.7	16.5	250.7
	1984	102.2		99.5	19.1	7.8	6.0	15.3	250.0
	1985	100.1		103.9	19.7	6.9	5.6	16.9	253.2
	1986	99.1		102.9	21.9	6.3	4.4	18.3	252.8
	1987	98.5		103.2	22.7	6.0	3.7	22.1	256.3
	1988	97.9		107.1	21.5	5.1	3.4	23.5	258.6

[1] Details may not sum due to rounding.
Source: IDB Country Studies Division.

Annex Table 4   BRAZIL. Income-Expenditure Matrix[1]
(Percentages of GNP)

	Year	Business Sector	Households	Government	Rest of World	Formation Capital	Total
Business Sector	1980	—	72.1	3.0	9.3	24.1	108.5
	1981	—	71.1	3.0	9.8	24.0	107.8
	1982	—	73.5	3.1	7.9	22.1	106.6
	1983	—	76.0	3.2	11.9	17.5	108.6
	1984	—	75.2	2.7	14.1	16.2	108.3
	1985	—	72.2	3.0	12.6	17.8	105.7
	1986	—	71.9	3.5	9.1	19.1	103.6
	1987	—	64.8	5.0	9.5	23.0	102.3
	1988	—	61.7	5.0	10.5	24.4	101.6
Households	1980	82.4	—	6.5	—	—	99.9
	1981	81.8	—	6.7	—	—	100.2
	1982	81.3	—	7.4	—	—	101.9
	1983	81.8	—	6.9	—	—	102.5
	1984	84.1	—	5.9	—	—	105.4
	1985	82.6	—	7.2	—	—	109.7
	1986	80.3	—	7.5	—	—	107.6
	1987	81.4	—	7.8	—	—	107.1
	1988	82.3	—	7.5	—	—	111.2
Government	1980	12.4	9.2	—	0.9	—	20.7
	1981	13.1	9.7	—	0.9	—	21.7
	1982	13.2	10.6	—	0.8	—	22.4
	1983	13.2	10.3	—	0.6	—	21.8
	1984	11.5	9.5	—	0.8	—	20.2
	1985	11.8	9.9	—	1.0	—	20.7
	1986	14.3	10.4	—	0.5	—	23.0
	1987	12.6	8.7	—	0.4	—	23.6
	1988	11.9	8.4	—	0.4	—	22.3
Rest of the World	1980	11.7	—	1.8	—	—	15.9
	1981	10.2	—	2.0	—	—	15.3
	1982	8.6	—	2.2	—	—	14.7
	1983	9.4	—	2.6	—	—	16.1
	1984	8.2	—	2.6	—	—	15.0
	1985	7.3	—	2.6	—	—	13.8
	1986	6.6	—	2.3	—	—	11.7
	1987	6.2	—	1.6	—	—	10.4
	1988	5.3	—	1.7	—	—	9.5

ANNEX   145

	1980	1.1							
	1981	1.3							
	1982	1.5							
	1983	2.3							
	1984	1.4							
	1985	1.6							
	1986	2.0							
	1987	−2.4							
	1988	−2.0							
Sources of Capital Formation	1980	19.7	18.6						24.1
	1981	20.7	19.4			2.3	2.9		24.0
	1982	19.3	17.8			0.4	3.7		22.1
	1983	18.6	16.3		−0.7	0.7	4.7		17.5
	1984	22.1	20.7		−0.9	−2.5	5.4		16.2
	1985	29.2	27.6		−2.6	−5.8	5.5		17.8
	1986	27.3	25.3		−4.0	−5.3	5.0		19.1
	1987	31.3	33.6		−5.5	−2.5	4.0		23.0
	1988	39.1	41.1		−11.0	−3.3	3.4		24.4
					−9.7	−5.2	3.4		
					−8.4				
					−12.9				
	1980		19.0			5.1			
	1981		19.8			4.1			
	1982		16.7			5.4			
	1983		14.6			2.9			
	1984		16.6			−0.3			
	1985		18.2			−0.3			
	1986		17.6			1.5			
	1987		22.9			0.1			
	1988		26.2			−1.8			
Total	1980	108.5	99.9		20.7	11.7	3.7	24.1	268.6
	1981	107.8	100.2		21.7	10.2	4.6	24.0	268.4
	1982	106.6	101.9		22.4	8.6	5.6	22.1	267.3
	1983	108.6	102.5		21.8	9.4	6.0	17.5	266.0
	1984	108.3	105.4		20.2	8.2	6.3	16.2	264.7
	1985	105.7	109.7		20.7	7.3	5.9	17.8	267.2
	1986	103.6	107.6		23.0	6.6	4.6	19.1	264.4
	1987	102.3	107.1		23.6	6.2	3.8	23.0	266.1
	1988	101.6	111.2		22.3	5.3	3.8	24.4	268.6

[1]Details may not sum due to rounding.
Source: IDB Country Studies Division.

BIBLIOGRAPHY

Abreu, Marcelo De Paiva. "Stability and Social Policy in Brazil: The Way Ahead." *Bulletin of Latin American Research* 6, 2 (1987).

Arida, Persio. "Economic Stabilization in Brazil." Paper presented at the Inter-American Economic Issues Seminar. The seminar was sponsored by the Latin American Program of the Woodrow Wilson International Center for Scholars, Smithsonian Institution, Washington, D.C., November 1, 1984.

―――, and André Lara-Resende. "Inertial Inflation and Monetary Reform in Brazil." Paper prepared for the conference "Inflation and Indexation," Institute of International Economics, Washington, D.C., December 6–8, 1984.

Bacha, Edmar Lisboa. "Preliminary Notes on the Economic Strategy of the New Brazilian Government." Mimeo. September 1985.

Baer, Werner. *The Brazilian Economy: Growth and Development*. New York: Praeger, Third Edition, 1989.

―――, and Paul Beckerman. "Indexing in Brazil." *World Development* 2, 10–12 (October-December 1974).

―――. *Industrialization and Economic Development in Brazil*. Homewood, Illinois: Richard D. Irwin, 1965.

―――. "The Resurgence of Inflation in Brazil, 1974–86." *World Development* 15, 8 (August 1987).

―――, and Joaquin J. M. Guilhoto. "Structural Changes in Brazil's Industrial Economy." *World Development* 15, 2 (1987).

Banco Central do Brasil. *Programa Econômico, Ajustamento Interno e Externo* (published on a quarterly basis since 1982).

―――. *Relátorio do Banco Central do Brasil*, 1988 (25), 1987 (24), and 1986 (23).

Bastos Marques, Maria Silvia, and Sérgio Ribeiro da Costa Werlang. "Moratória Interna, Dívida Pública e Juros Reais." Rio de Janeiro: Instituto Brasileiro de Economia, Fundação Getúlio Vargas, 1988.

Bresser Pereira, Luis, and Yoshiaki Nakano. *The Theory of Inertial Inflation: The Foundation of Economic Reform in Brazil and Argentina*. Boulder/London: Lynne Reinner Publishers, 1987.

Cardoso, Eliana. "Debt Cycles in Brazil and Argentina." Paper presented at the conference on "Financing Latin American Growth: Prospects for the 1990s," sponsored by the National Autonomous University of Mexico, Washington University, and the Jerome Levy Economics Institute, Annandale on the Hudson, New York, October 1988.

Cline, William R. *International Debt and the Stability of the World Economy, Policy Analyses in International Economics 4*. Distributed by MIT Press/Cambridge, London: Institute for International Economics, 1983.

Costa, Ramónaval Augusto. "Salário e Pobreza." Brasília: Departamento de Economia, Universidade de Brasília, 1988.

Cutolo dos Santos, Sérgio, and Carlos Alberto Ramos. "Mercados de Trabalho no Setor Público Federal: Subsídios para o Trabalho (versão preliminar)." Mimeo. Brasília, 1988.

Dias Carneiro, Dionisio, and Pedro Bodin de Moraes. "Inflation and the Development of the Brazilian Financial System." Rio de Janeiro: Catholic University of Rio de Janeiro, 1986.

———, and Rogerio F. Werneck. "Investment Behavior and Recession in Brazil." Rio de Janeiro: Catholic University of Rio de Janeiro, 1986.

———. "Passivo do Governo e Déficit Público no Período 1970/85." In Lozardo, Ernesto, et al. *Déficit Público Brasileiro: Política Econômica e Ajuste Estrutural*. Rio de Janeiro: Editora Paz e Terra, 1987.

Dornbusch, Rudiger, and Mario Henrique Simonsen. "Inflation Stabilization with Incomes Policy Support: A Review of the Experience in Argentina, Brazil and Israel." Paper presented for the Group of Thirty, New York, October 2–3, 1986.

"Economic Report of the President," Washington, D.C.: U.S. Government Printing Office, 1989.

Fields, G. S. "Who Benefits from Economic Development?—A Reexamination of Brazilian Growth in the 1960s." *The American Economic Review*, September 1977.

Fishlow, Albert. "Brazilian Size Distribution of Income." *The American Economic Review* (Papers and Proceedings of the Eighty-Fourth Annual Meeting of the American Economic Association). May 1972.

Flôres de Lima, Beatriz. *Criptoeconomia ou Economia Subterrânea*. Estudos Especiais, IBRE 5. Rio de Janeiro: Instituto Brasileiro de Economia, Editora da Fundação Getúlio Vargas, 1985.

França, Paulo Oscar. "Déficit Público: Política Econômica de Ajuste Estructural." Mimeo. Brasília, November 1985.

———. "Reforma Financiera e Estabilização Econômica." *Conjuntura Econômica* 39, 11 (November 1985).

———. "Uma Proposta de Solução Para a Crise Financeira e Gerencial do Estado." Mimeo. Brasília. (December 1987).

Fundação Instituto Brasileiro de Geografia e Estatística—IBGE, *Estatísticas Históricas do Brasil* (3 volumes), 1986.

———. Diretoria de Pesquisas, Departamento de Emprego e Rendimento. *Pesquisa Nacional por Amostra de Domicílios*, 1979, 1981, 1983–87.

Goldsmith, Raymond W. *Brasil 1850–1984, Desenvolvimento Financeiro Sob um Século de Inflação*. São Paulo: Banco Bamerindus do Brasil, S.A., e Editora Harper & Row do Brasil, Ltda.

———. *Financial Structure and Development*. New Haven: Yale University Press, 1969.

Hanson Costa, Margaret, Lia Marcia Alt Pereira, and Carlos Roberto Lavalle da Silva. "Medidas do Déficit Público: Variações em Torno dos Principais Conceitos." Rio de Janeiro: Fundação Getúlio Vargas, Centro de Estudos Fiscais, 1988.

Inter-American Development Bank. *External Debt and Economic Development in Latin America*. Washington, D.C., 1984.

——— . *Socioeconomic Report of Brazil*. Document GN-1236-1. August 1978.
Jaguaribe, Hélio, et. al., *Brasil 2000: Para um Novo Pacto Social*. São Paulo: Editora Paz e Terra, 1986.
Knight, Peter T. "Brazilian Socioeconomic Development: Issues for the Eighties," *World Development* (November/December 1981).
———, and Constantine Lluch, Dennis Mahar, Thomas W. Merrick, and Ricardo Moran. *Brazil: Human Resources Report*. Washington: World Bank, 1979.
———, F. Desmond McCarthy, and Sweder van Wijnbergen. "Escaping Hyperinflation." *Finance and Development* (December 1986).
———, and Ricardo Moran. *Brazil: Poverty and Basic Needs Series*. World Bank monograph, 1981.
Langoni, Carlos Geraldo. *A Economia de Transformação*. Rio de Janeiro: Coleção Brasil em Questão, 1975.
———. "Bases Institucionais da Economia Brasileira." Brasília: Banco Central do Brasil, 1981.
Lemgruber, Antonio Carlos. "Qual é o Déficit Público No Brasil." *Carta Econômica* 3. Banco Boa Vista (1987).
———. "A Inflação Brasileira e a Teoria da Inercia." *Carta Econômica* 7, 4 (1988).
Longo, Luiz Aranhado, et al. *O Combate à Inflação no Brasil: Uma Política Alternativa*. Rio de Janeiro: Editora Paz e Terra, 1984.
Lopes, Franciso. "Inflation and External Debt Problems in Latin America." Rio de Janeiro: Catholic University of Rio de Janeiro, 1985.
———. "Inflação Inercial, Hiperinflação e Desinflação: Notas e Conjeturas." *Revista da Anpec* 7, 8 (1984).
———. *O Desafio da Hiperinflação: Um Busca da Moeda Real*. Rio de Janeiro: Editora Campus, 1989.
Maynard, Geoffrey, and Willy Van Ryckeghem. "Stabilization Policy in an Inflationary Economy." In Gustav F. Papanek (ed.), *Development Policy—Theory and Practice*, Cambridge, Massachusetts: Harvard University Press, 1968.
Medeiros, Paulo de Tarso. "Poupança e Poupança Financeira." *Conjuntura Econômica* 39, 7 (1985).
Meyer, Arno, and Maria Silvia Bastos Marques. "Mecanismos de Redução da Dívida Externa dos Países em Desenvolvimento." Rio de Janeiro: Instituto Brasileiro de Economia, Fundação Getúlio Vargas, 1988.
Ministerio de Minas e Energia. *Sumário Mineral*. Brasília, 1986.
Modiano, Eduardo Marco. "O Choque Argentino e o Dilema Brasíleiro." Texto para Discussão 112. Rio de Janeiro: Pontifícia Universidade Católica de Rio de Janeiro, 1985.
Modigliani, Franco, and Tommaso Podoa-Schioppa. "The Management of an Open Economy with '100% Plus' Wage Indexation." *Essay in International Finance 130*. Princeton, N.J.: International Finance Section, Department of Economics, Princeton University, 1978.
Nogueira Batista, Jr., Paulo. *Da Crise Internacional à Moratória Brasileira*. Rio de Janeiro: Editora Paz e Terra, 1988.

———. "Formação de Capital e Transferência de Recursos ao Exterior." *Revista de Economia Política* 7, 1 (1987).
Paláez, Carlos Manuel. *Economia Brasileira Contemporânea: Origens e Conjuntura Atual.* São Paulo: Editora Atlas, 1987.
Pfefferman, Guy. "The Social Cost of Recession in Brazil." Mimeo. Washington, D.C.: World Bank, 1986.
Polak, Jacques. *Financial Policies and Development*, Paris: Development Center of the Organization for Economic Cooperation and Development, 1989.
Presidência da Republica. *Projeto do I Plano Nacional de Desenvolvimento da Nova República, 1986-89.* Brasília, 1985.
República Federativa do Brasil, *Projecto do II Plano Nacional de Desenvolvimento* (1975-79). Brasília, 1974.
Rodrigues Alves, Silvio. "Por que o Governo é Deficitário." OPÇÂO. 1987.
Rufatt, Adolfo. Paper on Macroeconomic Analysis 2. Washington, D.C.: Country Studies Division, Inter-American Development Bank, 1985.
Secretaria de Planajamento da Presidência da República. *Brasil: Programa de Estabilização Econômica.* Brasília, 1986.
Secretaria de Orçamento e Contrôle de Empresas Estatais. *Relatório Anual da SEST.* Brasília: Secretaria de Planajamento da Presidência da República, 1988.
Simonsen, Mario Henrique. *A Experiência Inflacionária no Brasil.* Rio de Janeiro: Instituto de Pesquisas e Estudos Sociais, 1964.
———. *Brasil 2001*, Rio de Janeiro: APEC Editora, 1969.
———. "Desindexação e Reforma Monetária," *Conjuntura Econômica*, novembro 1984.
———(ed.). *O Mercado Brasileiro de Capitais*, Documento EPEA 2, 1965.
Tyler, William G. "The Anti-Export Bias in Commercial Policies and Export Performance: Some Evidence from the Brazilian Experience." *Journal of the Kiel Institute of World Economics* 119, 1 (1983).
Werneck, Rogério L. Furquim. "Public Sector Adjustment to External Shocks and Domestic Pressures in Brazil, 1970-85." Texto para Discussão 163. Rio de Janeiro: Pontifícia Universidade Católica de Rio de Janeiro, 1986.
———. "Poupança Estatal, Dívida Externa e Crise Financeira do Setor Publico." *Pesquisa e Planajamento Econômico* (December 1986).
———. "Retomada do Crescimento e Esforço de Poupança: Limitações e Possibilidades." *Pesquisa e Planajamento Econômico* 17, 1 (1987).
———. "Uma Contribuição à Definicão dos Objetivos e das Formas de Controle das Empresas Estatais no Brasil." Texto para Discussão 196. Rio de Janeiro: Pontifícia Universidade Católica do Rio de Janeiro, 1988.
Williams, John (ed.). *Inflation and Indexation: Argentina, Brazil and Israel.* Washington, D.C.: Institute for International Economics, 1985.
World Bank. *Brazil: A Macroeconomic Evaluation of the Cruzado Plan.* Washington, D.C., 1988.
———. *Brazil, Country Economic Memorandum.* (Report No. 4674-BR), August 22, 1983.

Zini, Jr., Alvara A. "Fundar a Dívida Pública." Texto de Discussão. São Paulo: Universidade de São Paulo, Faculdade de Economia e Administraçao, Instituto de Pesquisas Econômicas, 1989.

———. "Termos de Troca e Taxa de Câmbio Real, no Longo Prazo." São Paulo: Departmento de Economia, FEA-USP, 1988.

Zottman, Luiz. "A Formação de Poupança Financiero no Brasil e Sua Capacidade para Gerar Acumulação e Absorção de Capital Fixo." Rio de Janeiro: Escola Superior de Guerra, Departamento de Estudos, 1988.

INDEX

A

Adjustment:
  domestic, 2–3, 7, 13–14, 16, 51, 53, 57, 59, 63, 71–72, 74–75, 79, 85, 109, 110, 113
  economic, 1–3, 72
  external, 2–3, 51, 53, 55, 74, 110, 113
  process, 2–3, 5, 10, 35, 37, 39, 41, 45, 53, 63, 71, 78, 88, 192
Alcohol, 12, 35, 38, 40, 43–44, 45, 108
Aluminum, 41, 43
Anti-export bias, 40, 46
Alves, Sílvio Rodrigues, 69n

B

Baer, Werner, 18n, 25n, 28n, 93n
Balance of payments, 1–2, 8, 9, 11, 16, 18, 33–39, 41, 43–44, 46, 53, 59, 63, 65, 73, 74, 78, 83, 87, 91, 98
Bank for International Settlements, 34
Bank of Brazil, 31
Batista, Paulo Nogueria, Jr., 28n, 80n
Brazilian Congress, 15, 112
Brazilian Institute of Capital Markets (IBMEC), 63n
Brazilian Institute of Geography and Statistics (IBGE), 85–86

C

Capital goods, 18, 40–41, 45–46, 57, 68, 98
Capital Markets Law, 21–23
Cardoso, Eliana, 28n
Central Bank Resolution,
  #63, 38
  #851, 40
Coffee, 17
Compensatory Financing Facility (CFF), 35
Constitution, 10, 15, 49, 103, 106–107, 112

Cruzado Plan, 5, 9, 10, 12, 45, 48, 67–68, 96–99, 102, 108, 110
Cruzado II, 99

D

Debt:
  crisis, 1–2, 4, 6, 13, 17, 24, 39, 51, 55, 89
  domestic, 6–8, 11, 14, 16, 24, 35, 69, 70, 75–76, 78, 80, 83, 95, 99, 104, 110
  external, 1–3, 5–6, 11, 29, 31, 33–34, 37–38, 45, 53, 63, 65, 69, 80, 99, 103, 105
  medium & long-term, 10, 28, 31, 33–36, 38, 102
  servicing, 2, 5, 10–11, 29, 31, 34, 59, 65, 67, 74, 80, 102, 105
Debt-equity auctions, 12, 105, 108
Decree Law 2.065, 85, 87
Deficit:
  fiscal, 7–8, 13, 15, 66, 72–73, 75–76, 78, 93, 99, 104, 109, 110, 112
  nominal, public sector, 76, 79
  operational, public sector, 8, 11, 76, 78–80, 91, 95, 104–105

E

Economically active population (EAP), 85–86
Employment, 6, 12–13, 86, 89, 98, 104, 109
Energy, 3–4, 27, 34, 40–41, 43–44, 65, 67
Exchange rate, 2, 8–9, 18, 35, 87–90, 93, 98–99
Expanded consumer price index (ECPI), 96
Exports, 1–6, 9, 20, 29, 31, 34, 36–41, 46, 48, 51, 67–68, 75, 77, 86, 89, 91, 99, 103
Extended Fund Facility (EFF), 31, 35, 73

F

Federal Savings Bank (CEF), 23
Ferro do Aço, 46n
Financial-interrelationships ratio, 21
First National Development Plan of the New Republic (I PND-NR), 46n
Flores de Lima, Beatriz Melo, 79n
Foreign exchange, 12, 17–18, 37, 39, 43–44, 46, 48, 63, 87, 108
França, Paulo, Oscar, 65n
Fundaçao Getulio Vargas, 23n, 85

G

Garlow, David, 111n
Goldsmith, Raymond W., 21n

H

Host-Madsen, Paul P., 138n
Housing Finance System (SFH), 22
Hydroelectric, 26, 28, 37, 40, 43, 65

I

Imports: 3–5, 8–9, 31, 33–38, 40–41, 43–46, 48, 51, 87, 98, 103
  restrictions, 3, 4, 40, 46, 73
  substitution, 1, 2, 5, 8, 17–18, 28, 38–41, 43, 45–46, 65, 75
Income distribution, 7, 15, 27, 66, 72, 85, 95
Indexation, 23–25, 75, 77, 88, 91, 93–94, 96, 110, 112
Industrialization, 1, 17–18
Inflation:
  hyper, 8, 13, 95–96, 107, 109
  inertial, 8–9, 25, 93, 95, 97, 110
Informatics, 49
Inputs, basic, 3, 40–41, 46, 48
Inter-American Development Bank (IDB), 48
Interest payment moratorium, 10, 12, 103–105, 108
International Monetary Fund (IMF), 8, 11, 33–37, 73–78, 83, 85, 89, 91, 94, 104–105
International reserves, 1, 11, 31, 33, 37, 83, 99, 105
Investment:
  fixed, 5, 6, 9, 25, 28, 68, 70, 77, 98, 103
  ratio, 4–6, 17, 51, 57, 63, 67–68, 72
  state enterprise, 4, 63, 67, 75
Itaipú, 40

J

Jaguribe, Hélio, 66n, 85n
Job Tenure Guarantee Fund (FGTS), 22, 97

L

Latin America, 1, 3–4, 20, 28, 39, 40, 44, 59
Law:
  #4.131, 38
  #6.078, 77
Lemgruber, Carlos, 76n
London Interbank Offer Rate (LIBOR), 31, 34, 36

M

Manufacturing, 3, 6, 20, 26, 46, 68
Market switching, 48
Medeiros, Paulo de Tarso, 25n
Minimum wage, 13, 77, 85, 87, 89, 90, 97, 109
Monetary correction, 6, 8–9, 14, 23–25, 69, 78, 80, 83, 89, 111

N

Nakano, Yoshiaki, 93n
National Alcohol Program (PROALCOOL), 44, 45
National Consumer Price Index (INPC), 76–77, 85–87
National Economic and Social Development Bank (BNDES), 23
National Housing Bank (BNH), 22
National Treasury Bill (BTN), 13, 109
New Cruzado Plan, 103–104, 108
Nonferrous metals, 43, 46
Non-monetary assets, 23
North-South Railway, 104
Nuclear program, 43, 65

O

Oil price shocks, 3, 8, 25, 27–28, 34, 39, 53, 55, 59, 75, 93–94
Overnight Market, 72

P

Paris Club, 36, 105
Passbook savings, 12, 97, 108
Pereira, Luis Bresser, 93n

INDEX

Petroleum, 3, 27–28, 34, 37, 40, 43–45, 98, 103
Polak, Jaques J., 46n
Privatization, 12–15, 109–110, 112
Programa de Integracao Social (PIS), 22–23
Public Sector Workers Patrimony Program (PASEP), 23
Public sector borrowing requirements (PSBR), 75–76, 78, 97, 102, 110

R

Readjustable Treasury Bond (ORTN), 9, 12, 23, 80, 97, 108
Rufatt, A., 135n

S

São Paulo Industrial Federation of Exporters (FIESP), 46
Savings:
  business, 70
  domestic, 2, 4, 6–7, 20, 23, 57, 71–72
  economic, 24–25, 71
  external, 4, 6–7, 18, 20, 24, 28, 51, 55, 57, 68, 71
  financial, 14, 21, 23, 25, 110
  government, 6, 14, 20, 24–25, 105
  household, 7, 70
  ratio, 25, 59, 68
Savings-investment identity, 53, 55, 57, 137–138
Siderbrás, 65
Simonsen, Mario H., 18n
SIMPAS, 107

State Secretariat for State Enterprises (SEST), 63
Subsidized credit, 75
Summer Plan, 12–13, 15–16, 108–109, 112–113

T

Tin, 43
Trade: 1–2, 11, 33, 48, 59
  balance, 9–10, 33, 41, 53, 98–99, 102–103
  deficit, 28, 33, 53
  surplus, 1–3, 9, 11, 13–14, 16, 33–34, 36–38, 43, 51, 53, 55, 73, 80, 95, 98, 105, 109–110, 113
Treasury Bill (LTN), 80
Tyler, William G., 48n

U

Unemployment, 3, 53, 77, 79, 86, 93–95
Uranium, 43

V

Velocity, 83

W

Wage policy, 2–3, 15, 74, 77, 83, 85, 86, 95, 112
Wernek, Rógerio, 65n, 80n
Williams, John, 93n
Working capital, 21, 88–89
World Bank, 48, 66